G000094144

Geography and History

1

Geography and History 1 is a collective work, conceived, designed and created by the Secondary Education department at Santillana, under the supervision of **Teresa Grence Ruiz**.

WRITERS

Martin Minchom

Álvaro Bellón Mena

Raquel Rubalcaba Bermejo

María Ángeles Fernández de Bartolomé

Pedro Adiego Sancho

Rosa López Pérez

Javier Velilla Gil

Francisco Javier Zabaleta Estévez

CLIL CONSULTANT

Elena del Pozo

EDITOR

Lesley Thompson

PROOFREADING

Joseph Candora

MANAGING EDITOR

Sheila Tourle

Do not write in this book. Do all the activities in your notebook.

Geography index

History index

About this book

The book is organised into 12 units. Every section of a unit helps the students to develop their key competences.

Opening double page: presentation of the unit

The **contents** of the unit are presented at the beginning.

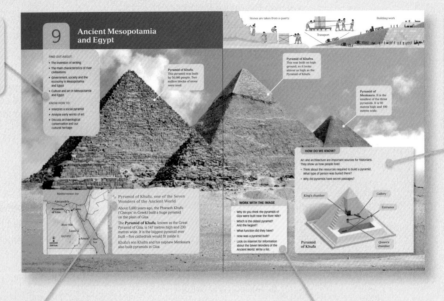

How do we know?: the student is introduced to the techniques and sources of geographers and historians.

A **CD symbol** shows that the text is recorded

The **Work with the image** section checks the student's understanding of the visual material and the text.

The content pages

Think about it invites the students to reflect about challenging concepts.

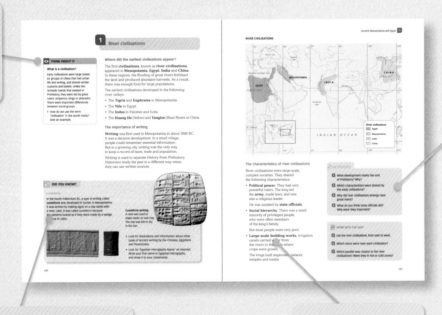

A series of **activities** cover all the main contents of the page.

The **Did you know?** section widens the students' range of knowledge.

The **main contents** are clearly presented.

Activity Round-up: learning to learn

This section always begins with a **summary** of the key ideas.

Numerous activities provide a full **round-up** of the unit, and encourage learner autonomy.

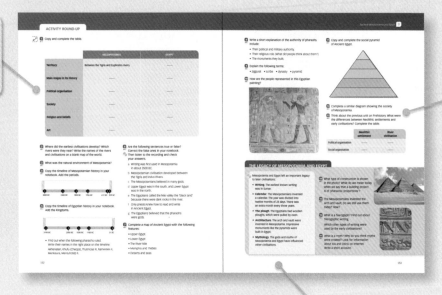

The **final section** analyses environmental problems in the Geography units, and our inheritance from the past in the History units.

Know how to...: key competences

The students develop **key skills** in Geography and History.

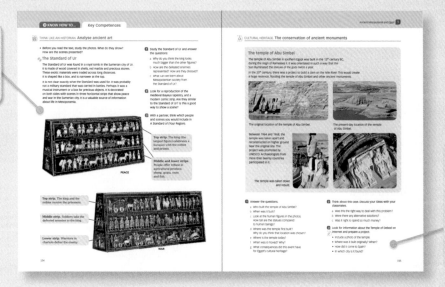

The students do individual activities, pairwork and **group projects**, making full use of internet resources.

Key Competences

  Linguistic competence

Competence in mathematics, science and technology

   Digital competence

Social and civic competence

Cultural awareness and expression

  Learning to learn

Initiative and entrepreneurship

1 Planet Earth

FIND OUT ABOUT:

- Why life exists on Earth
- The Earth's movement and its consequences
- How maps represent the Earth
- Latitude and longitude

KNOW HOW TO:

- Use a scale
- Locate a place on a map
- Use a map of time zones

"I see Earth!"

Today, we all know what the Earth looks like from space. But until the 20th century, no-one was sure.

In 1961, the astronaut Yuri Gagarin became the first person to see the Earth from space. His first words were: "I see Earth! It is so beautiful!" Since Gagarin's flight, hundreds of men and women have gone into space.

Artificial satellites now collect images of the Earth all the time. Satellite images are important in meteorology, environmental conservation, military intelligence, and many other fields.

HOW DO WE KNOW?

Maps are representations of the Earth's surface. One of the first world maps was made by Ptolemy, a Greek geographer and astronomer, in the second century AD.

- Where is the Iberian Peninsula?
- Which continents are shown?
- Why is America missing?

? WORK WITH THE IMAGE

- What does the Earth look like from space? Why do we call it the "blue planet"?
- Who was Yuri Gagarin?
- How do we use the information provided by satellites?

The Earth and the Solar System

ACTIVITIES

1. List the planets in order of distance from the Sun. (Begin with the nearest planet.) Which is the largest planet? Which is the smallest planet?

2. What is the meaning of the following terms?
   - Solar System
   - orbit
   - satellite

The Solar System

The **Solar System** consists of a single star, the **Sun**, and the planets that orbit it. The Sun is a huge mass of hot gases, which sends out energy to the rest of the Solar System. There are eight planets: **Mercury, Venus, Earth, Mars, Jupiter, Saturn, Uranus** and **Neptune**.

Our own planet, the **Earth**, is the fifth biggest planet in the Solar System. It has a surface area of 510 million square kilometres (km^2). It is the third closest planet to the Sun, which is 150 million km away.

Most planets in the Solar System have one or more **satellites**, which are astronomical bodies that orbit them. The Earth only has one satellite: the **Moon**.

THE SOLAR SYSTEM

THE BIOSPHERE

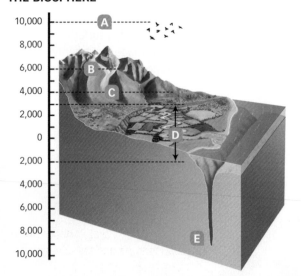

A Limit of the flight of birds. B Limit of life in the tropical zone.
C Limit of life in the temperate zone. D Most living things.
E Lowest limit of life.

The biosphere: life on Earth

The Earth is the only planet in the Solar System where life exists. The following conditions make this possible:

- The Earth has the ideal **temperature** for life. It is the right distance from the Sun so it is not too hot or too cold.

- The **atmosphere** is a layer of gases that protects the Earth from the Sun's radiation. It contains essential gases, like oxygen.

- **Water** is necessary for all living things.

The **biosphere** is the ecological system in which life exists. Nearly all living things are found between an altitude of 3,000 metres (m) above sea level, and 2,000 m below sea level.

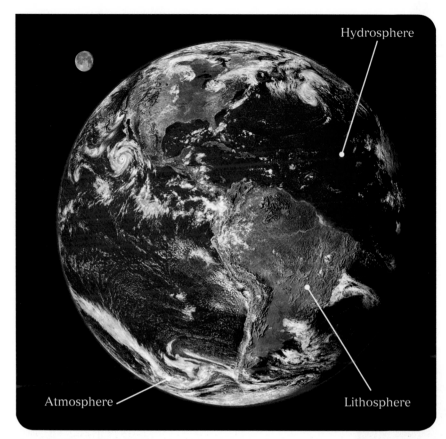

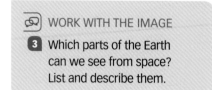

WORK WITH THE IMAGE
3 Which parts of the Earth can we see from space? List and describe them.

The Earth seen from space.

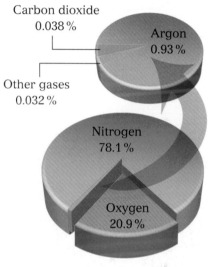

Gases in the atmosphere at the Earth's surface.

The outer structure of the Earth

The Earth's surface is made up of three parts: a layer of gases and clouds, large bodies of water, and land.

- **The atmosphere** is the layer of gases that surrounds the Earth. It consists of nitrogen (78%), oxygen (21%), and carbon dioxide and other gases (1%).

- **The hydrosphere** is all the water that exists on our planet: oceans and seas, rivers and lakes, ice, groundwater and water vapour.

- **The lithosphere** is the Earth's solid outer layer. It consists of the continents and submerged land under the oceans and seas.

WORK WITH THE CHART
4 Which two gases make up most of the atmosphere?

ACTIVITIES

5 Match the two columns. Listen and check your answers.

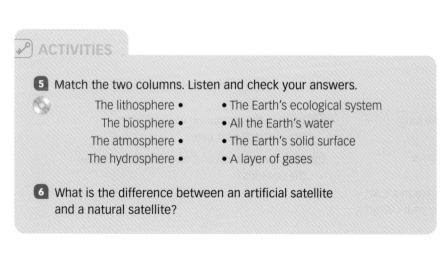

The lithosphere •	• The Earth's ecological system
The biosphere •	• All the Earth's water
The atmosphere •	• The Earth's solid surface
The hydrosphere •	• A layer of gases

6 What is the difference between an artificial satellite and a natural satellite?

THINK ABOUT IT

Imagine that our planet had both an atmosphere and liquid water – but extreme temperatures. Would life on Earth be possible in those circumstances?

The movement of the Earth

Rotation and revolution

Like other objects in the Solar System, the Earth moves all the time. It has two types of movement:

- **Rotation** on its own axis.
- **Revolution** around the Sun.

Rotation

The Earth spins continually on its own **axis** in a west-to-east direction. It takes 24 hours to complete one rotation.

The rotation of the Earth causes the alternation of **day** and **night**. The Earth is spherical so the Sun cannot illuminate the whole planet simultaneously. Consequently, it is always day on only one side of the Earth's surface, where it receives the Sun's rays. On the other side, it is night.

Revolution

At the same time as the Earth rotates on its axis, it also moves around the Sun in an **elliptical orbit**. It takes the Earth 365 days and six hours to complete one revolution. As a calendar year only has 365 days, there is a **leap year** every four years, when we add an extra day to the month of February.

The Earth is **tilted** so the angle of the Sun's rays changes in each hemisphere during the year. This causes the **seasons**.

ROTATION OF THE EARTH

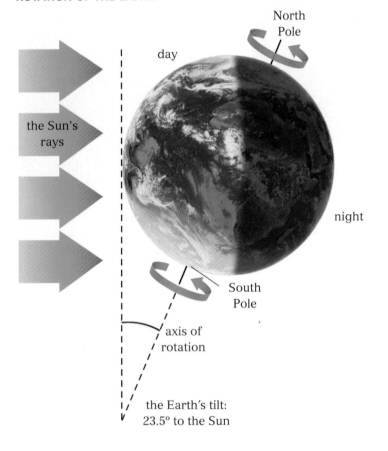

the Sun's rays

day

North Pole

night

South Pole

axis of rotation

the Earth's tilt: 23.5° to the Sun

ACTIVITIES

1. What is the rotation of the Earth? How long does it take?
2. Why does the rotation of the Earth cause the alternation of day and night?
3. Does the length of day and night change more at the Equator or at the poles during the year? Why?
4. What is the revolution of the Earth? How long does it take?
5. Why does the revolution of the Earth cause the seasons?

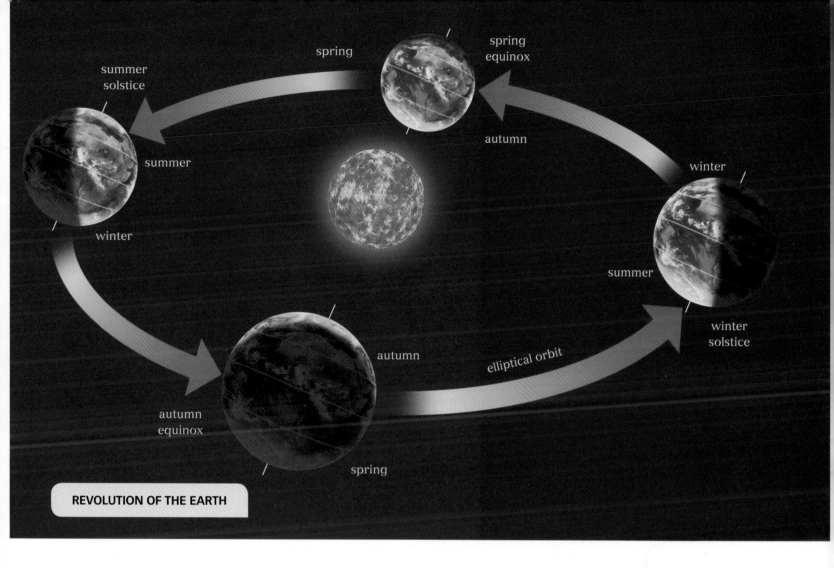

REVOLUTION OF THE EARTH

The seasons

At the Equator, the Sun's rays reach the Earth vertically all the year round so there is little difference between the seasons.

However, further from the equator, the seasons are reversed in the two hemispheres:

- In **summer**, the Sun's rays reach one hemisphere almost vertically. At the same time, it is **winter** in the other hemisphere. For example, it is summer in Spain when it is winter in Chile.

- In **spring** and **autumn**, the Sun's rays reach both hemispheres at a similar angle.

The four seasons begin at the solstices and equinoxes:

- Summer and winter: at the two **solstices** (around 21 June and 21 December), the Sun's rays are vertical at one of the tropics. Days are long and warm in one hemisphere, but short and cold in the other.

- Spring and autumn: at the two **equinoxes** (around 21 March and 23 September), the Sun's rays are vertical at the equator. Both hemispheres receive the same amount of sunlight, and day and night are equally long.

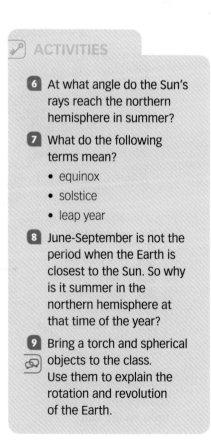

ACTIVITIES

6 At what angle do the Sun's rays reach the northern hemisphere in summer?

7 What do the following terms mean?
- equinox
- solstice
- leap year

8 June-September is not the period when the Earth is closest to the Sun. So why is it summer in the northern hemisphere at that time of the year?

9 Bring a torch and spherical objects to the class. Use them to explain the rotation and revolution of the Earth.

How do we represent the Earth?

A globe.

Globes and maps

The Earth is spherical. However, it is not a perfect sphere because it is flat at the poles. We call this shape a **geoid**.

- **Globes** are accurate representations of the Earth because they have a similar shape to our planet.
- **Maps** provide information about a small area, a country, a region or the whole world. However, maps have a flat surface but our planet is three-dimensional. Consequently, they distort shapes and distances.

The main features of a map

A map has the following features: a title, a scale, a key, an arrow pointing north, and a grid of imaginary lines (parallels and meridians).

An **arrow** pointing north shows orientation.

Texts give us place names and other information.

The **title** tells us what the map is about.

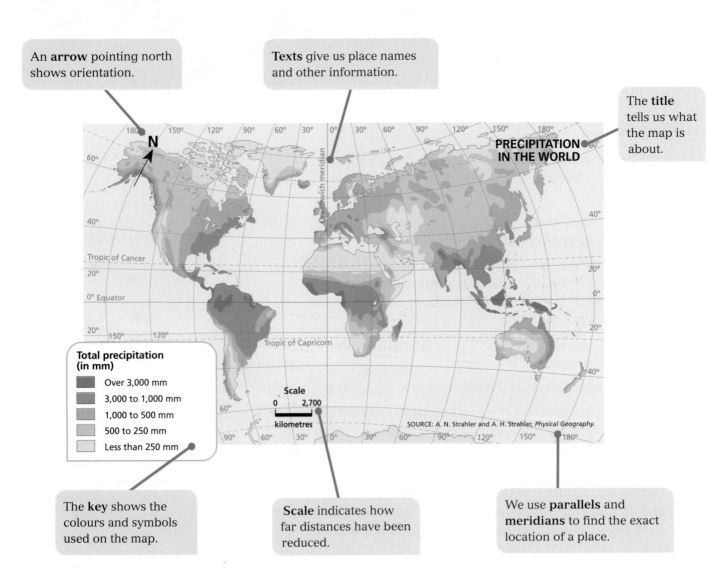

PRECIPITATION IN THE WORLD

Total precipitation (in mm)
- Over 3,000 mm
- 3,000 to 1,000 mm
- 1,000 to 500 mm
- 500 to 250 mm
- Less than 250 mm

Scale
0   2,700
kilometres

SOURCE: A. N. Strahler and A. H. Strahler, *Physical Geography*.

The **key** shows the colours and symbols used on the map.

Scale indicates how far distances have been reduced.

We use **parallels** and **meridians** to find the exact location of a place.

Types of maps

There are two main types of maps.
They give us different kinds of information:

- **Topographic maps** show the main features of the natural environment, like mountains and rivers. They also include man-made features, such as cities and roads.

- **Thematic maps** provide visual information on a particular subject, for example climate or population. They often use colours, symbols and text.

⟳ WORK WITH THE MAPS

1. What types of relief can you see on the topographic map?

2. What type of information does the thematic map give us?

3. What is the difference between a topographic map and a thematic map?

A TOPOGRAPHIC MAP

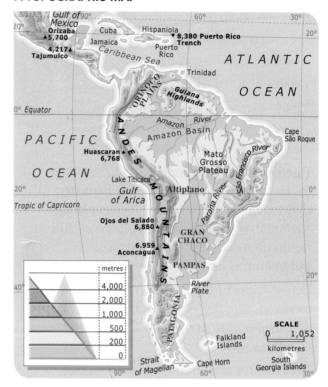

A THEMATIC MAP

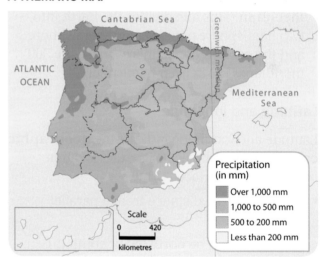

⚷ DID YOU KNOW?

Orientation in nature

We establish direction by using the **cardinal points**: north, south, east and west. If we are lost in the countryside without a compass, map or GPS, we can use the position of the Sun for orientation. The Sun rises in the east and sets in the west. At night-time, the North Star always indicates north.

- Look on internet for a map of star constellations. Can you find the North Star? (First, look for the Big Dipper.) Try to identify it in the night sky tonight.

⚷ ACTIVITIES

4. Name two ways of representing the Earth. What are the advantages and disadvantages of each one?

5. Make a list of the main parts of a map. What type of information do we get from each of the following?
   - map key
   - scale
   - parallels and meridians

6. Investigate the colours and symbols used on maps. Look for one example of each of the following:
   - a line
   - a symbol
   - a green area
   - a blue area
   - a very small circle

7. Do you use maps in your own life? Are they printed on paper, or displayed on an electronic screen? In which situations do we use each kind of map?

Parallels and meridians

Parallels and meridians form a grid of imaginary lines that help us to find the exact location of a place on Earth.

- **Parallels** are imaginary circles running in an east-west direction. The **Equator** (0°) divides the Earth into two **hemispheres**: the northern hemisphere and the southern hemisphere. There are 90 parallels between the Equator and each pole.

  Other important parallels, from north to south, are: the **Arctic Circle**; the **Tropic of Cancer**; the **Tropic of Capricorn**; the **Antarctic Circle**.

- **Meridians** are imaginary semicircles running in a north-south direction from the North Pole to the South Pole. The **prime meridian** (0°) is also called the **Greenwich meridian**. This line divides the Earth into two hemispheres: the western hemisphere and the eastern hemisphere. There are 360 meridians: 180 in each hemisphere.

Latitude and longitude

Latitude and longitude indicate the **geographic coordinates** of a place – its exact location on the Earth's surface.

- **Latitude** is the distance from a parallel to the Equator:
  - Latitude can be north (N) or south (S).
  - Parallels show latitude.
  - It is measured in degrees (°), minutes (') and seconds (").
  - Its values go from 0° at the Equator to 90°.

- **Longitude** is the distance from a meridian to the Greenwich meridian:
  - Longitude can be east (E) or west (W).
  - Meridians show longitude.
  - It is measured in degrees (°), minutes (') and seconds (").
  - Its values go from 0° at the Greenwich meridian to 180°.

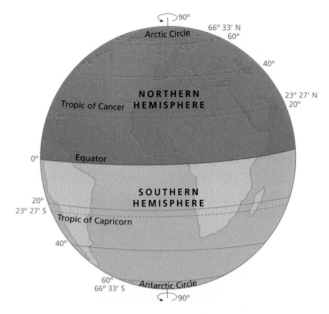

Parallels: the Equator divides the Earth into the northern and southern hemispheres.

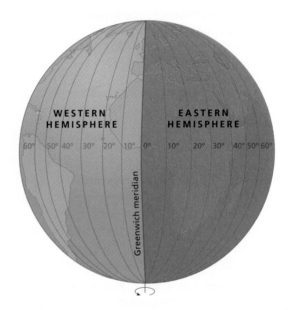

Meridians: the Greenwich meridian divides the Earth into the western and eastern hemispheres.

◉ THINK ABOUT IT

We put latitude before longitude when we give the geographic coordinates. For example, Rio de Janeiro (Brazil) is in the southern hemisphere and west of the Greenwich meridian. Its approximate geographic coordinates are latitude 22° south (S) and longitude 43° west (W). Its exact geographic coordinates are 22° 54' 10" S, 43° 12' 27" W.

- Is it sometimes useful to give approximate figures? Why?

How do we locate a place on a map?

We can locate a place on a map if we have its **geographic coordinates**: its latitude and longitude.

Latitude is shown in numbers on the left and right of the map.

Longitude is shown in numbers at the top and bottom of the map.

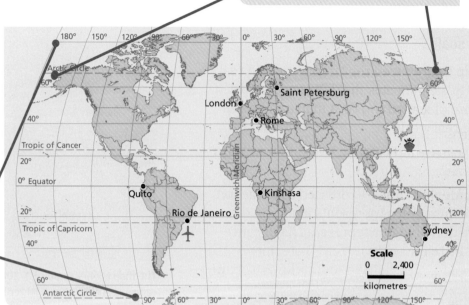

An example: Saint Petersburg

1. The map shows it is near the 60° parallel in the northern hemisphere. So its latitude is 60° north.

2. It is near the 30° meridian in the eastern hemisphere. So its longitude is 30° east.

3. Its geographic coordinates are therefore 60° N, 30° E.

DID YOU KNOW?

GPS

GPS (Global Positioning System) is a satellite navigation system. Each GPS receiver is in contact with several satellites. It gives highly accurate calculations of latitude and longitude.

• When and where do you think GPS is used?

ACTIVITIES

1 Copy the table in your notebook. Complete it with the missing information.

City	Latitude	Longitude
Saint Petersburg	60° N	30° E
	21° S	38° W
London		
	32° S	150° E
Rome		
Quito		
Kinshasa		

2 Imagine that a ship is in difficulty west of the Canary Islands. Is it necessary to know its geographic coordinates before rescuing it? Why?

3 Look for the ship and the plane on the map. Then copy and complete the sentences in your notebook.

- ○ The lost ship is in the ..... hemisphere and its approximate coordinates are ..... It was going to 20° S, 120° E. Its direction should be .....
- ○ The rescue plane is in the ..... hemisphere, and its approximate coordinates are .....
- ○ Its direction will be ..... towards the ship.

5   How do we use scale on a map?

Map scale

A map is a reduced representation of a real area. Scale indicates the difference between the size of something on a map and its size in the real world.

Scale can be indicated in two different ways on a map:

- **Numeric scale** is expressed as a fraction. The numerator represents a unit on the map. The denominator represents its distance in the real world.

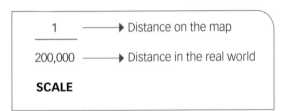

In this case, a scale of 1/200,000 means that 1 cm on the map is equal to 200,000 cm on the ground.

Numeric scale can be written in three ways:

A $\dfrac{1}{200,000}$ **B** $1/200,000$ **C** $1:200,000$

- **Graphic scale** (bar scale) shows the equivalent distance on a bar divided into equal segments, usually 1cm. The bar looks like a small ruler. The numbers on the bar indicate the actual distance that each segment represents.

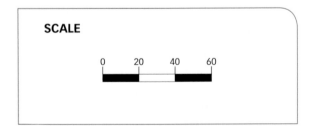

In this case, 1 cm on the map represents 20 km in the real world.

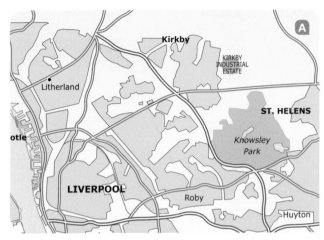

The map is on a **scale of 1/200,000**. This means that the region is 200,000 times larger than this representation.

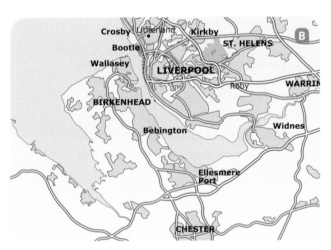

The map is on a **scale of 1/600,000**. In the real world, the region is 600,000 times larger than in this representation. That is why this map does not show many details.

ACTIVITIES

1 Compare the maps.

  a Study Maps A and B. These show Merseyside – the region around Liverpool (England). With a partner, find Litherland and the Kirkby Industrial Estate on map A. Use a ruler to measure the distance on the map. Then calculate the distance in kilometres.

  b Compare maps A and B. Why is Widnes only on map B?

How to use scale to calculate distances

a **Interpret the map scale.** The scale on this map is 1/8,250,000. So 1 cm on the map is equivalent to 82.5 km (or 8,250,000 centimetres) in the real world.

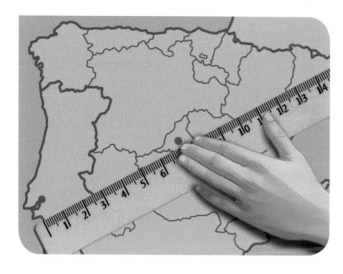

b **Measure the distance you wish to calculate.** For example, use a ruler to measure the distance between Madrid and Lisbon. (In this case, it is 6 cm.)

c **Do the calculations.** Work out the figure that is proportional to six centimetres. x represents the distance that you want to calculate:

$$\frac{1}{8,250,000} = \frac{6 \text{ cm}}{x}$$

$$x = \frac{8,250,000 \times 6}{1}$$

$$x = 49,500,000 \text{ cm}$$

d **Change centimetres into kilometres.**

49,500,000 cm = 495 km.

The distance between Madrid and Lisbon is 495 km if we go in a straight line.

ACTIVITIES

2 You are going on a car trip around Europe.

a Look at the map and the scale.

b Calculate the distance in a straight line between each city.

c Copy and complete the table.

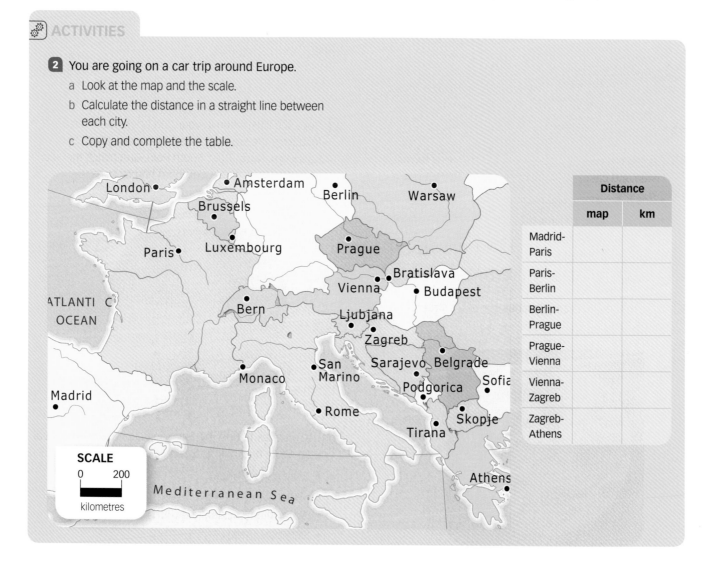

	Distance	
	map	km
Madrid-Paris		
Paris-Berlin		
Berlin-Prague		
Prague-Vienna		
Vienna-Zagreb		
Zagreb-Athens		

SCALE
0   200
kilometres

1 Copy and complete the diagram.

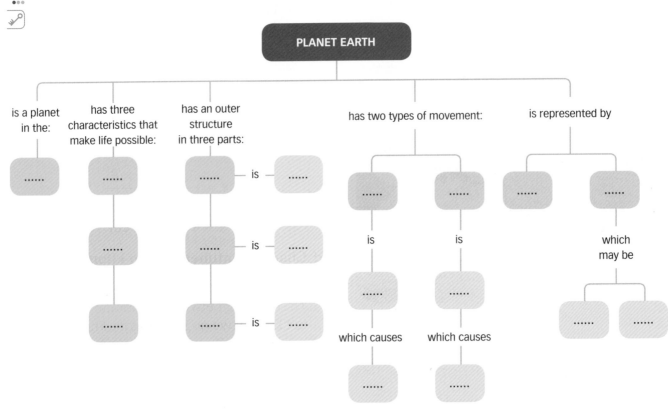

PLANET EARTH

is a planet in the:

has three characteristics that make life possible:

has an outer structure in three parts:

has two types of movement:

is represented by

which may be

which causes

which causes

2 What is the biosphere?

3 Explain the difference between the following terms. Listen and check your answers.

- The hydrosphere and the lithosphere
- Numeric scale and graphic scale
- Parallel and meridian
- Latitude and longitude
- Solstice and equinox

4 Look at the photo and describe the outer structure of the Earth.

5 Copy the illustration in your notebook. Label the following: the Equator, Tropic of Cancer, Tropic of Capricorn, North Pole, South Pole, Greenwich meridian, northern hemisphere, southern hemisphere.

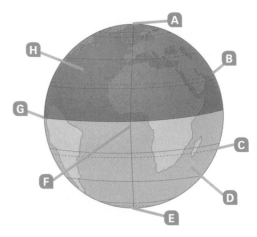

6 Use an atlas to find the following capitals on a political map. Work out their geographic coordinates.

- Cairo (Egypt, Africa)
- Madrid (Spain, Europe)
- Washington (United States, America)
- Singapore (Asia)

7 Copy and complete this table on the Earth's movements in your notebook. Then answer the questions.

	Rotation	Revolution
What type of movement is it?	....	....
How long does it take?	....	....
What does it cause?	....	....

a Why do day and night alternate on Earth?

b What would happen to Earth if rotation did not occur?

c What causes the seasons? How important are they for life on our planet?

d What are leap years? Why do they occur?

8 Visit the world on the internet.

a Use an internet search engine to find 'Google Maps'.

b Type your own address in the box at the top. Click on "Satellite" for a satellite image of your house. Click on "Maps" to see what your neighbourhood looks like on a map.

c Using Google Maps, make a "virtual" visit to Helsinki, Cairo and Rio de Janeiro. Do they look similar to each other?

9 Look at the map and answer the questions.

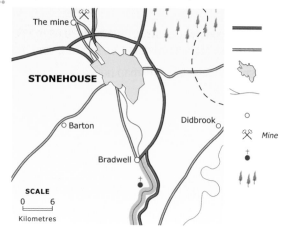

a What do you think the symbols mean?

b Use the scale to calculate the distance between Barton and Bradwell.

c Is this a topographic map or a thematic map?

10 Which of the following conditions are necessary for life on Earth?

- The Earth is not too near and not too far from the Sun.
- It has one satellite: the Moon.
- It has an atmosphere.
- The water cycle takes place.

ExoMars Rover.

SPACE EXPLORATION

We have learned a lot about the universe, but many things remain to be discovered. That is why many scientific missions are carried out. For example:

- **BepiColombo** is a mission of the European Space Agency (ESA) and the Japan Aerospace Exploration Agency to the planet Mercury.

- **ExoMars** is a mission of the ESA and the Russian Federal Space Agency to study life on Mars.

- **Ulysses** (1990-2009) was a joint mission of the North American agency NASA and the ESA to collect data on the Sun.

- The **Hubble Space Telescope** orbits the Earth and makes detailed observations of the Solar System.

- The **Rosetta** spacecraft landed a robot on comet 67P in 2014.

11 Why do you think that so many space missions are jointly organised by various countries?

12 Why is so much money invested in space research?

13 Why do you think the Canary Islands are a good place to observe the night sky? Find out about the "Instituto de Astrofísica de Canarias" by using an internet search engine to look for their website.

REAL LIFE SKILLS. **Use a city map**

City maps (also known as **street plans**) help us to find our way around a city.
They have to include a lot of detail, so they are very large scale representations.

- Which Spanish city does the map below represent?

> Street plans are divided by vertical and horizontal lines. We can find a place by looking for the letter at the top and the number at the side.

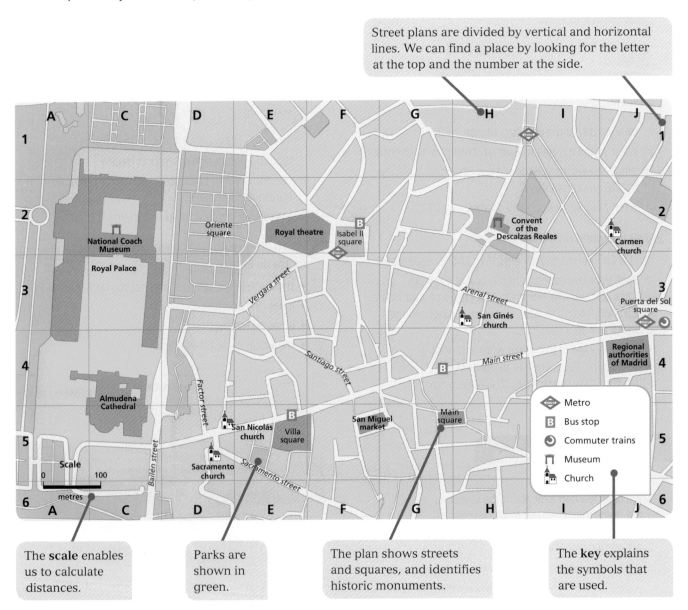

> The **scale** enables us to calculate distances.

> Parks are shown in green.

> The plan shows streets and squares, and identifies historic monuments.

> The **key** explains the symbols that are used.

1 Find the places on the city map:

   a   Look at D5 and H2. Which buildings are on these squares?

   b   What are the references for San Ginés Church and Carmen Church?

   c   Can you find a museum? Is it near a metro station?

2 Use the scale.

   a   What is the scale of this map?

   b   What is the distance in a straight line from the Convent of the Descalzas Reales to the Royal Theatre?

3 Work in groups, and choose your role. You are a foreign tourist (A), or you live in Madrid (B).

Think about the language we use for directions: *How do I get to...?, Turn right..., Go straight ahead...*

   a   A is in the main square and asks B for directions. B explains how to get to the Royal Theatre.

   b   B then uses the map to suggest other places that are worth visiting. A and B talk about how to get there.

PRACTICAL KNOWLEDGE. **Why do we change the time when we travel?**

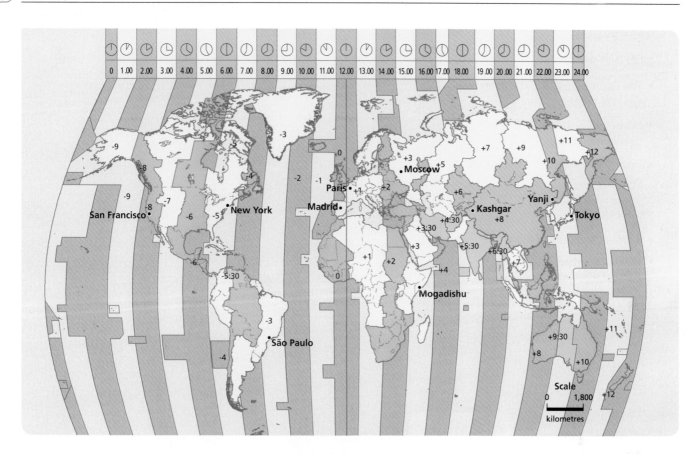

Time zones

As a result of the Earth's rotation, it is daytime on one side of the Earth when it is night-time on the other.

Time zones were created to make the time around the world correspond to the position of the Sun.

The Earth is a sphere (360°), and takes 24 hours to rotate on its axis. It takes one hour to move the equivalent of 15° because 24 × 15 = 360. Consequently, the Earth is divided into 24 time zones, which go from pole to pole. It is the same time everywhere inside a time zone.

Time zones are measured from the **Greenwich meridian**:

- If we go **east**, we move the clock forward by one hour as we go through each time zone.

- If we go **west**, we move the clock back by one hour as we go through each time zone.

Time zones are influenced by political factors.

- Some countries, like China and Argentina, have the same time across the whole country, even though they are in more than one time zone.

- Other countries, such as the United States, have several time zones.

1 Look at the map and answer the questions.

a You take a flight from Madrid at 10 am, and arrive in New York eight hours later. What time do you arrive?

b You fly from San Francisco to Paris. How many time zones will you cross? Do you put your watch forward or back when you arrive?

c Look at China on the map. If the Sun rises at 5 am in Kashgar, what time does it rise in Yanji?

d Why do they say "and one hour earlier in the Canary Islands" in the Spanish media?

2 Find out the time in the following cities using internet. (Type the key words "world clock" in an internet search engine.)

- London (United Kingdom)
- Mumbai (India)
- Lima (Peru)
- Casablanca (Morocco)

2 The Earth's relief

FIND OUT ABOUT:

- The Earth's crust and the main types of relief
- How relief is formed and which agents modify it
- How the world's relief influences our lives

KNOW HOW TO:

- Read a relief map of the world
- Compare a relief map and a population map

Cloud of water vapour

 Surtsey, the birth of an island

1963

In November 1963 some fishermen were on a boat near the south coast of Iceland. Suddenly, they saw smoke rising from the water. At first, they thought that a ship was on fire. Then they realized that a volcanic eruption was beginning on the ocean floor.

In the months that followed, an island was formed from volcanic lava.

1963-1967

Eruptions continued for another four years. By 1967 the island had a surface area of 2.7 km².

Since 1967

Since 1967, erosion has reduced the surface area of the island. Each year its surface area falls by 2 cm.

2008

In 2008 UNESCO declared Surtsey a World Heritage Site. It is an incredible laboratory where scientists investigate the formation of an ecosystem. Today, it has plant life and a number of animal species, such as seals, sea birds and insects.

1963 >   1967 >   2008 >

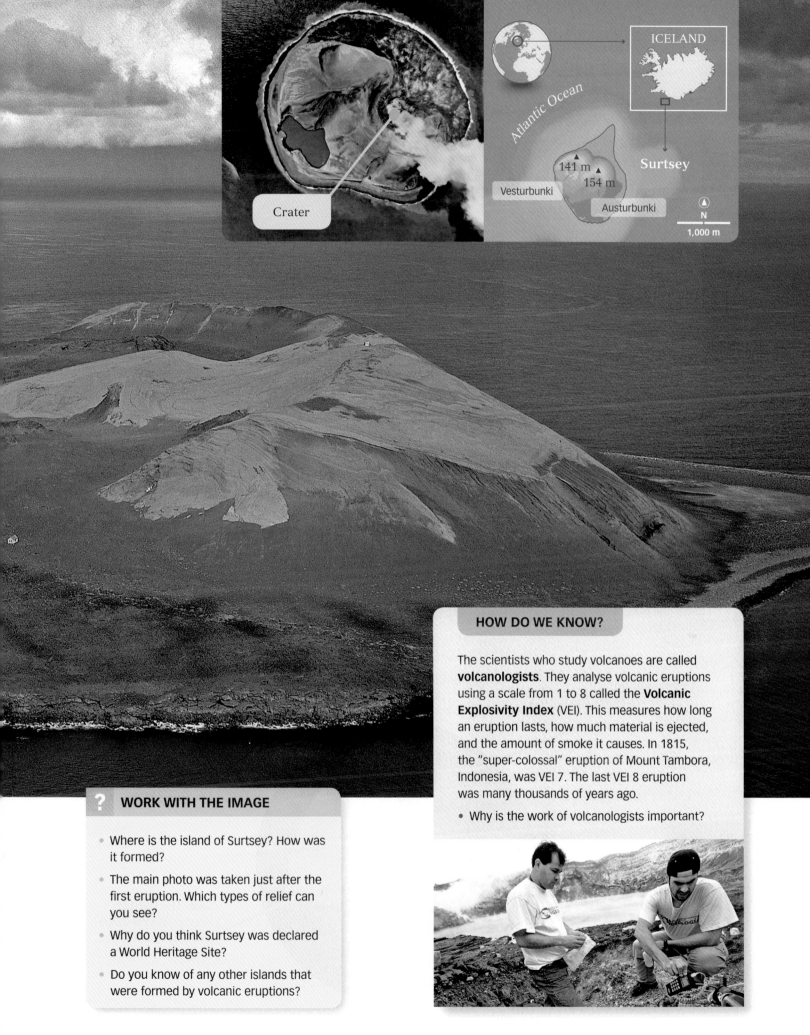

Crater

ICELAND

Atlantic Ocean

Surtsey

141 m

154 m

Vesturbunki

Austurbunki

N

1,000 m

HOW DO WE KNOW?

The scientists who study volcanoes are called **volcanologists**. They analyse volcanic eruptions using a scale from 1 to 8 called the **Volcanic Explosivity Index** (VEI). This measures how long an eruption lasts, how much material is ejected, and the amount of smoke it causes. In 1815, the "super-colossal" eruption of Mount Tambora, Indonesia, was VEI 7. The last VEI 8 eruption was many thousands of years ago.

• Why is the work of volcanologists important?

? WORK WITH THE IMAGE

• Where is the island of Surtsey? How was it formed?

• The main photo was taken just after the first eruption. Which types of relief can you see?

• Why do you think Surtsey was declared a World Heritage Site?

• Do you know of any other islands that were formed by volcanic eruptions?

1 The Earth's crust

The structure of the Earth

The Earth has three layers:

- The **crust** is the Earth's surface.
  It is only 1 % of the Earth's volume.
  It is a thin, solid layer of rock.

- The **mantle** is the middle layer.
  It occupies almost 85 % of the Earth's volume.
  It is made up of various materials,
  including liquid rock or **magma**.

- The **core** is the deepest layer.
  The outer core is liquid,
  but the inner core is solid.

The Earth's temperature increases with depth.
The temperature in the core reaches
over 5,000 degrees Centigrade (°C).

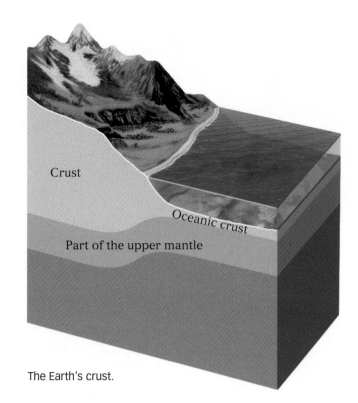

Crust

Oceanic crust

Part of the upper mantle

The Earth's crust.

WORK WITH THE ILLUSTRATIONS

1. What are the layers of the Earth, beginning with the deepest? How deep is each layer?

2. Does the Earth's crust have the same depth under the oceans as under the continents?

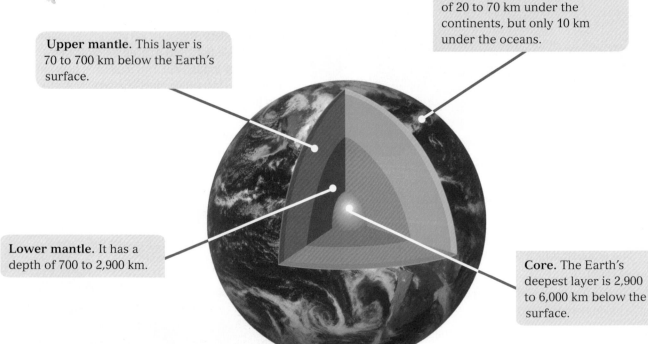

Upper mantle. This layer is 70 to 700 km below the Earth's surface.

Crust. This layer has a depth of 20 to 70 km under the continents, but only 10 km under the oceans.

Lower mantle. It has a depth of 700 to 2,900 km.

Core. The Earth's deepest layer is 2,900 to 6,000 km below the surface.

The internal structure of the Earth.

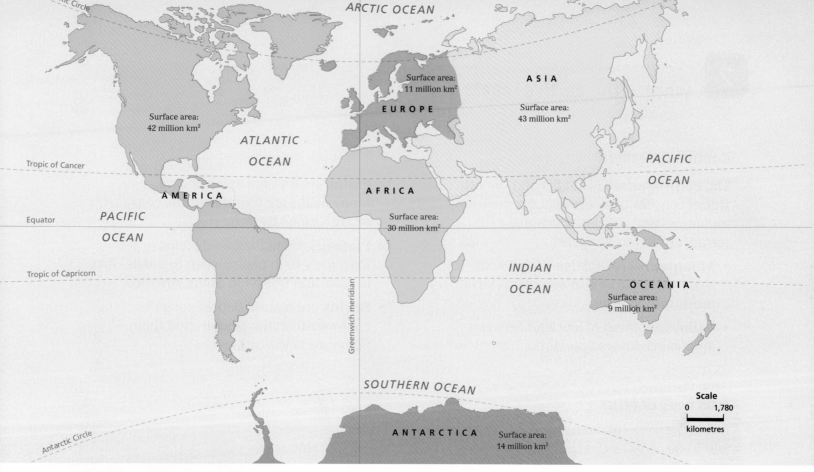

THE OCEANS AND CONTINENTS

Oceans and continents

Most of the Earth is **covered by water**. About 71% of the Earth's surface is **submerged land** under the oceans and seas. The **dry land** of the continents makes up the remaining 29% of the Earth's surface.

The **continents** are very large land masses, surrounded by oceans and seas. From the largest continent to the smallest, the six continents are **Asia**, **America**, **Africa**, **Antarctica**, **Europe** and **Oceania**. Most of the Earth's dry land is in the northern hemisphere.

Oceans are vast masses of saltwater. The five oceans are connected to each other:

- The **Pacific Ocean** is the largest and deepest ocean.
- The **Atlantic Ocean** is the second largest ocean.
- The **Indian Ocean** has no natural frontier separating it from the Atlantic.
- The **Southern Ocean** is mainly frozen for much of the year.
- The **Arctic Ocean** is also mainly frozen. It is the smallest ocean.

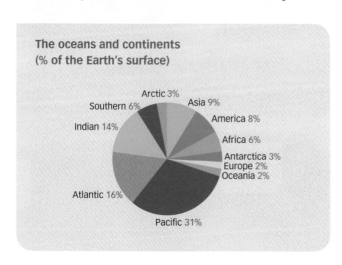

The oceans and continents (% of the Earth's surface)

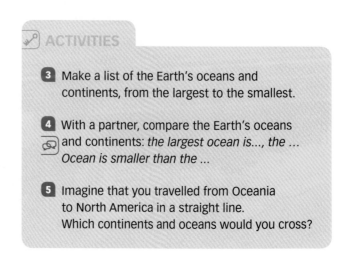

ACTIVITIES

3. Make a list of the Earth's oceans and continents, from the largest to the smallest.

4. With a partner, compare the Earth's oceans and continents: *the largest ocean is..., the ... Ocean is smaller than the ...*

5. Imagine that you travelled from Oceania to North America in a straight line. Which continents and oceans would you cross?

Continental relief

The Earth's surface is not flat and smooth. **Relief** consists of all the features, such as mountains and valleys, which make the terrain around us so varied.

- **Mountains** are high landforms with steep sides. Groups of mountains form **mountain ranges**.

- **Valleys** are areas of low land between mountains. Rivers flow through many valleys.

- **Plains** are low, flat areas of land. Many plains are found near the coast, or are formed by large rivers.

- **Plateaus** are high, raised plains. Extremely high plateaus are found in Tibet in Asia, and Bolivia in South America.

- **Basins** are natural depressions that are lower than the land around them. Some are below sea level.

MAIN TYPES OF RELIEF

Coastal relief

In high coastal areas, there are **cliffs**, which are steep rock formations. Many **beaches** are found in flat, coastal areas. The following landforms are found in coastal regions:

- A **peninsula** is an area of land that is mainly surrounded by water.

- An **isthmus** connects a peninsula to a continent.

- A **cape** is a strip of land that extends into the sea.

- An **island** is an area of land surrounded by water on all sides.

- A **gulf** is an area of the sea that is partly surrounded by land. A **bay** is a small gulf.

Relief on the ocean floor

Relief on the ocean floor is as varied as continental relief:

- A **continental shelf** is a large plateau that surrounds a continent, reaching a depth of 200 m. A **continental slope** leads down from the continental shelf into the deeper part of the ocean.

- **Abyssal plains** are vast plateaus at a depth of 3,000-7,000 m. **Mid-ocean ridges** are long mountain ridges that are found on the abyssal plains. Some of the peaks of underwater mountains rise above the ocean's surface and form islands.

- **Ocean trenches** are long, deep cracks in the ocean floor. The deepest ocean trench is Challenger Deep (11,000 m) in the Pacific Ocean.

ACTIVITIES

1 What is the difference between a plain and a plateau, and between an island and a peninsula?

2 What are underwater mountain ridges called?

3 How similar is continental relief to relief on the ocean floor?

4 Investigate the vocabulary used in Spanish to refer to groups of mountains. Is there more than one term?

5 Make five cards. Write the word for one landform on each card, and put the corresponding definition on the other side.

In small groups, read out your definitions to your classmates. Ask them to say which landform it describes. Then show them the other side of the card.

6 Investigate the living beings that inhabit the abyssal plains. What are extremophiles?

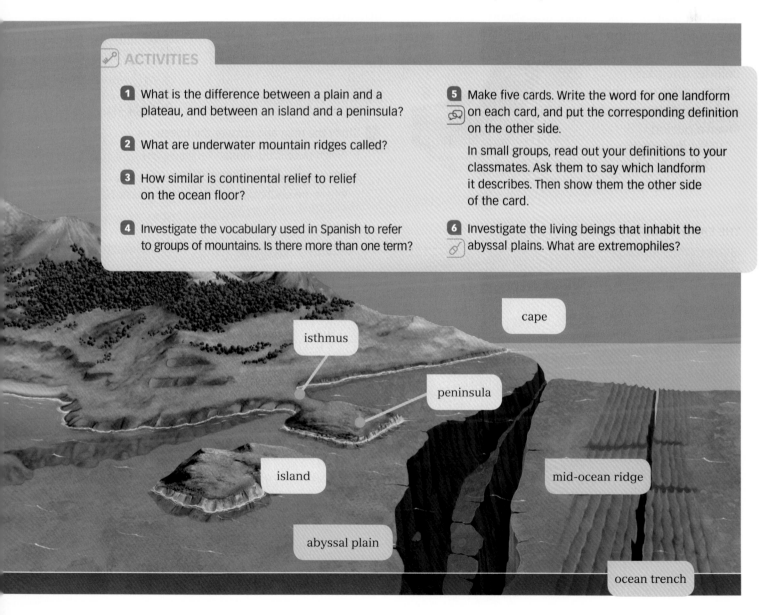

isthmus

cape

peninsula

island

mid-ocean ridge

abyssal plain

ocean trench

Continental drift and tectonic plates

According to the theory of **continental drift**, a single super-continent (Pangaea) broke up to form smaller continents many millions of years ago. Consequently, modern continents look like pieces of a gigantic jigsaw puzzle. For example, if we study the outlines of Africa and South America we can see that they were once joined together.

The Earth's crust is divided into great blocks called **tectonic plates** that move apart or slide against each other.

The Earth's internal forces work continually on these plates, which move at a speed of two to ten centimetres per year. When two plates collide, one plate slides under the other and pushes it upwards. Over a period of time, mountain ranges are formed.

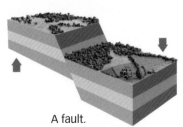

A fault.

Faults and folds

As a result of the movement of the Earth's mantle, the Earth's crust is under continuous pressure near the boundaries of tectonic plates. This causes faults and folds:

- **Folds** are created when the rock is not too rigid to bend.
- The Earth's crust sometimes breaks when the rock is extremely rigid. This causes a **fault**, and land is pushed upwards or downwards.

A fold.

WORK WITH THE MAP

1 Study the map and answer the questions.

  a Which plate is the Iberian Peninsula on?

  b Which plate are the Canary Islands on?

  c Where are earthquakes and volcanoes found?

THE EARTH'S TECTONIC PLATES

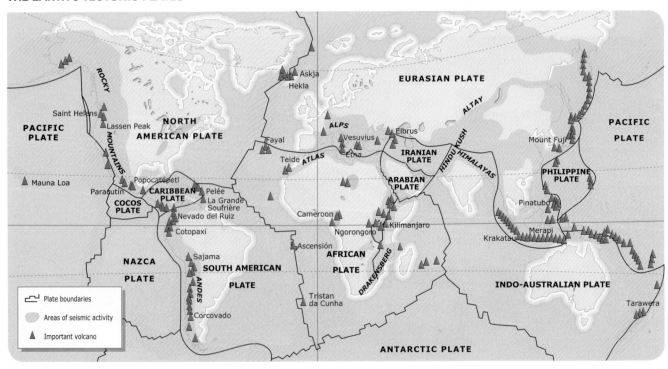

Volcanoes

A **volcano** is a crack in the Earth's crust.

Most volcanoes are found near the boundaries of tectonic plates, where the Earth's crust is weakest.

During an eruption, **magma** (hot liquid rock) rises to the Earth's surface. It goes up the volcano's main channel, or **vent. Lava** (the name for magma on the Earth's surface), ash and gases are all ejected. They are pushed through an opening in the volcano called a **crater**.

Lava and rocks accumulate around the volcano and form a **cone**. Volcanic eruptions under the sea may form islands, like the Canary Islands.

Earthquakes

Earthquakes are violent movements of the Earth's crust. They usually occur along the boundaries of tectonic plates, where the plates slide against each other.

During an earthquake, energy is released in **seismic waves** from a point under the Earth's surface called a **hypocentre** (or focus). The **epicentre** is the closest point on the Earth's surface. This is where the earthquake is at its strongest.

An earthquake on the ocean floor may cause a **tsunami**, which is a series of huge waves.

THE ERUPTION OF A VOLCANO

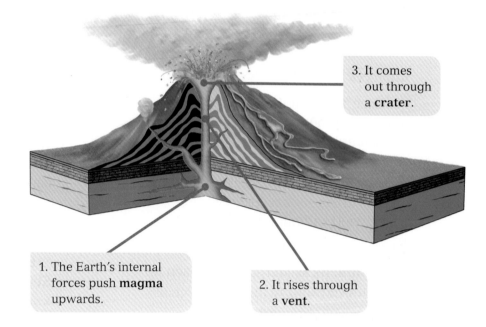

3. It comes out through a **crater**.

1. The Earth's internal forces push **magma** upwards.

2. It rises through a **vent**.

A tsunami causes enormous damage in coastal areas.

 ACTIVITIES

2 What are tectonic plates?

3 Describe a volcanic eruption. Use the following terms:

- crater
- magma
- cone
- lava
- vent

4 What are the main consequences of earthquakes and volcanic eruptions for the people who live in the area? Make notes on your own ideas, and then look for information in encyclopedias or on internet.

5 Look on internet for information about the tsunami which took place in Japan on 11 March 2011.

- What caused it?
- Which regions did it affect?
- What were the consequences?

6 Find out about the San Andreas Fault:

- Where is it?
- Has it caused any earthquakes?
- What are the future consequences of its movement?

How does relief change?

Changes in relief

We have seen that the Earth's relief is basically formed by its **internal forces**. For example, the movement of tectonic plates causes the formation of mountain ranges.

But relief is also shaped by **external forces** on the Earth's surface: temperature, water, wind and human action.

There are three processes:

- **Erosion**: rocks and soil are broken up and moved around by external agents.

- **Transportation**: the eroded material is transported by agents like water and wind.

- **Deposition**: the material is deposited in areas where **sediments** accumulate.

Water

Water plays an extremely important role in erosion, transportation and deposition:

- **Rivers** erode materials in their steep upper slopes, where they create river valleys and canyons. Then rivers transport the eroded materials along their middle course. They deposit **sediment**, which accumulates in low areas. For example, deltas are triangular deposits of sediment near river mouths.

- **Seas** and **oceans**: waves and currents wear away the coast and create cliffs. Sea water transports eroded material and deposits it on the coast, where it forms beaches.

- **Rain water** and **groundwater** dissolve rocks like limestone, creating remarkable caves and landscapes.

Torcal de Antequera (Málaga). Rainwater has dissolved the limestone to create this strange, irregular landscape.

The Grand Canyon (USA). This canyon was formed by the Colorado River. It is 446 km long, reaches a width of 29 km, and is over 1.5 km deep.

Étretat (France). Ocean waves and currents pull rocks away from the coast, and steep cliffs are formed.

Wind

The **wind** transports particles of sand and soil and deposits them in a different place. This explains the formation of sand dunes.

Temperature

There is a great difference between daytime and night-time **temperatures** in mountains and deserts. Water enters the cracks in rocks and then freezes. As water expands when it freezes, the changes in temperature can break the rocks.

Living things

Living things change relief. For example, rocks and soil are fragmented by tree roots and the tunnels that animals dig.

Human beings influence the landscape greatly through activities like agriculture and mining. We sometimes make the terrain flatter to build roads or housing estates. Today, the Earth's relief has many **man-made** features, such as reservoirs.

White Sands, New Mexico (USA).
Winds form these unusual dunes.

👁 THINK ABOUT IT

Most people in the world live in low areas. Only a small minority live on steep mountainsides.

However, we adapt the natural environment to our needs. For example, we build terraces on mountainsides for agriculture, or build ski stations in the mountains to promote winter tourism. There is a significant impact on the environment when we build a tunnel through mountains, or a port on the coast.

• Think about the region where you live. What do you think it looked like many centuries ago? Which features of its relief have been changed by human intervention?

🔧 ACTIVITIES

1 Explain how relief is modified. What are the main external agents?

2 Do you think more than one external agent can modify relief at the same time? How?

3 Which photos on this double page show relief that was formed by water?

4 Investigate. What are stalactites and stalagmites?

5 Look at the photo of the Grand Canyon. What do you think this landscape looked like when the canyon began to form over 15 million years ago? What was it like 5 million years ago?

6 Investigate human activities that influence relief. Decide which activities are beneficial, and which ones are harmful to the environment.

Summarize your conclusions in a table with two columns in your notebook.

1 Copy and complete the diagram.

```
                            ┌─────────────┐
                            │   RELIEF    │
                            └─────────────┘
        ┌───────────────────────┼───────────────────────┐
   takes the following      is formed by the        is changed by
        forms:                 action of            the action of

                            ┌──────────────┐         ┌──────┐
                            │internal forces│         │ ...... │
                            └──────────────┘         └──────┘
 On continents  On the coast  Under oceans    which cause          such as

  ┌──────┐   ┌──────┐   ┌──────┐    ┌──────┐              ┌──────┐     ┌────────────┐
  │ ...... │   │ ...... │   │ ...... │    │ ...... │—which are—│ ...... │     │ temperature │
  └──────┘   └──────┘   └──────┘    └──────┘              └──────┘     └────────────┘

  ┌──────┐   ┌──────┐   ┌──────┐    ┌──────┐              ┌──────┐     ┌──────┐
  │ ...... │   │ ...... │   │ ...... │    │ ...... │—which are—│ ...... │     │ ...... │
  └──────┘   └──────┘   └──────┘    └──────┘              └──────┘     └──────┘

  ┌──────┐   ┌──────┐   ┌──────┐    ┌──────┐              ┌──────┐     ┌──────┐
  │ ...... │   │ ...... │   │ ...... │    │ ...... │—which are—│ ...... │     │ ...... │
  └──────┘   └──────┘   └──────┘    └──────┘              └──────┘     └──────┘

  ┌──────┐   ┌──────┐   ┌──────┐    ┌──────┐              ┌──────┐     ┌──────┐
  │ ...... │   │ ...... │   │ ...... │    │ ...... │—which are—│ ...... │     │ ...... │
  └──────┘   └──────┘   └──────┘    └──────┘              └──────┘     └──────┘

  ┌──────┐   ┌──────┐   ┌──────┐
  │ ...... │   │ ...... │   │ ...... │
  └──────┘   └──────┘   └──────┘
```

2 Copy and complete the diagram.

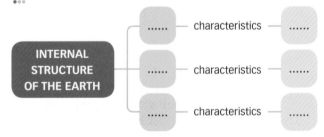

```
                    ┌──────┐ — characteristics — ┌──────┐
                    │ ...... │                    │ ...... │
 ┌──────────────┐   └──────┘                    └──────┘
 │   INTERNAL   │   ┌──────┐ — characteristics — ┌──────┐
 │  STRUCTURE   │   │ ...... │                    │ ...... │
 │ OF THE EARTH │   └──────┘                    └──────┘
 └──────────────┘   ┌──────┐ — characteristics — ┌──────┐
                    │ ...... │                    │ ...... │
                    └──────┘                    └──────┘
```

3 Explain the difference between the following terms.

Listen and check your answers.

- Fault and fold
- Hypocentre and epicentre
- Plain and basin
- Cape and gulf
- Plateau and abyssal plain

4 What types of relief are shown in the photo?.

5 Label a blank world map with the following landforms.

Mountain ranges	Plateaus and plains	Capes and gulfs	Islands
• Himalayas	• Bolivian Altiplano	• Cape of Good Hope	• Greenland
• Andes	• Tibetan Plateau	• Gulf of Guinea	• Madagascar
• Atlas Mountains	• Great European Plain	• Cape Horn	• Australia
• Balkans	• Mato Grosso	• Gulf of Mexico	• British Isles
• Rocky Mountains	• Great Plains	• Bay of Bengal	• Borneo

6 Study relief maps of the continents in an atlas or on the internet. Complete fact files on Europe, Asia, Africa and America. Include one or more examples of each landform.

Landforms	Continent
Mountain ranges	......
Peaks	......
Plains and plateaus	......
Peninsulas	......
Capes	......
Gulfs	......

7 Look for information about the following:
• The Richter Scale
• The Ring of Fire

8 Compare the map of tectonic plates with the relief map of the world. Is there a connection between tectonic plates and the formation of mountain ranges? Why?

9 Does the water of a river cause more erosion in some places than in others? Why does this happen?

10 What is the scale of the map of world relief in this unit? Is it a large scale map or a small scale map?

NATURAL HAZARDS: Earthquakes

Scientists around the world try to predict earthquakes. They monitor the movement of the Earth's tectonic plates all the time. But they cannot say exactly when an earthquake will occur.

What do I do if there's an earthquake?

• **Inside a building:** keep away from walls and windows; take shelter under a desk or table; do not take the lift; turn off the gas, water and electricity after the earthquake.

• **Outside:** keep away from electric wires and the walls of buildings; cover your head for protection against falling objects.

• **On the coast:** go to high ground. Do not stay too near the sea in case there are tidal waves.

In regions where earthquakes are frequent, buildings have seismic shock absorbers.

11 Which parts of Spain have most seismic activity? Investigate on internet.

12 Prepare a table with two columns under the headings *Do* and *Don't*. Write recommendations about how people should behave during an earthquake. Include your own suggestions: *Look for…, Don't panic!*

TECHNICAL SKILLS. **Read a topographic profile**

A **topographic profile** is a representation of the relief of a region. It shows the different altitudes found on a topographic map. It is like viewing a region from the side if we could cut a slice through the surface of the Earth.

Look at this topographic profile. It shows the route that the cyclists took during the Tour of Spain in 2011.

The **vertical axis** shows altitude.

The types of **relief** are identified.

The **map** shows the location of the topographic profile.

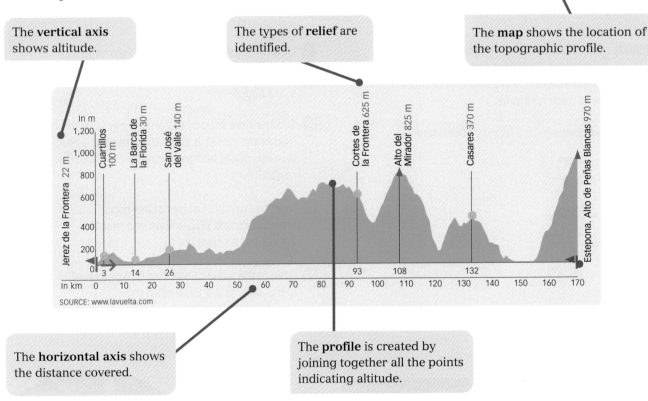

SOURCE: www.lavuelta.com

The **horizontal axis** shows the distance covered.

The **profile** is created by joining together all the points indicating altitude.

We can get information from a topographic profile in several ways:

- **Establish the orientation.**
  - Check the orientation on the map.
- **Identify the places.**
  - Find towns and cities.
  - Look for landforms like mountains, valleys and rivers.
  - Check their altitude.
- **Describe the profile.**
  - Where does the profile start and finish?
  - What distance is shown?
  - What are the altitudes?
  - What is the relief like?

1 Establish the location.
   a Which region is shown?
   b What distance will the cyclists cover? (Look at the horizontal axis.)

2 Identify the places.
   a Does the race go through any towns or villages?
   b Which mountains does it cross? Which is the highest?
   c Is this a flat or mountainous stage?
   d What do the symbols on the diagram represent?

3 It is the day before this stage of the race is held. Write a short news item about tomorrow's race using the future tense: *Tomorrow, the cyclists will... Next, they will...*

Mention:
   - The distance.
   - The names of places.
   - The difficulty of the stage.

THINK LIKE A GEOGRAPHER. **Compare relief and population maps**

Before you study the maps, discuss with a partner:

• Where is China? What are its frontiers?

• What do you know about the country? (Size, population, economy…)

THE RELIEF OF CHINA

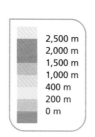

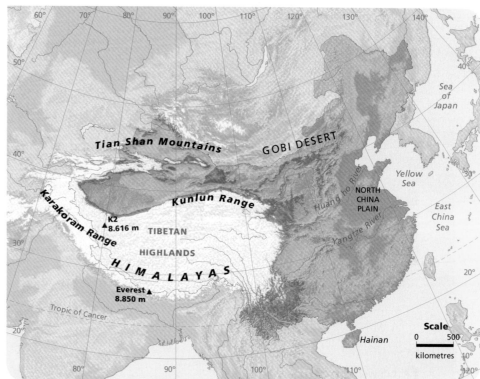

POPULATION DENSITY IN CHINA

1 Where are most of the plains in China? Where are the most mountainous regions?

2 How high are the Himalayas?

3 What does orange represent on the map of population density? What does yellow represent?

4 Where are the least densely populated parts of the country? Are they on the plains or in mountainous regions?

5 Explain why most of China's population is in the south and east of the country.

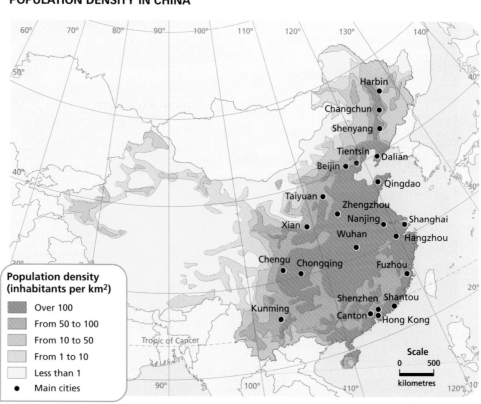

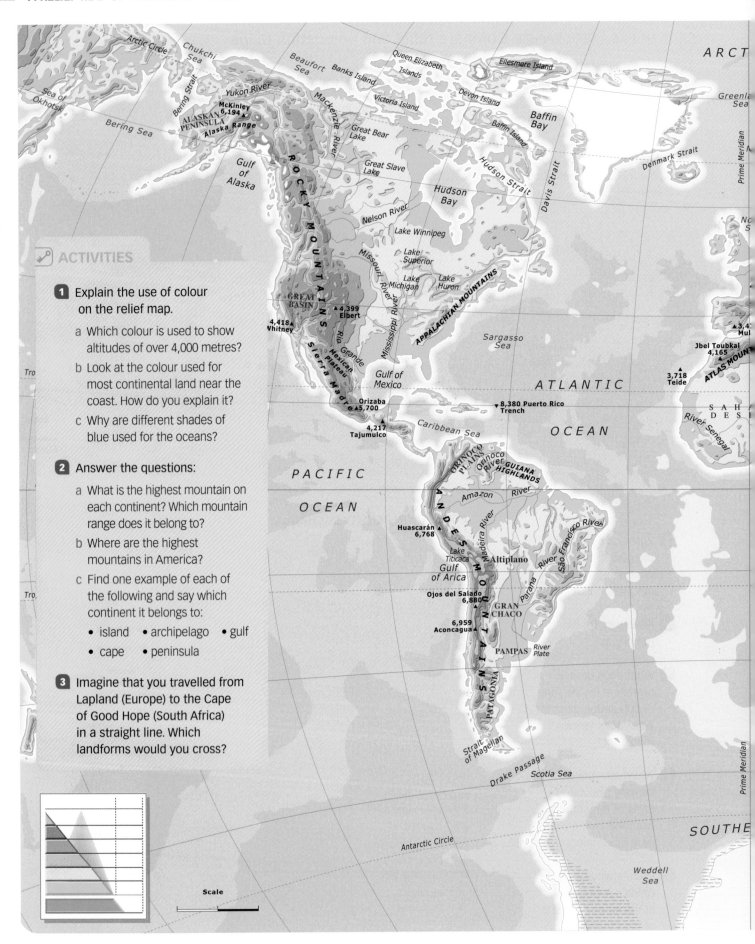

ACTIVITIES

1 Explain the use of colour on the relief map.

a Which colour is used to show altitudes of over 4,000 metres?

b Look at the colour used for most continental land near the coast. How do you explain it?

c Why are different shades of blue used for the oceans?

2 Answer the questions:

a What is the highest mountain on each continent? Which mountain range does it belong to?

b Where are the highest mountains in America?

c Find one example of each of the following and say which continent it belongs to:

- island
- archipelago
- gulf
- cape
- peninsula

3 Imagine that you travelled from Lapland (Europe) to the Cape of Good Hope (South Africa) in a straight line. Which landforms would you cross?

Scale

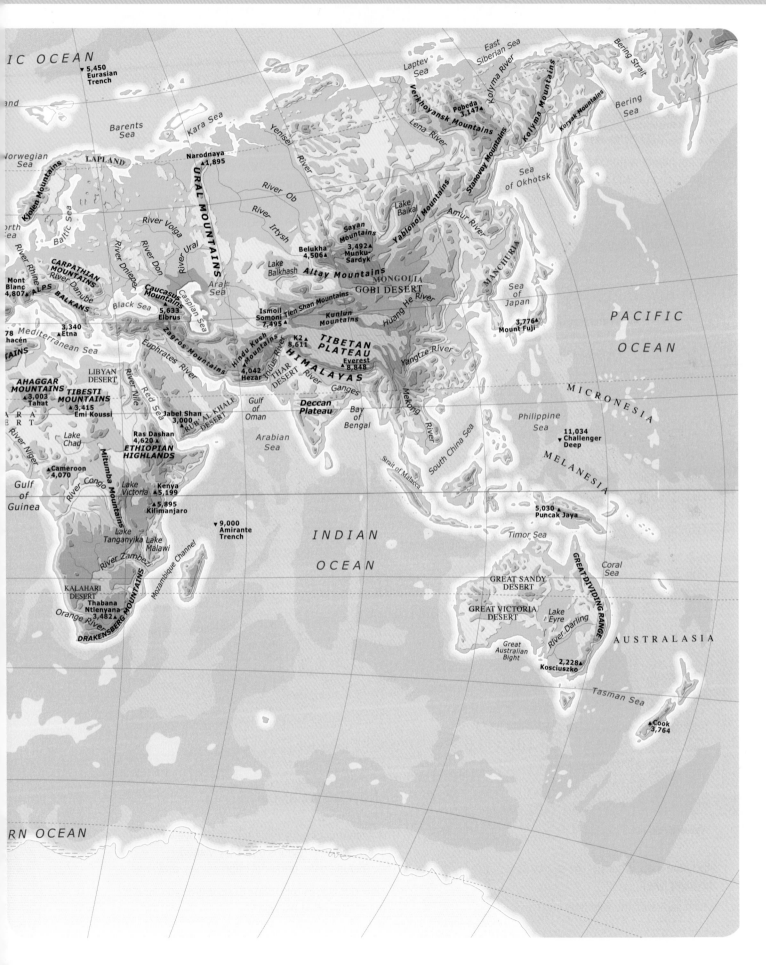

IC OCEAN

▼ 5,450
Eurasian
Trench

Norwegian
Sea

Barents
Sea

Kara Sea

Laptev
Sea

East
Siberian Sea

Kolyma River

Bering Strait

LAPLAND

Kjølen Mountains

Narodnaya
▲ 1,895

Yenisei River

Verkhoyansk Mountains

Lena River

Pobeda
3,147 ▲

Kolyma Mountains

Koryak Mountains

Bering
Sea

River Ob

River Volga

River Irtysh

Lake
Baikal

Stanovoy Mountains

Yablonoi Mountains

Amur River

Sea
of Okhotsk

North
Sea

Baltic Sea

River Ural

River Don

River Dnieper

URAL MOUNTAINS

Aral
Sea

Lake
Balkhash

Belukha
4,506 ▲

Sayan
Mountains

3,492 ▲
Munku-
Sardyk

Altay Mountains

MONGOLIA

MANCHURIA

Sea
of
Japan

CARPATHIAN
MOUNTAINS

River Danube

Mont
Blanc
4,807 ▲

ALPS

BALKANS

Caucasus
Mountains

Caspian Sea

Black Sea

Ismoil
Somoni
7,495 ▲

5,633
Elbrus

Tien Shan Mountains

Kunlun
Mountains

GOBI DESERT

Huang He River

3,776 ▲
Mount Fuji

PACIFIC

OCEAN

78

Mediterranean Sea

hacén

3,340
▲ Etna

AINS

Zagros Mountains

Euphrates River

Hindu Kush
Mountains

4,042
Hezar

K2
8,611 ▲

Indus River

TIBETAN
PLATEAU

Everest
8,848 ▲

Yangtze River

HIMALAYAS

MICRONESIA

AHAGGAR
MOUNTAINS

▲ 3,003
Tahat

TIBESTI
MOUNTAINS

▲ 3,415
Emi Koussi

LIBYAN
DESERT

River Nile

Red Sea

Jabel Shan
3,000

RUB' AL-KHALI DESERT

Gulf
of
Oman

THAR
DESERT

Ganges River

Deccan
Plateau

Bay
of
Bengal

Mekong River

Philippine
Sea

11,034
Challenger
Deep

MELANESIA

River Niger

Lake
Chad

Ras Dashan
4,620 ▲

ETHIOPIAN
HIGHLANDS

Arabian
Sea

South China Sea

Cameroon
▲ 4,070

Gulf
of
Guinea

Mitumba Mountains

River Congo

Lake
Victoria

Kenya
▲ 5,199

▲ 5,895
Kilimanjaro

Strait of Malacca

5,030 ▲
Puncak Jaya

INDIAN

Amirante
Trench
▼ 9,000

Lake
Tanganyika

Lake
Malawi

OCEAN

Timor Sea

GREAT SANDY
DESERT

Coral
Sea

GREAT DIVIDING RANGE

River Zambezi

Mozambique Channel

KALAHARI
DESERT

Thabana
Ntlenyana
▲ 3,482

DRAKENSBERG MOUNTAINS

Orange River

GREAT VICTORIA
DESERT

Lake
Eyre

River Darling

AUSTRALASIA

Great
Australian
Bight

2,228 ▲
Kosciuszko

Tasman Sea

RN OCEAN

▲ Cook
3,764

FIND OUT ABOUT:

- Where water is found
- Continental water: rivers, lakes, groundwater and glaciers
- The course and flow of a river
- Oceans and seas
- The importance of water in our lives

KNOW HOW TO:

- Analyse a map of the world's oceans and seas
- Discuss the problem of water pollution

The sources of the Nile

In the 19th century, many parts of inland Africa were still unexplored. In 1858, and again in 1862, the explorer John Hanning Speke reached the lake that he called Lake Victoria. He realised that he had discovered the main source of the River Nile.

John Hanning Speke

I looked proudly on the flowing water because it confirmed my idea – that the Nile was fed by the abundant water of the great mountains of East Africa.

THE SOURCES
OF THE NILE

HOW DO WE KNOW?

The accounts of early explorers and travellers tell us about the regions that they visited. They include data, personal impressions, drawings…

- How detailed is this map? Does it give you an idea of what the Nile was like?

? WORK WITH THE IMAGE

- Study the map. Where is the source of the River Nile?
- Which sea does the Nile flow into?

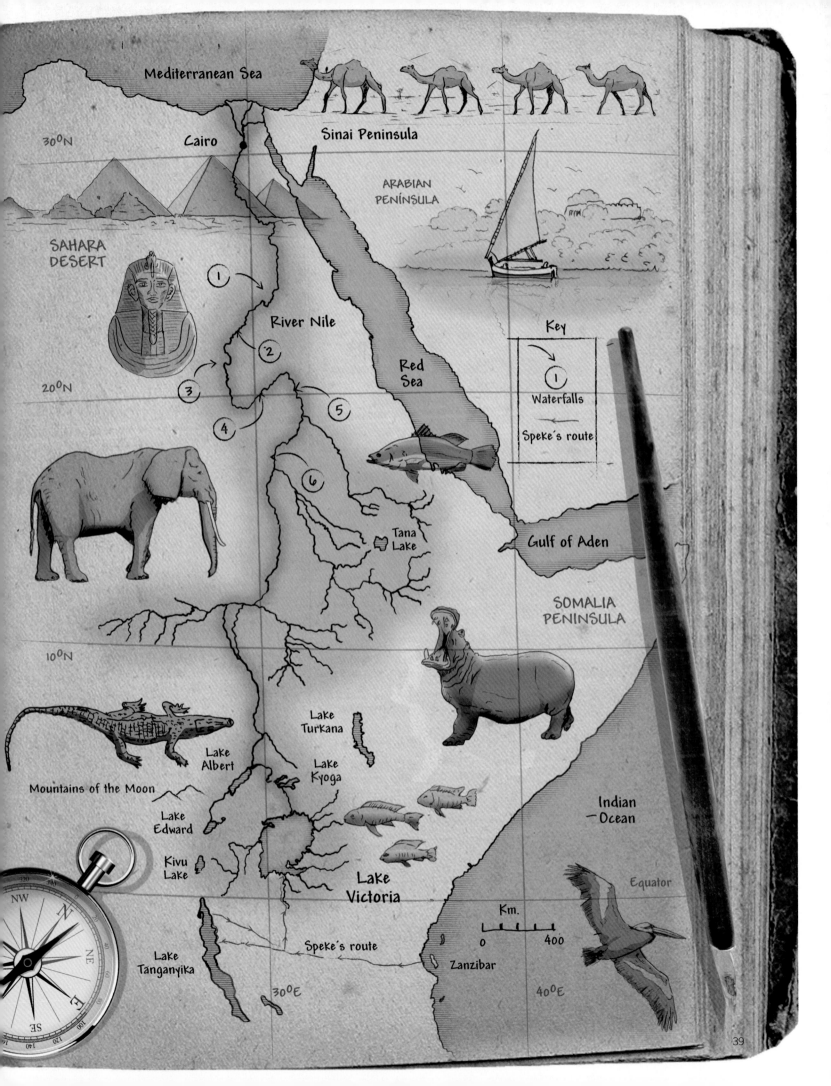

Mediterranean Sea

Sinai Peninsula

Cairo

ARABIAN
PENÍNSULA

30°N

SAHARA
DESERT

①

River Nile

②

③

④

⑤

⑥

20°N

Red
Sea

Key

①
Waterfalls

← Speke's route

Tana
Lake

Gulf of Aden

SOMALIA
PENINSULA

10°N

Lake Turkana

Lake
Albert

Lake
Kyoga

Mountains of the Moon

Lake
Edward

Indian
Ocean

Kivu
Lake

Lake
Victoria

Equator

Km.

0   400

NW

N

NE

Speke's route

Zanzibar

Lake
Tanganyika

SE

30°E

40°E

39

The water cycle

About 71% of the Earth's surface is covered by water. That is why the Earth is sometimes called the "blue planet".

The amount of water on Earth is always the same. But water changes **state**. At different times, it may be found as a **liquid**, a **solid** or a **gas** (water vapour).

In its different states, water moves continually between the oceans, the atmosphere and the Earth. This process is called the **water cycle**.

THE WATER CYCLE

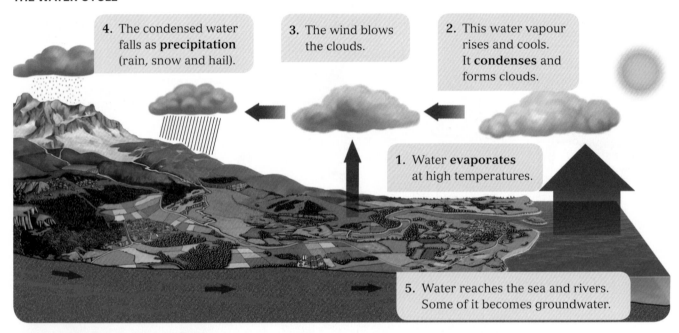

4. The condensed water falls as **precipitation** (rain, snow and hail).

3. The wind blows the clouds.

2. This water vapour rises and cools. It **condenses** and forms clouds.

1. Water **evaporates** at high temperatures.

5. Water reaches the sea and rivers. Some of it becomes groundwater.

WORK WITH THE DIAGRAM

1. Study the diagram of the water cycle. What do the following terms mean?

- evaporation
- condensation
- precipitation

2. What are the different types of precipitation?

3. Discuss the diagram with a partner. Describe the process of the water cycle to each other.

Seawater and continental waters

Seawater forms 97% of the water on Earth, and is found in oceans and seas. It has a high level of **salinity** (the amount of salt dissolved in water).

Continental water is found in rivers, lakes and the ice and snow in glaciers. It is also found beneath the Earth's surface as **groundwater**. It is fresh water, which has a lower level of salinity than saltwater. Less than 3% of the Earth's water is fresh water, and only a small proportion of it can be used for human consumption.

👁 THINK ABOUT IT

Fresh water is found in many places on Earth. Why can't we use it all for drinking water?

Rivers

A **river** is a continuously moving body of water that flows into an ocean, a sea or another river. It is formed by precipitation, or melting ice and snow.

The river flows all the way from its **source** to the **river mouth**. A river that flows into another river (and not the sea) is called a **tributary**.

The area occupied by the main river and its tributaries is known as a **river basin**.

THE WORLD'S MOST IMPORTANT RIVERS

WORK WITH THE MAP

4 Study the map and answer the questions:

a Find the following rivers on the map: Colorado, Niger, Paraguay, Rhine, Indus and Darling.

b Which continents do they flow through?

ACTIVITIES

5 Look for information on the Ganges River.

Prepare a fact file with information on its sources, river mouth, length and tributaries.

The **Mississippi** is the river with the highest flow in North America. Its tributaries include large rivers like the Ohio and the Arkansas. Its river basin has more than 25,000 km² of navigable water.

The **Danube** is the second longest river in Europe. It is 2,880 km long, and most of it is navigable. Its source is in the Black Forest in Germany.

The **Yangtze** is the longest river in Asia (over 6,300 km). It passes through some spectacular landscapes, like the famous Three Gorges.

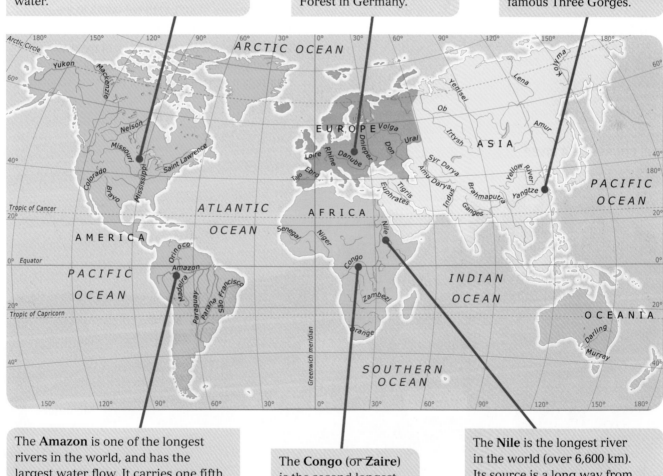

The **Amazon** is one of the longest rivers in the world, and has the largest water flow. It carries one fifth of all the fresh water flowing into the oceans. It lowers the salinity and changes the colour of the Atlantic Ocean up to 200 km from the coast.

The **Congo** (or Zaire) is the second longest river in Africa. In some areas, it is 16 km wide.

The **Nile** is the longest river in the world (over 6,600 km). Its source is a long way from the coast. There is an enormous delta where it flows into the Mediterranean Sea.

2

The course and flow of a river

The course of a river

There are three stages in the **course** of a river:

- The **upper course** is near the **source** of a river. Most rivers begin in mountainous areas, where the water flows rapidly down steep slopes. The river causes erosion by removing and transporting rocks, and forms narrow mountain valleys.

- The **middle course** is flatter. The water flows more slowly, and transports material such as earth and stones. It creates bends called **meanders**.

- The **lower course** is where abundant water flows, especially if the river is joined by tributaries. The river flows slowly and deposits material. It reaches the **river mouth**.

In its lower course, a river shapes the landscape in different ways:

- It spreads mud and other material across a wide, flat area. A fertile **alluvial plain** is formed.

- An **estuary** forms at the river mouth, where the river flows into the sea. The river sometimes deposits the sediment (sand and stones) in a triangular area near the river mouth, called a **delta**.

> ### 👁 THINK ABOUT IT
>
> When we discuss the direction of a river, we look towards the river mouth, with our backs to the source. The right bank of the river is then on our right.
>
> - Which places are on the left bank of the river nearest your school? Look on a map for a river in your region if there isn't a river near your school.

THE COURSE OF A RIVER

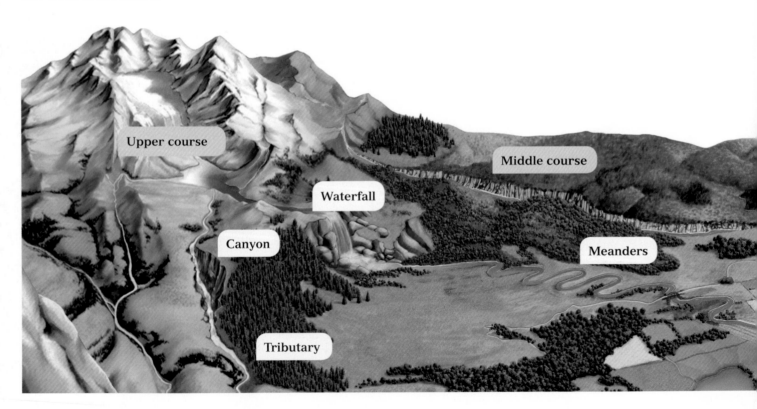

Upper course

Middle course

Waterfall

Canyon

Meanders

Tributary

The flow of a river

The **flow** of a river is the amount of water that it carries. This varies at different times of the year.

- Rivers fed by **melting ice** and **snow** have a higher flow in the spring.
- Rivers fed by high **precipitation** have an abundant flow in the rainy season.
- Some rivers in the Mediterranean or desert regions are dry for most of the year. Water only flows in these rivers when it rains.

A river has a **regular water flow** when approximately the same amount of water flows throughout the year. An **irregular water flow** is when the amount of water varies greatly from one season to another.

The long profile of a river

A **long profile** is a kind of graph that gives us a lot of information about a river: its length, the places it flows past, and its altitude in a particular region.

ACTIVITIES

1 Explain the difference between the upper course, middle course and lower course of a river.

2 Think about all the ways that human beings use rivers. Compare your ideas with your classmates.

WORK WITH THE MAP

3 Study the long profile of the River Nile and answer the questions.

a Where is the source of the river? What altitude is it at?

b How long is the river?

c Which places does it go past?

d Which sea does it flow into?

THE LONG PROFILE OF THE RIVER NILE

Places are indicated by a **point**.

The **blue line** shows the river.

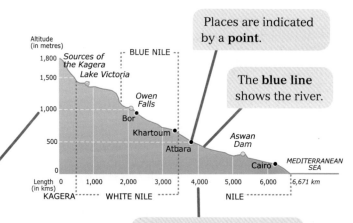

The **vertical axis** shows the altitude from the source to the river mouth.

The **horizontal axis** shows the length of the river.

Lower course

Alluvial plain

Delta

Estuary

Lakes

Lakes are permanent masses of water that have accumulated in inland basins. Most lakes contain fresh water. A lake that contains saltwater is called an **inland sea**.

The water in lakes comes from various sources:

- **Precipitation**. The volume of water varies greatly if the region has both a rainy season and a dry season.

- **Rivers**, **groundwater** and **melting ice** from glaciers.

WORK WITH THE MAP

1 Which continents are the following lakes found on? Michigan, Maracaibo, Tanganyika, Ladoga, Aral Sea, Constance.

THE WORLD'S BIGGEST LAKES

The **Great Lakes** (Lakes Ontario, Erie, Huron, Michigan and Superior) originate in glaciers. Lake Superior is the largest fresh water lake in the world.

The **Caspian Sea** is the largest lake in the world. It contains saltwater, and is 28 m below sea level.

Lake Baikal is the deepest lake in the world. There are several islands on the lake.

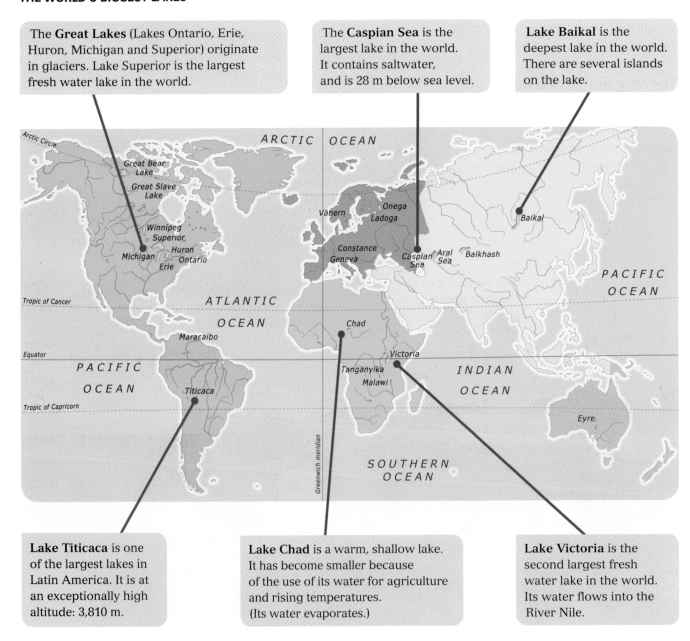

Lake **Titicaca** is one of the largest lakes in Latin America. It is at an exceptionally high altitude: 3,810 m.

Lake Chad is a warm, shallow lake. It has become smaller because of the use of its water for agriculture and rising temperatures. (Its water evaporates.)

Lake Victoria is the second largest fresh water lake in the world. Its water flows into the River Nile.

Groundwater

Groundwater is water that is stored beneath the Earth's surface. It makes up nearly a quarter of the Earth's fresh water.

Most groundwater comes from precipitation. After rainfall, water filters through the soil. If there is a layer of impermeable rock (like granite), the water cannot go any further. It then forms a large store of underground water called an **aquifer**.

Groundwater is a very valuable resource. It can be brought to the surface with wells, and used for agriculture in dry regions. However, an aquifer should never be overexploited because it can take centuries to fill up again.

AN AQUIFER

Aquifer

Well

Impermeable rock

Glaciers

A GLACIER

The **ice caps** and **glaciers** hold most of the Earth's fresh water. **Glaciers** are masses of ice created by the accumulation of snow. They are found near the poles and on high mountain peaks.

Some coastal glaciers break up when ice melts in the summer. They form **icebergs**, which are masses of floating ice.

Today, glaciers cover over 10 % of the Earth's surface.

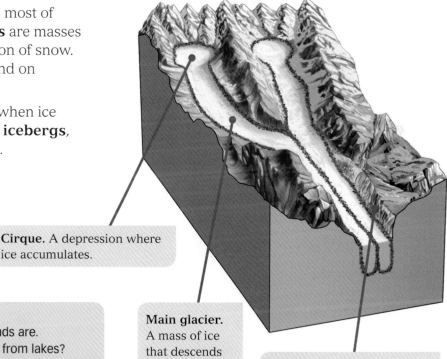

Cirque. A depression where ice accumulates.

Main glacier. A mass of ice that descends the mountain.

Moraine. Deposits of rocks.

ACTIVITIES

2 Find out what marshes and ponds are. In what ways are they different from lakes?

3 Can all the water in lakes, groundwater and glaciers be used as drinking water?

4 Investigate on internet the proportion of an iceberg that is underwater. Use a computer program to represent it in a diagram.

5 Discuss how we should use groundwater with your classmates. Suggest alternative sources of drinking water.

◉ THINK ABOUT IT

The ice caps store huge amounts of water. But they are melting because of global warming. What consequences will this have for the future of the population living in coastal areas? Discuss your ideas with your classmates.

Oceans and seas

Oceans and seas hold nearly all the world's liquid water.

- **Oceans** are huge masses of water that surround the continents, and separate them from each other.

- **Seas** are smaller than oceans, and are partly enclosed by land.

There is salt in all oceans and seas, but they do not all have the same **salinity**. High temperatures make water evaporate rapidly from warm, closed seas. Consequently, they have a higher salt content than cold, open seas.

ACTIVITIES

1 Which has a higher level of salinity, the Red Sea or the Baltic Sea? Why?

WORK WITH THE MAP

2 Study the map and make notes:

a Identify the world's oceans. Which continents do they border?

b Find one sea on each continent.

c Test your partner: *Which continents border the (Indian Ocean)? Is the (North Sea) in Asia?*

THE EARTH'S OCEANS AND MOST IMPORTANT SEAS

DID YOU KNOW?

Bathymetric charts

These maps show the depth of oceans and seas.

The are similar to relief maps.

Light blue shows shallower water.

Dark blue shows deeper water

| 0 m |
| 200 m |
| 2,000 m |
| 4,000 m |
| 6,000 m |

Currents, tides and waves

In oceans and seas, water is in continual movement because of currents, tides and waves:

- **Ocean currents** are large masses of water that cross the oceans in a similar way to rivers.

  - A **warm current** has a higher temperature than the water around it.

  - A **cold current** is colder than the surrounding water.

  Marine currents have great influence on the **climate** of coastal regions.

- **Tides** are the daily rise and fall of the water level in oceans and seas. They are caused by the gravitational forces of the Moon and the Sun. It is **high tide** when the water level rises and **low tide** when it falls.

- **Waves** are movements of the surface of the water caused by the wind. Although waves appear to move forward, they actually go up and down in a circular motion. Their shape changes when they come into contact with the sea bed.

The importance of oceans and seas

Oceans and seas are very important to human beings:

- They provide us with **food**.

- They provide us with **raw materials** and **energy**. Large quantities of gas and oil are found beneath the ocean floor.

- They attract **tourism** to coastal areas, where they create jobs.

- They are used for **transport**. They transport both people and goods.

ACTIVITIES

3 What are the three types of movement of water in oceans and seas? Explain how they occur.

4 Look on internet for information about one ocean or sea. Find out the ways in which it is important to the people who live near it.

THE MOVEMENT OF WAVES

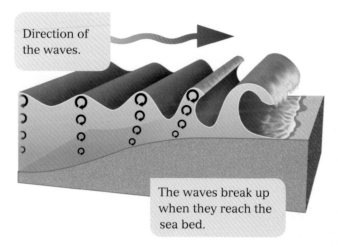

Direction of the waves.

The waves break up when they reach the sea bed.

A

B

High tide (A) and low tide (B). The tide takes over six hours to rise and the same length of time to fall.

1 Copy and complete the diagram.

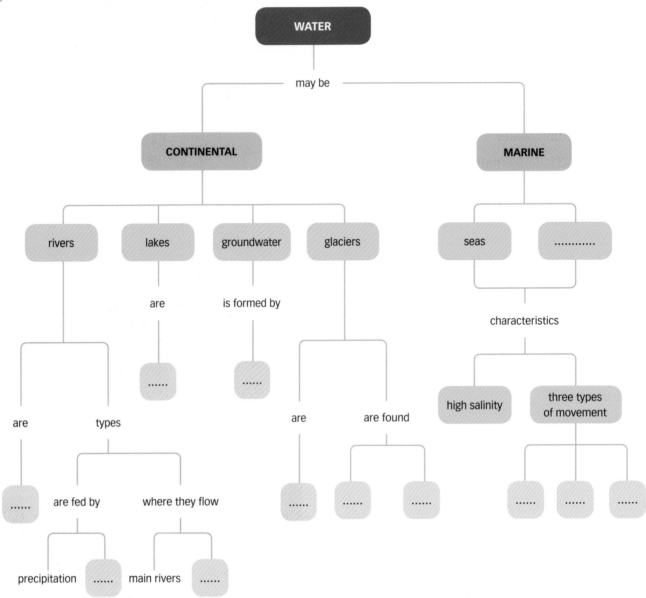

2 Are the following sentences true or false? Correct the false ones in your notebook. Listen to the recording and check your answers.

a Groundwater is saltwater that is found beneath the Earth's surface.

b A river basin is the area occupied by a river and its tributaries.

c A river flows slowly in its upper course, where it forms alluvial plains.

d Warm, closed seas have higher salinity than cold, open seas.

3 Copy and complete the table.

COURSE OF A RIVER		
Parts	**Where?**	**Description**
Upper	......	......
Middle	......	......
Lower	......	......

In which course are the following features found?
- waterfall
- delta
- meander
- alluvial plain

48

4 Label a blank map of the world with the following seas and rivers.

Seas	Rivers	
• Caribbean	• Amazon	• Rhine
• Mediterranean	• Yangtze	• Volga
• Coral Sea	• Mississippi	• Indus
• North Sea	• Danube	• Nile
• Arabian Sea	• Congo	• Orinoco

5 Explain the difference between the following terms:

- Delta and estuary
- Lake and inland sea
- Current and tide
- Ocean and sea
- Glacier and iceberg

6 Look for information about the following rivers on internet or in encyclopaedias. Prepare a fact file on each river:

- Amazon (America)
- Congo (Africa)
- Danube (Europe)
- Yangtze (Asia)

Sources:
Tributaries:
Flows into:
Other information:

7 Look at the photos and answer the questions.

- What can you see in the first photo? In which season was it taken?
- Why was the scene so different a few months later?
- Does this water course have a regular or irregular water flow?

WATER POLLUTION

Many kinds of human activity pollute our rivers and seas:

- Industries produce toxic waste, which is deposited in rivers and seas.
- In some regions, urban waste is not purified properly.
- Agricultural pesticides filter down into groundwater.
- Oil tankers collide against rocks, and release oil on our coasts.

8 Look for more information and photos on two of these problems. Are there other types of water pollution?

Prepare a short report in three parts.

A: Causes. Explain why water pollution is such a serious problem in the world.

B: The nature of the problem. Examine two or three specific cases.

C: Consequences. Discuss what we can all do about it.

THINK LIKE A GEOGRAPHER. **Analyse sea currents, climate and population**

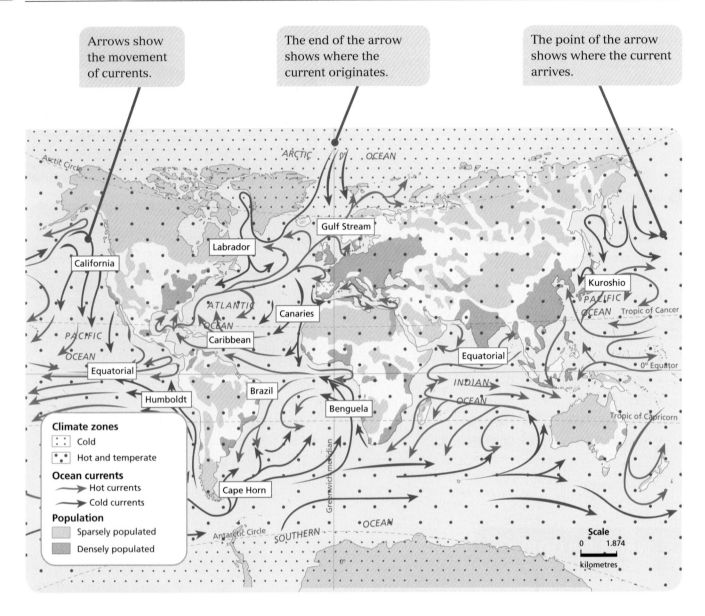

Arrows show the movement of currents.

The end of the arrow shows where the current originates.

The point of the arrow shows where the current arrives.

Climate zones
- ⠿ Cold
- ⠿ Hot and temperate

Ocean currents
- → Hot currents
- → Cold currents

Population
- ⬜ Sparsely populated
- ⬛ Densely populated

Scale
0   1.874
kilometres

1 Analyse the symbols.

a What do the blue and red arrows indicate?

b How is orange used?

c How are warm and temperate climates shown?

d How are cold climates shown?

2 Analyse the map.

a Where are the greatest concentrations of population?

b Are they found in cold climates? Or warm and temperate climates?

c Where do warm currents originate?

d Where do cold currents originate?

3 Answer the following questions:

a Does the place of origin of water affect its temperature?

b Europe is one of the most densely populated regions in the world. Which currents influence its climate?

c Does the Gulf Stream cause temperatures to rise or fall in the areas it reaches?

d What is the influence of the Canaries Current?

e Look at south-east Asia. Is there a connection between the following?
- ocean currents
- population density
- climate

THINK ABOUT THE ENVIRONMENT. **The Three Gorges Dam**

Before you begin: What did you learn about China in earlier units?
What information does the photo on this page give us?

 A huge hydroelectric project

The Three Gorges Dam is an enormous hydroelectric dam on the Yangtze River in China. The idea of building a dam was an old one. But finally, construction began in 1994 and the dam was completed in 2012. It was named after the Three Gorges, a famous area of natural beauty on the Yangtze River.

According to the Chinese government, the Three Gorges Dam is an exceptional engineering achievement. It is a huge power station that generates enormous amounts of electricity. It regulates the water level in the Yangtze River, and controls flooding. (This is important because great cities like Shanghai are located near the river.) As a result of the dam, large ships can now navigate along the Yangtze River.

However, environmentalists have criticised the project. They argue that it does not control the water level very well. Large quantities of waste are dumped in the water. Moreover, the dam is in an earthquake zone. An earthquake could destroy the dam and cause flooding in a highly populated region.

There have been other problems, too. The natural beauty of the Three Gorges was affected when water levels rose. Archaeological sites were flooded. Human rights campaigners were also concerned about the human cost of the dam. Over a million people who lived in the region were forced to leave their homes.

1 Read the text and answer the questions:

a What is the Three Gorges Dam?

b When was it built?

c How did it get its name?

2 Analyse the situation.

a What does the Chinese government think about the Three Gorges Dam?

b What are the benefits of the dam?

c What problems has it caused?

3 Using internet resources, find out more about the dam.
Look for texts, photos, maps and links to videos.
Think about the extra information that you will look for.
For example:

- Where is the dam?
- How big is it? Are other dams bigger?
- What measures has the government taken?

4 Share your material with your classmates.
Discuss the impact of the project on the environment, economy, culture and society of the region.

4 Climate

How will climate change affect us?

Over the last century, average temperatures on Earth have risen by more than 0.6° C. Global warming has been caused by human activity, such as the burning of oil and coal, deforestation and the use of chemicals in industry. This has caused an increase in harmful gases in the atmosphere.

If temperatures continue to rise, the polar caps and glaciers will melt, and sea levels will rise. Some regions will turn into deserts…

HOW DO WE KNOW?

In recent years, the sea level has risen by several centimetres. Today, satellite technology measures the level of glaciers and seas against other points of reference.

- Can satellite technology measure the amount of water in a lake?
- What will happen if the sea level rises?

? WORK WITH THE IMAGE

- What are the causes of climate change?
- In your opinion, what are its most important consequences?
- What can we do about this problem?

Rising sea levels.

Changes in the natural cycle of plants and animals.

Increase in global temperatures.

Consequences of climate change

Greater risk of flooding.

Desertification and water scarcity.

Melting of the polar ice caps.

Rambla Salada (Murcia). Summer droughts are characteristic of the Mediterranean climate.

The layers of the atmosphere

The **atmosphere** consists of a layer of gases surrounding the Earth up to an altitude of more than 1,000 km. It is composed of **oxygen**, **nitrogen** and other gases. The atmosphere regulates the Earth's temperature. It prevents the Earth from getting too cold at night, and allows heat to circulate from warm to cold regions.

The **troposphere** and **stratosphere** are the two layers of the atmosphere closest to the Earth's surface.

- The **troposphere** is the lowest layer, and is in contact with the Earth's surface. It is composed of air and water vapour. **Precipitation** takes place in the troposphere.

- The **stratosphere** is the layer above the troposphere. It contains the **ozone layer**, which absorbs harmful radiation from the Sun.

Climate and weather

- **Weather** is the state of the atmosphere at a particular time. In many places, this changes from one day to another. For example, we are referring to the weather when we say: 'It is raining in Manchester today, but it is expected to be dry tomorrow'. **Meteorology** is the study of weather conditions.

- **Climate** is the typical state of the atmosphere over a long period of time. For example, we are talking about climate when we say: 'Summers are very warm in Greece'. **Climatology** is the study of the climate.

A WEATHER MAP

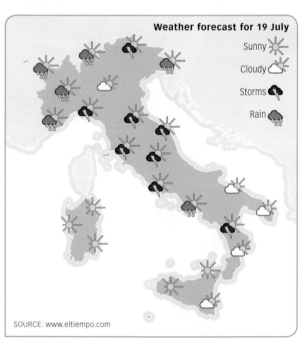

Weather forecast for 19 July

Sunny
Cloudy
Storms
Rain

SOURCE: www.eltiempo.com

🔗 WORK WITH THE MAP

1 Study this weather map, and check the names of cities and regions on a map of Italy. Discuss the weather forecast with a classmate: *It will be sunny in (Palermo). What will the weather be like in (Turin)? There will be storms...*

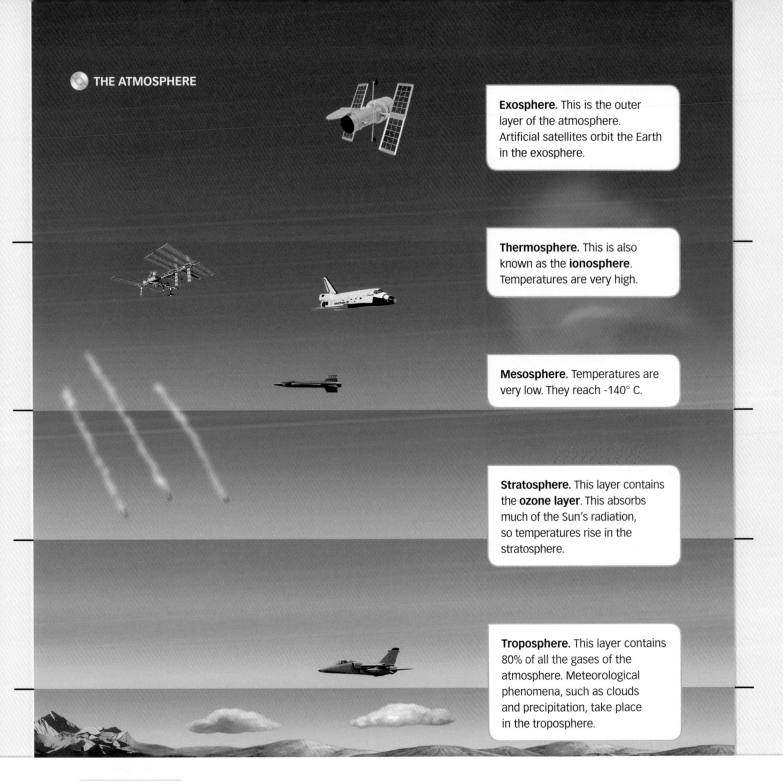

THE ATMOSPHERE

Exosphere. This is the outer layer of the atmosphere. Artificial satellites orbit the Earth in the exosphere.

Thermosphere. This is also known as the **ionosphere**. Temperatures are very high.

Mesosphere. Temperatures are very low. They reach -140° C.

Stratosphere. This layer contains the **ozone layer**. This absorbs much of the Sun's radiation, so temperatures rise in the stratosphere.

Troposphere. This layer contains 80% of all the gases of the atmosphere. Meteorological phenomena, such as clouds and precipitation, take place in the troposphere.

ACTIVITIES

2 What is the atmosphere? Why is it so important?

3 Compare climate and weather.

  a Write three short sentences referring to climate or the weather. For example: *It's raining in (Málaga) today.* In groups, ask your classmates to say whether you are talking about climate or the weather.

  b Then discuss the weather today. Decide if it is typical of the climate in your region.

WORK WITH THE ILLUSTRATION

4 Study the illustration and answer the questions:

  a What are the characteristics of each layer of the atmosphere?

  b Which layer contains the ozone layer?

  c Where do meteorological phenomena take place?

DID YOU KNOW?

Extreme temperatures

Temperatures of over 55° C have been recorded in Libya and Tunisia (Africa) and Death Valley (California, USA).

The coldest temperature ever recorded was in Antarctica: −89° C.

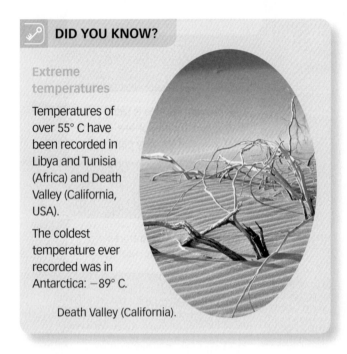

Death Valley (California).

THINK ABOUT IT

When we study the temperature of a place we need the following information:

- **Maximum and minimum temperatures.** The highest and lowest temperatures over a period of time.

- **Temperature variation.** The difference between maximum and minimum temperatures.

- **Average monthly temperature.**

- **Average annual temperature.**

Factors which influence temperature

Temperature is the amount of heat in the atmosphere. It is measured with a thermometer, and expressed in degrees Centigrade (° C). On maps, **isotherms** are the lines that join areas with the same temperature.

Temperatures are not the same everywhere in the world. They vary according to latitude, altitude and distance from the sea:

- **Latitude.** Temperatures are higher near the Equator, where the Sun's rays reach the Earth vertically. They decrease as we move towards the poles.

- **Altitude.** Temperatures are usually higher in low areas. They decrease by an average of 6.4° C for each thousand metres in altitude.

- **Distance from the sea.** The sea makes coastal climates milder. Inland climates are hotter in summer and colder in winter than coastal climates.

ACTIVITIES

1 What is temperature? How is it measured?

2 With a partner think of one place on the Iberian Peninsula, and another on a Spanish island. Which factors affect their temperatures?

THE EARTH'S CLIMATE ZONES

Cold zone
Temperate zone
Hot zone
Temperate zone
Cold zone

AVERAGE ANNUAL TEMPERATURES AROUND THE WORLD

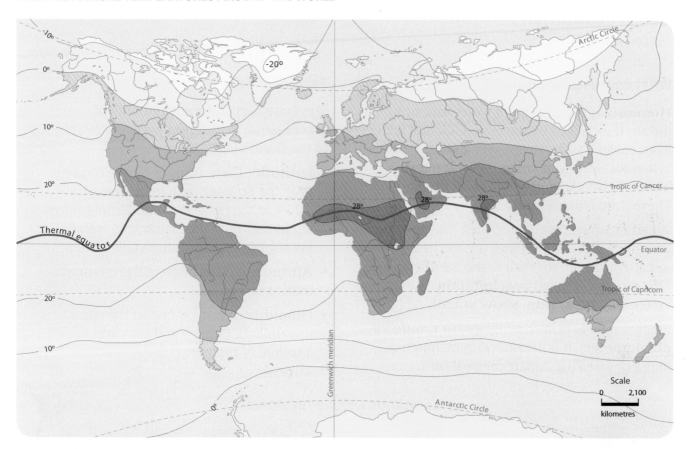

📖 WORK WITH THE MAP

3. Look at the map of Average Annual Temperatures with a partner. Find one region with very high temperatures. Find another region with very low temperatures. How do you explain the differences?

4. What do you think the 'thermal equator' is?

👁 **THINK ABOUT IT**

Find out the weather forecast for tomorrow in the capital of your Autonomous Community.

• Are the temperatures typical of this time of the year?

Climate zones

The Earth is divided into five main climate zones:

• There is a **hot zone** between the Tropic of Cancer and the Tropic of Capricorn. The Sun's rays reach the Earth at a vertical angle all year round so temperatures are always high. There is very little difference between the seasons.

• There are two **temperate zones** between the tropics and the polar circles. The Sun's rays reach the Earth at a greater angle than in the hot zone. Consequently, temperatures are mild and vary with the seasons.

• There are two **cold zones** within the polar circles. The Sun's rays reach the Earth at an oblique angle all year round. Consequently, temperatures are always very low.

🔑 ACTIVITIES

5. Copy and complete the table with information about the main climate zones.

Climate zone	Where?	Temperatures
......	......	......
......	......	......
......	......	......
......	......	......
......	......	......

3

Precipitation

What causes precipitation?

Humidity is the amount of water vapour in the air. It is caused by the evaporation of water from oceans, lakes, rivers, wetlands and plants. When water vapour cools, it **condenses**: it becomes liquid and forms small drops. These drops form **clouds**.

When the drops get colder, their size and weight increase. When they are too heavy to remain in the air, they fall to the Earth's surface. This process is called **precipitation**. Water may fall as **rain**, **snow** or **hail**.

Precipitation is measured by a **rain gauge** (or **pluviometer**). It is expressed in millimetres (mm), or litres per square metre (L/m²).

Factors affecting precipitation

There are very different amounts of precipitation in different parts of the Earth's surface:

- **Latitude**. There is more rain in regions near the Equator than in the temperate zones or the polar regions. Temperatures are higher near the Equator so water evaporates rapidly. It then falls as rain.

- **Altitude**. It rains more in the mountains than in low areas.

- **Humidity**. It rains more on the coast than inland. Oceans and seas are a source of humidity.

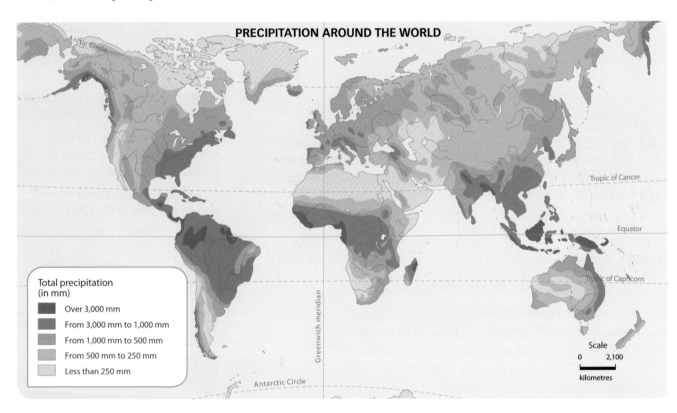

PRECIPITATION AROUND THE WORLD

Total precipitation (in mm)

- Over 3,000 mm
- From 3,000 mm to 1,000 mm
- From 1,000 mm to 500 mm
- From 500 mm to 250 mm
- Less than 250 mm

Scale
0   2,100
kilometres

WORK WITH THE MAP

1 Compare the map of Precipitation Around The World to a political atlas.

a Find three countries where annual precipitation is over 3,000 mm.

b Find three countries where annual precipitation is between 250 and 500 mm.

c What is the wettest part of Spain?

Types of rainfall

Convectional rain is found in hot and temperate climates.

2. Water vapour cools as it rises.

3. As the water vapour cools, it condenses and forms drops. The drops form clouds. Rain falls to the Earth.

1. The Sun heats the ground and water evaporates.

Orographic (relief) rain is found in mountainous regions.

3. Clouds form. It rains on the side of the mountain that the humid air has reached.

2. The air is forced to rise. It cools.

1. Humid air reaches a mountain.

Frontal rain occurs at the **front** (or boundary) between a mass of warm air and a mass of cold air.

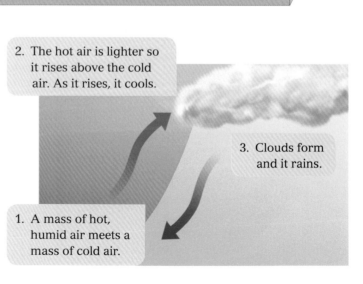

2. The hot air is lighter so it rises above the cold air. As it rises, it cools.

3. Clouds form and it rains.

1. A mass of hot, humid air meets a mass of cold air.

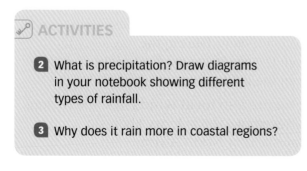

ACTIVITIES

2 What is precipitation? Draw diagrams in your notebook showing different types of rainfall.

3 Why does it rain more in coastal regions?

1 What is atmospheric pressure?

2 Complete the sentences:

a ..... is an area of high pressure.

b ..... is an area of low pressure.

c Hot air weighs ..... than cold air.

d Pressure is ..... in low areas.

3 Look at this photo. Does it show an anticyclone or a depression over northern Spain?

4 Investigate the trade winds. Which direction do they blow in? Is their direction important for navigation? Make notes on your findings.

5 With a partner, discuss what the picture of sea breezes shows.

SEA BREEZES

Atmospheric pressure

Atmospheric pressure is the weight of the air on the Earth's surface. It is measured by a **barometer**, and is expressed in millibars (mb). It varies according to altitude and temperature:

- **Altitude**. Atmospheric pressure is lower in high, mountainous areas.

- **Temperature**. Hot air weighs less than cold air.

Pressure affects atmospheric conditions:

- **Anticyclones** are areas of high pressure. They cause dry, stable weather and clear skies.

- **Depressions** are areas of low pressure. They cause unstable weather, rain and storms.

Wind

Wind is a mass of moving air. It is caused by differences in atmospheric pressure. Air moves from areas of high pressure to areas of low pressure.

Wind speed is measured by an **anemometer**, and is expressed in kilometres per hour (km/h). A **weather vane** shows the direction of the wind.

There are different types of wind:

- **Prevailing winds** always blow in the same direction. For example, **trade winds** blow from the tropics towards the equator.

- **Seasonal winds** change direction according to the season. In Asia, **monsoon** winds blow from the Indian Ocean towards the continent in summer, carrying rain. In winter, they blow from the continent towards the sea.

- Some winds, like **sea breezes**, change direction daily. During the day, they blow from the sea to the land. At night, they blow from the land out to sea again.

- There are also **local winds** in some regions. For example, the hot, dry khamsin wind blows across North Africa.

Weather maps

A **weather map** shows atmospheric pressure at sea level:

- A series of lines called **isobars** connect areas that have the same atmospheric pressure.

- The letter **H** shows a **high pressure area** (or anticyclone). The weather is usually stable and dry.

- The letter **L** shows a **low pressure area** (or depression). There are often storms and rain.

- **Fronts** are shown as continuous lines. (Blue lines are cold fronts, and red lines are warm fronts.) The weather is often unstable.

🔍 WORK WITH THE MAP

6 Study the map and answer the questions:

  a Locate the following on the map:
  - fronts
  - depressions
  - anticyclones

  b What is the weather like in the regions shown on the map?

A WEATHER MAP

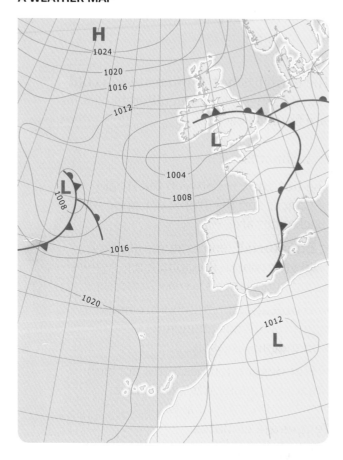

🔑 DID YOU KNOW?

Tropical cyclones and tornadoes

A **tropical cyclone** is a very strong wind that rotates at a speed of up to 300 km per hour. It causes great storms.

Cyclones occur in tropical latitudes. They are also known as **hurricanes**. In Asia, they are called **typhoons**.

A **tornado** is a column of air that spins rapidly. Tornadoes can move considerable distances, and they cause great damage. They are frequent in some parts of the United States.

- Cyclones and tornadoes cause natural disasters. What other natural disasters occur? What consequences do they have for the people who live in a region?

5 The Earth's climates

The Earth has **hot**, **temperate** and **cold** climate zones. However, different climates are found in each zone.

Hot climates

The **hot zone** is between the Tropic of Cancer and the Tropic of Capricorn. Its climates are:

- **Equatorial**: temperatures are high all year round. Precipitation is regular and abundant.

- **Tropical:** temperatures are high. Precipitation is abundant in the rainy season.

- **Hot desert:** temperatures are high and precipitation is very scarce.

Temperate climates

The **temperate zones** are between the tropics and the polar circles. There are four seasons because of the inclination of the Sun's rays:

- **Mediterranean**: summers are hot and winters are mild. Precipitation is irregular and mainly occurs in winter. **Humid sub-tropical** climates have similar temperatures to the Mediterranean climate, but precipitation is greater.

- **Oceanic**: temperatures are mild all year, and precipitation is abundant.

- **Continental**: summers are hot and winters are very cold. Precipitation mainly occurs in the summer.

Cold climates

- **Polar**: temperatures are extremely low near the poles, and precipitation is very scarce, usually in the form of snow.

- **Mountain**: temperatures are low, and precipitation is seasonal.

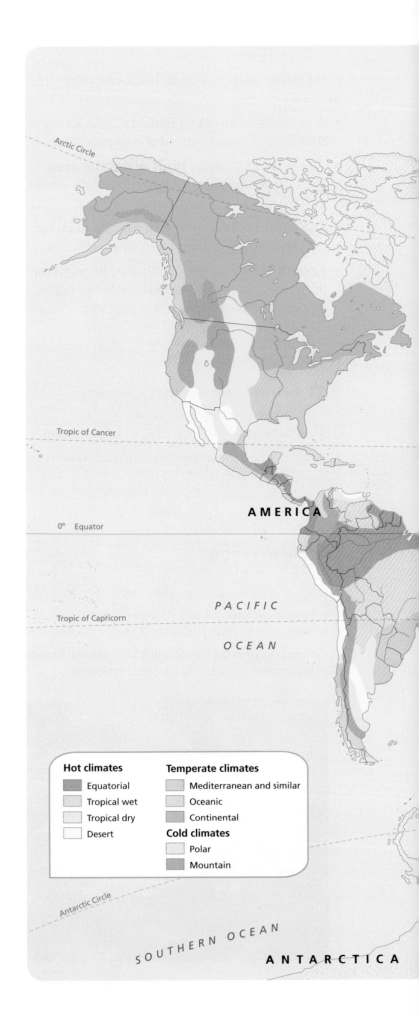

Hot climates
- Equatorial
- Tropical wet
- Tropical dry
- Desert

Temperate climates
- Mediterranean and similar
- Oceanic
- Continental

Cold climates
- Polar
- Mountain

Arctic Circle
Tropic of Cancer
0° Equator
Tropic of Capricorn
Antarctic Circle

AMERICA
PACIFIC
OCEAN
SOUTHERN OCEAN
ANTARCTICA

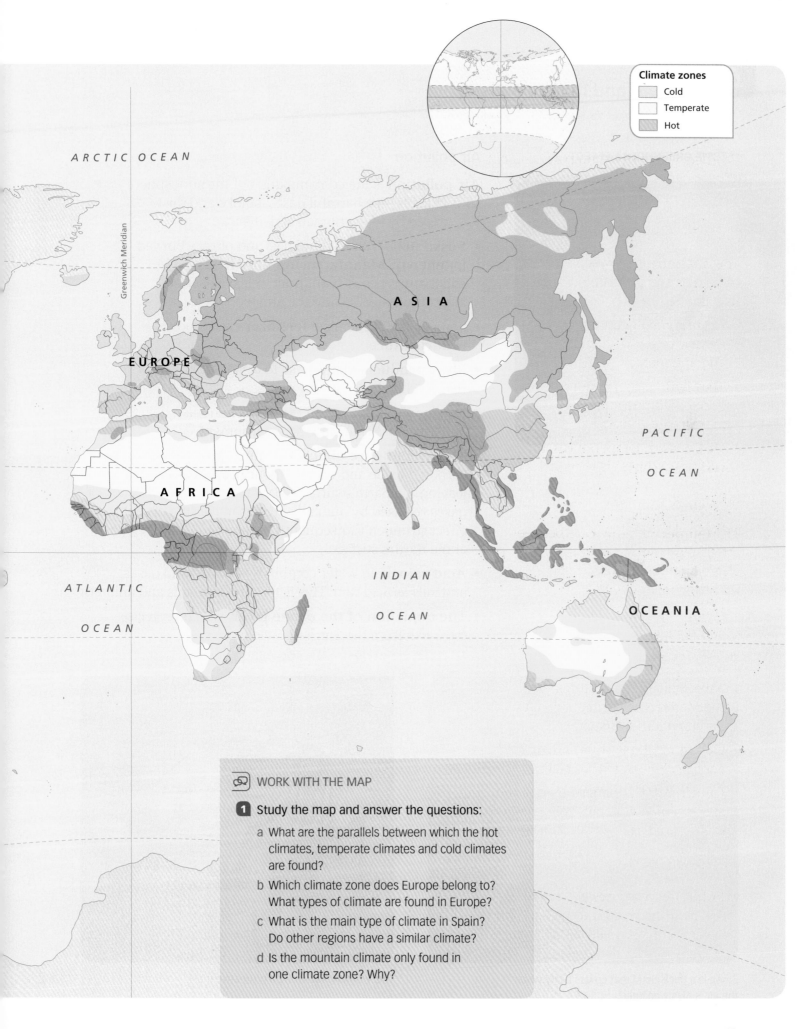

Climate zones

- Cold
- Temperate
- Hot

ARCTIC OCEAN

Greenwich Meridian

ASIA

EUROPE

AFRICA

PACIFIC

OCEAN

INDIAN

OCEAN

ATLANTIC

OCEAN

OCEANIA

WORK WITH THE MAP

1 Study the map and answer the questions:

a What are the parallels between which the hot climates, temperate climates and cold climates are found?

b Which climate zone does Europe belong to? What types of climate are found in Europe?

c What is the main type of climate in Spain? Do other regions have a similar climate?

d Is the mountain climate only found in one climate zone? Why?

THE GREENHOUSE EFFECT

Air pollution

Air pollution is the contamination of the atmosphere by pollutants, like harmful gases, smoke and dust. It is caused by many human activities:

- **Fossil fuels** (coal, natural gas, and oil) are burned for **energy. Manufacturing industries**, and many types of **transport**, release gases like carbon dioxide into the atmosphere.

- Some harmful chemical **fertilizers** are used in **agriculture**.

- Many **products** that we use to clean our houses release chemicals into the air.

Air pollution causes health problems in human beings. But it also causes harm to the environment:

- **The greenhouse effect** is a natural process: a mixture of carbon dioxide and water vapour prevents solar heat from leaving the Earth's surface. However, the concentration of gases released by human activities makes the greenhouse effect stronger. Consequently, temperatures are rising at the Earth's surface.

- **Acid rain**. Rain water combines with harmful gases, and falls as acid rain. This is harmful to plants and animals.

- **The depletion of the ozone layer**, which protects the Earth from the Sun's ultraviolet rays.

Smog is a thick cloud that covers a city when the air is highly polluted.

This woman is wearing a protective mask.

Global warming and climate change

Global warming is the increase of average temperatures on the Earth's surface.
In the 20th century, average temperatures on Earth increased by 0.6 %.

Greenhouse gases are present naturally in the atmosphere. However, the burning of fossil fuels (for example coal) has greatly increased the amount of carbon dioxide in the atmosphere.

Global warming has serious consequences:

- **Climate change**. Climates will become more extreme and less predictable. There will be flooding in some regions, and drought in others. Some regions will become very hot, and others will be very cold.

- The **melting of the polar ice caps**.
  In the last century, the sea level has risen by 15-20 cm. If this continues, some coastal regions will be covered by water.

Scientists say that it is essential to reduce the emission of greenhouse gases. In 1997, the **Kyoto Protocol** was an international treaty to reduce greenhouse gases in the atmosphere. Since then, international negotiations have continued on ways to deal with this problem.

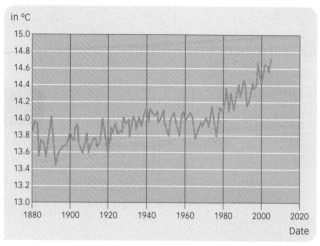

The temperature of the atmosphere.

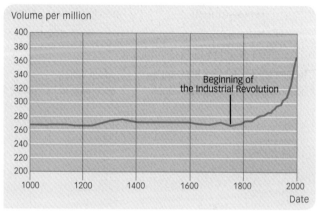

World emissions of carbon dioxide.

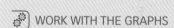

ACTIVITIES

1. Define the following terms, and explain how they are connected:
   - greenhouse effect
   - global warming
   - climate change

2. What do you think your region will be like in the year 2050 if global warming continues?

3. Find out if there have been any recent international negotiations over climate change. What is the attitude of the United States and China?

WORK WITH THE GRAPHS

4. What is the link between the two graphs?

👁 THINK ABOUT IT

How does climate affect our lives?

Some regions are densely populated, while others are sparsely populated. Climate is an important factor influencing human settlement. For example, extreme cold prevents plants from growing because the soil is frozen. Agriculture is difficult in areas where there is little precipitation. Living conditions are not healthy in hot tropical forests. On the other hand, many people live near the coast in temperate zones, where the climate is mild.

People adapt to their environments in many ways. For example, they build houses with the right types of materials to keep out the cold. By using modern technology, they dig deep wells to find water in dry areas.

- In groups, choose one sparsely populated part of the world (for example, a rainforest, desert or very cold region). Find out who lives there, and how they adapt to the conditions. Share your findings with the rest of the class.

1 Copy and complete the diagram.

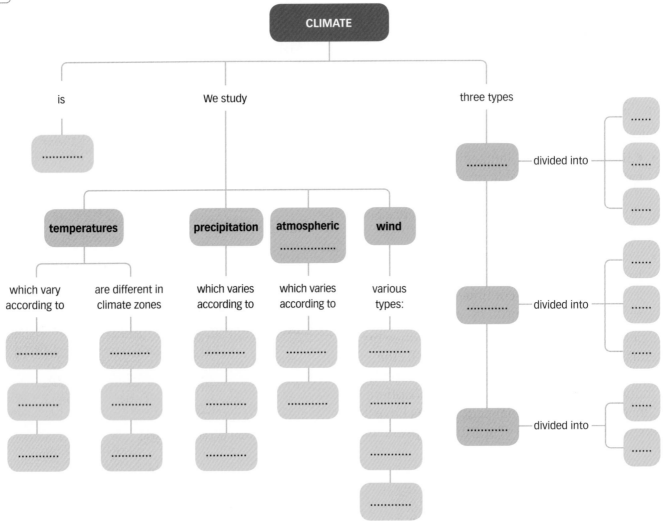

```
                           CLIMATE

        is           We study              three types

     ┌────────┐                         ┌────────┐          ┌──────┐
     │ ...... │                         │ ...... │─divided──│ .... │
     └────────┘                         └────────┘  into    ├──────┤
                                                            │ .... │
  ┌──────────┬──────────┬───────────┬────────┐              ├──────┤
temperatures precipitation atmospheric  wind                │ .... │
             ........                                        └──────┘

which vary  are different  which varies  which varies  various
according   in climate      according    according     types:
to          zones           to           to
  ┌────┐    ┌────┐         ┌────┐       ┌────┐       ┌────┐   ┌──────┐
  │....│    │....│         │....│       │....│       │....│   │ .... │
  └────┘    └────┘         └────┘       └────┘       └────┘   ├──────┤
  ┌────┐    ┌────┐         ┌────┐       ┌────┐       ┌────┐ ┌────────┐─divided──┤ .... │
  │....│    │....│         │....│       │....│       │....│ │ ...... │  into    ├──────┤
  └────┘    └────┘         └────┘       └────┘       └────┘ └────────┘          │ .... │
  ┌────┐    ┌────┐         ┌────┐                    ┌────┐                     └──────┘
  │....│    │....│         │....│                    │....│
  └────┘    └────┘         └────┘                    └────┘   ┌────────┐          ┌──────┐
                                                    ┌────┐    │ ...... │─divided──│ .... │
                                                    │....│    └────────┘  into    ├──────┤
                                                    └────┘                        │ .... │
                                                                                  └──────┘
```

2 Which of the Earth's climate zones does each letter represent?

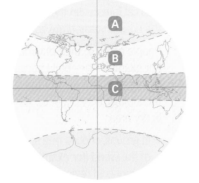

3 Define the following terms:

- The atmosphere
- Atmospheric pressure
- Clouds
- Precipitation

4 Copy and complete the table in your notebook.

	Definition	Unit of measurement	Measuring device
Temperature	......	......	......
Precipitation	......	......	......
Atmospheric pressure	......	......	......
Wind	......	......	......

5 Explain the difference between the following terms. Listen and check your answers.

- Troposphere and stratosphere
- Climate and the weather
- Anticyclone and depression

6 Explain how the following factors influence temperatures and precipitation:

- Latitude
- Altitude
- Distance from the sea

7 Investigate the following types of natural disaster. Make notes about them in a table, and look for illustrations.

	Tropical cyclones	Droughts	Flooding
Definition	......	......	......
Causes	......	......	......
Consequences	......	......	......

8 Study this weather map and answer the questions:

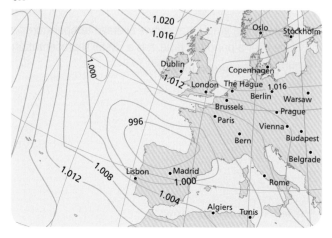

- Can you see an anticyclone? Where is it?
- Is the weather more stable in Madrid or Berlin?
- Can we say anything about the climate in Paris?

9 Copy and complete the text. Listen to the recording and check your answers.

Air pollution is the ░░░░░░ of the atmosphere by pollutants, such as harmful gases. It is caused by many human activities. There are many causes of air pollution. For example, many types of transport release gases like ░░░░░ ░░░░░ into the atmosphere. Many products that we use to clean our houses release chemicals into the air.

Air pollution causes harm to the environment. The concentration of gases released by human activities makes the ░░░░░ ░░░░░ stronger so temperatures are rising at the Earth's surface.

GLOBAL WARMING

It is very important that governments reach agreements to reduce the emission of harmful gases and prevent global warming.

But as individuals there are a lot of things that we can do. For example:

- Use public transport.

- Conserve energy by switching off the light when we're not in the room.

- Avoid waste by practising the 'Three R's': Reduce, Reuse and Recycle.

10 Find out what the 'Three R's' are. How can you practise them in your daily life?

11 Think about ways we can reduce global warming, and organize a debate with your classmates.

TECHNICAL SKILLS. **Make a climograph**

A climograph is a graph that shows average temperatures and precipitation in a place over a period of time. It is a useful representation of its climate.

• Study this climograph for Kiev.

The **title** gives the place.

The **left vertical axis** shows **temperatures** over regular periods.

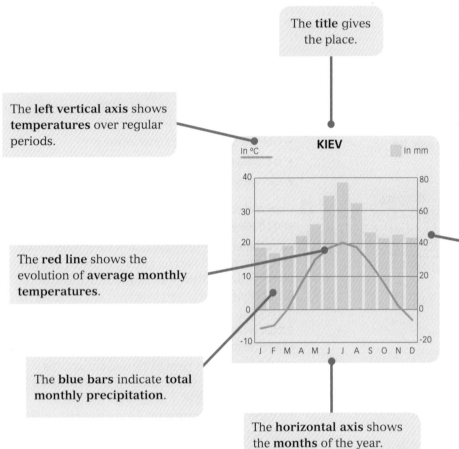

KIEV

In °C ___ In mm

The **red line** shows the evolution of **average monthly temperatures**.

The **right vertical axis** shows **precipitation** at regular periods.
The scale for precipitation is twice that for **temperatures**. For example, 5°C is at the same height as 10 mm.

The **blue bars** indicate **total monthly precipitation**.

The **horizontal axis** shows the **months** of the year.

How do we read a climograph?

a **Find the place.** Which hemisphere is it in? At what latitude?

b **Look at the temperatures.** Does the place have a hot, temperate or cold climate?

• If temperatures are above 20° C all the year round, it has a hot climate.

• If they vary between the seasons, it has a temperate climate.

• If they are always low, it has a cold climate.

c **Check precipitation.** Add up the precipitation for all the months to establish total annual precipitation. The climate is humid if the figure is above 1,000 mm. It could be an equatorial, tropical, oceanic or mountain climate.

However, the climate is very dry if the annual figure is less than 300 mm. It is a desert or polar climate.

d Next, check if precipitation is **more or less the same** throughout the year or if it falls at a certain time of the year. Dry months are when the bar showing precipitation is below the graph for temperature. For example:

• In an equatorial climate, the climate is hot and wet, and precipitation is regular all the year round. However, precipitation varies in a tropical climate.

• In temperate climate zones, dry summer months are characteristic of the Mediterranean climate. It is an oceanic climate if the graph shows that summers are wet. It is a continental climate if precipitation is regular all the year round.

STUDY THE EXAMPLE

Look at the climograph for Kiev on the previous page.

Average temperatures vary during the year. Precipitation is slightly over 500 mm, and is greater in the summer.

The climate is temperate because the changes in temperature show that it has different seasons.

We know it is a continental climate because precipitation is not very heavy, and the summer months are the rainiest.

- Now use the information in the table to make a similar climograph for Bangkok, in Thailand.

Month	T (°C)	P (mm)
J	26	10.6
F	27.6	28.2
M	29.2	30.7
A	30.1	71.8
M	29.6	189.4
J	29	151.7
J	28.6	158.2
A	28.5	187
S	28.1	319
O	27.7	230
N	26.9	57
D	25.5	9.4

NOW ANALYSE YOUR CLIMOGRAPH

- First, locate Bangkok on a map. What are its geographic coordinates? Is it in the northern hemisphere or the southern hemisphere?
- What are the temperatures like?
- Which are the warmest months? And the coldest?
- Does it have seasons?
- Add the precipitation for each month and calculate total annual precipitation. Is it abundant?
- How is precipitation distributed throughout the year?
- Finally, classify the climate of Bangkok. Explain your conclusions.

PLAN A TRIP

You are planning your holidays. Choose a place on a different continent and think about the following questions.

- What month do you usually go away on holiday?
- What activities do you enjoy: going on the beach, rock climbing, visiting museums…?
- Find out about the climate of the place you have chosen. What is the climate like in the month when you will travel? Is it the right type of place for the activities you have chosen?
- In conclusion: is this the right tourist destination for you?

5 Natural landscapes

The Amazon rainforest: the threat to biodiversity

The Amazon rainforest is the largest tropical forest in the world. Its biodiversity is extraordinary: it is home to millions of animal and plant species.

But the rainforest is in danger: trees are cut down for wood, land is used for agriculture and grazing, and new roads are built.

Large scale deforestation has dramatic consequences. The soil becomes less fertile, and carbon dioxide is released into the atmosphere. Biodiversity is greatly reduced.

The lungs of the world

The Amazon rainforest is sometimes called the "Lungs of the world" because it cleans up the air that we breathe. The trees absorb the carbon dioxide released by planes, cars and power stations.

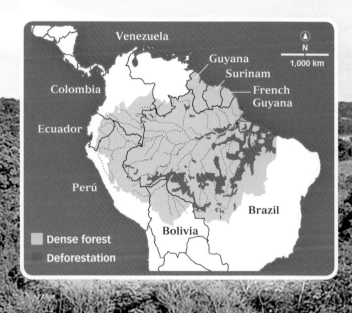

Venezuela
Guyana
Surinam
French Guyana
Colombia
Ecuador
Perú
Brazil
Bolivia

N
1,000 km

■ Dense forest
■ Deforestation

HOW DO WE KNOW?

In the past, it was difficult to have exact figures for deforestation. But today there is an official programme in Brazil called the **Real Time Deforestation Detection System**. This collects and compares satellite images every month. Now we are sure that the area covered by the Amazon rainforest is getting smaller.

Deforestation in the world
Millions of hectares

🌱 Tropical forest   🌱 Temperate forest

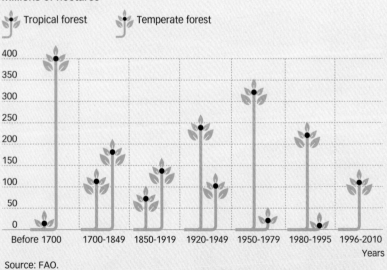

400
350
300
250
200
150
100
50
0

Before 1700   1700-1849   1850-1919   1920-1949   1950-1979   1980-1995   1996-2010
Years

Source: FAO.

? WORK WITH THE IMAGE

- Where is the Amazon rainforest?

- What is biodiversity?

- What is deforestation? What are its causes and consequences?

- What can we do about the problem of deforestation?

Natural landscapes

A **natural landscape** is a large area where specific types of climate, relief, vegetation and soil are found.

Natural landscapes are found in hot, temperate and cold climate zones, depending on their **latitude**:

- In **hot climates**, landscapes include rainforests, savannahs and hot deserts.

- In **temperate climates**, Mediterranean, oceanic and continental landscapes are found.

- In **cold climates**, landscapes include tundra and perpetual ice.

> 👁 **THINK ABOUT IT**
>
> Look at the photos and illustrations in this unit. Are there any landscapes that have not been affected by humans? Think about the question again as you work through the unit.

Natural landscapes and human settlement

Human **settlement** is far denser in some regions than in others. It is influenced by several factors:

- **Climate**. Only a few people live in deserts because water is so scarce. There is little human settlement in very cold climates.

- **Relief**. Most of the world's population lives at a fairly low altitude. Flat, coastal regions are often densely populated.

- **Water**. River valleys are densely populated. Abundant water is available for human consumption and agriculture.

Some natural landscapes are practically uninhabited. But **technology** can be used to overcome natural obstacles. For example, irrigation carries water into dry, desert land.

A NATURAL LANDSCAPE

Humanized landscapes

Most of the world's landscapes have been changed by human intervention. **Humanized landscapes** are found in nearly all parts of the world:

- **Rural landscapes**. We cut down trees and build terraces on mountain sides to provide more land for agriculture. Reservoirs and canals improve our water supply.

- **Urban landscapes**. Human settlements have many **man-made** features. For example, land is made flatter in the places where towns are built.

- **Economic activity**. Industry, mining and tourism all transform natural landscapes.

Threats to the environment

Today, many landscapes around the world are threatened by **pollution**, **deforestation**, **over-exploitation** of natural resources, and other problems caused by human activity.

Several international organisations promote the goal of **sustainable development**. They encourage people to use the natural resources that they need, but without causing long-term damage to the environment.

ACTIVITIES

1 Look for the area near your school on Google Maps (using the "satellite" option). In what ways has the landscape changed?

WORK WITH THE ILLUSTRATIONS

2 Compare the humanized landscape at the bottom of this page with the natural landscape on the previous page.

  a Make notes on the changes that have taken place.

  b Discuss your ideas with a partner.

A humanized landscape. Can you see any man-made features?

A HUMANIZED LANDSCAPE

DISTRIBUTION OF RAINFORESTS

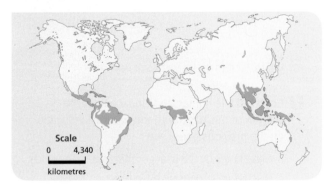

Scale
0   4,340
kilometres

THE EQUATORIAL CLIMATE

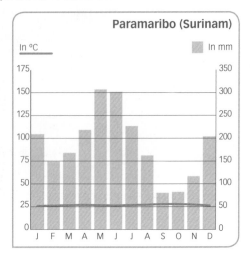

Paramaribo (Surinam)

In °C   In mm

 WORK WITH THE MAP AND GRAPH

1. Study the map and the graph, and answer the questions:

   a Which continents have rainforests?

   b Describe the temperatures and precipitation in Surinam.

DID YOU KNOW?

Pygmies

Pygmies live in communities in central Africa. Most of them are only 1.25 m to 1.45 m in height. They obtain their food from hunting and gathering plants in the rainforest. Their way of life has been badly affected by war, poverty and deforestation.

What are rainforests?

Equatorial **rainforests** are found in regions close to the equator. The **equatorial climate** has the following characteristics:

- **Temperatures** stay very high throughout the year.

- **Precipitation** is abundant and regular.

Dense and varied **vegetation** grows in rainforests because of their heat and humidity. They are home to an extremely wide range of plant and animal species, especially insects and birds.

The layers of a rainforest

A rainforest is divided into several layers:

- At the top layer, a few very tall trees called **emergents** reach a height of over 40 metres.

- In the middle layer, trees are about 25 metres tall. They form a **canopy** of thick leaves and branches, which prevents the light from reaching the ground.

- On the **forest floor**, only a few plants like ferns adapt to the lack of sunlight. Some plants climb up the stems and branches of other plants to receive more light.

 WORK WITH THE ILLUSTRATION

2 Study the illustration of the rainforest and answer the questions:

a Which layers of vegetation are found in a rainforest?

b Which is the darkest layer? Why?

Rainforests in danger

Rainforests do not have large populations because of their heat and humidity. Traditionally, native peoples live by gathering plants and hunting. The Indian tribes of the Amazon Rainforest, and the Pygmies in central Africa, are examples of hunter-gatherers.

Today, the world's rainforests are **in danger**. Many trees are being cut down for wood. The land is then used for agriculture, or to build new towns. Natural resources are being over-exploited.

 ACTIVITIES

3 Look for more information on rainforests in encyclopaedias and on internet. Complete a fact file with the following information:

Vegetation	Fauna	Human occupation
......	......	......
......	......	......
......	......	......
......	......	......
......	......	......

4 Investigate a native people living in a rainforest. Write a short text about them, similar to the one on pygmies on the opposite page.

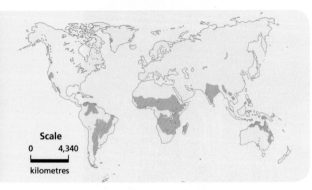

Scale
0   4,340
kilometres

DRY TROPICAL CLIMATE

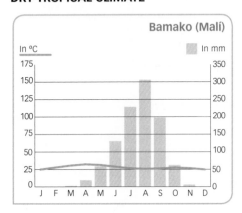

Bamako (Malí)

WET TROPICAL CLIMATE

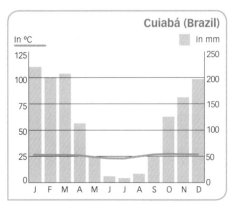

Cuiabá (Brazil)

⚙ WORK WITH THE MAP AND GRAPHS

1 Study the map and the graphs, and answer the questions:

a On which continents are tropical landscapes found?

b What are temperatures like in dry tropical and wet tropical climates?

c Is the equatorial climate similar to the tropical climate?

3 A tropical landscape: the savannah

The tropical climate

The tropics are the regions close to the Tropic of Cancer and the Tropic of Capricorn. The **tropical climate** has the following characteristics:

- **Temperatures** are always high.
- **Rainfall** is heavy, but irregular. There is a rainy season and a dry season.

Depending on precipitation, we can distinguish between a **dry** tropical climate and a **wet** tropical climate

Tropical landscapes

Tropical landscapes include the savannah, the tropical rainforest, and the hot desert. Tropical rainforests are similar to equatorial rainforests, but their vegetation is less dense.

In tropical regions, most people live on the coast or near the rivers.

The savannah

A **savannah**, or grassland, is a vast plain found in tropical regions. It has tall, green grass in the rainy season, but becomes very dry and brown in the dry season. There are a few scattered shrubs and trees. African savannahs have abundant **fauna**. There are **herbivores**, like giraffes and zebras, and **predators**, such as lions and cheetahs.

Agriculture, stock farming, the lack of water, and soil erosion threaten the savannah. When a savannah loses its plant life, it turns into a desert. This process is called **desertification**.

Steppes are found near deserts. In steppes, the dry season lasts for over nine months a year. They are similar to savannahs, but the grass is shorter.

The savannah.

4 The desert

The desert climate

There is very little precipitation in desert landscapes – less than 250 mm per year. There are both hot deserts and cold deserts:

- **Hot deserts** are found in tropical regions. During the day, temperatures are always high and can be over 50° C. At night they fall very sharply, to below 0° C.

- **Cold deserts** are found in temperate zones. Very hot summers are followed by very cold winters. Temperatures sometimes fall below −10° C.

Desert landscapes

Vegetation and animal life are scarce in deserts because of the **lack of water**. However, animals such as camels and plants like cacti have adapted to dry conditions. Date palms and other plants grow near **oases**, which are isolated areas where groundwater rises to the surface.

The human impact

Deserts are almost **uninhabited**. However, some nomads live in deserts, like the Tuaregs in the Sahara.

Oil and **natural gas** exploitation has led to the growth of a number of towns and cities in desert regions.

Tuaregs in the Sahara Desert.

DESERT CLIMATE

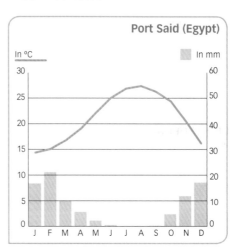

THE MAIN DESERTS IN THE WORLD

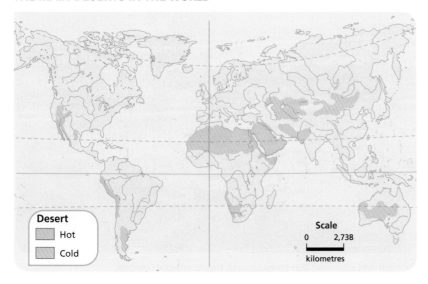

Desert
- Hot
- Cold

Scale
0   2,738
kilometres

ACTIVITIES

2 What are the main characteristics of hot deserts? And cold deserts?

3 What is an oasis? Why is it so important to people who live in deserts?

WORK WITH THE MAP

4 Look for the names of two hot deserts and two cold deserts shown on the map. Share your information in groups.

MEDITERRANEAN LANDSCAPES

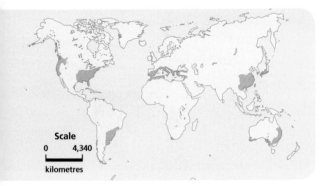

Scale
0   4,340
kilometres

THE MEDITERRANEAN CLIMATE

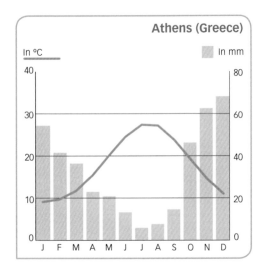

Athens (Greece)

In ºC   In mm

The Mediterranean climate

The Mediterranean climate is found in the regions surrounding the Mediterranean Sea. However, other parts of the world have a similar climate:

- **Temperatures** are high in the summer, and mild in winter.
- **Precipitation** is not heavy, and mainly falls in spring and autumn. Summers are very dry, and drought is a serious problem.

Mediterranean landscapes

Rivers have an irregular flow. They carry very little water in the summer. However, at other times they overflow and cause flooding.

Trees such as holm oaks and pine trees grow in Mediterranean forests. There are also shrubs, and aromatic plants such as lavender and rosemary.

The human impact

In Europe, Mediterranean landscapes have changed considerably:

- **Inland**, forests have been cut down. They have been replaced by wheat fields, olive trees and pasture for livestock.
- In **coastal regions**, fruit and vegetables have been grown for a very long time. In recent decades many areas have been transformed by tourism.

Tourism has changed the landscape in many coastal regions.

WORK WITH THE MAP AND GRAPH

1 Study the map and the graph and answer the questions.

a In which parts of the world is the Mediterranean climate found?

b What is the average temperature in Athens?

c What is total annual precipitation in Athens? Which are the driest months?

A MEDITERRANEAN LANDSCAPE

An inland Mediterranean landscape.

A coastal Mediterranean landscape.

WORK WITH THE IMAGES

2 Look at the top picture. How has human intervention changed the landscape?

3 What are the differences between the Mediterranean landscapes on this page?

4 Discuss the photo of the coast with a partner. What do you think this landscape looked like 100 years ago?

👁 THINK ABOUT IT

Mediterranean landscapes are extremely humanized. Why do you think this is the case?

• How do people's lives change?

The oceanic climate

The **oceanic climate**, also known as the **maritime climate**, is mainly found in coastal regions in temperate zones:

- **Temperatures** are mild all the year round because the ocean is not far away.
- **Precipitation** is heavy and regular. It rains in all seasons. Consequently, rivers always have an abundant, regular flow.

Oceanic landscapes

Oceanic landscapes are usually very green.
Their vegetation is abundant because of regular rainfall.

- **Deciduous forests** are found. Deciduous trees, such as oaks and beeches, lose their leaves in the autumn.
- There are **moors** in areas where the soil is poor. Bushes and short grasses grow on the moors.
- The grass in **meadows** is used as pasture for animals.

The human impact

Oceanic landscapes are very densely populated.
The natural landscape has been completely transformed by human intervention. For example, large cities and **industrial landscapes** are found in north-west Europe and many other regions.

Forests have been cut down to obtain timber, or to make space for farmland, roads, factories and towns.

OCEANIC LANDSCAPES

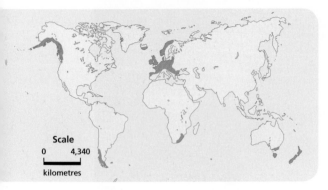

Scale
0   4,340
kilometres

THE OCEANIC CLIMATE

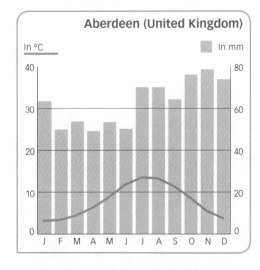

Aberdeen (United Kingdom)
In °C   In mm

Moors in southern France.

⚙ WORK WITH THE MAP AND GRAPH

1 Study the map and the graph, and answer the questions.

a Which parts of the world have an oceanic climate?

b What is the difference in temperature between the hottest and the coldest month in Aberdeen?

c Is there a season when it doesn't rain in Aberdeen?

AN OCEANIC LANDSCAPE

A deciduous forest. Were these two photos taken at the same time of the year?

DID YOU KNOW?

Deciduous forests

There is abundant fauna in deciduous forests. Plant stems and leaves are eaten by deer. Many animals, including squirrels and boars, eat the acorns from oak trees. In some parts of the world, there are predators like lynxes, foxes and bears.

Each autumn, leaves fall to the ground and decay. The soil becomes rich in nutrients. However, the soil is so fertile that it is also good for crops. As a result, many forests are cut down and the land is used for agriculture.

- Where is the wood or forest closest to your school? Is it a deciduous forest?

- Which trees, plants and animals are found there?

- Do you think the forest will still be there in a hundred years' time?

The continental climate

The continental climate is found in the temperate climate zone of the northern hemisphere:

- **Temperatures** vary greatly. Winters are extremely cold, while summers are hot.
- **Precipitation** is scarce, and generally occurs in the summer.

In many places, rivers are frozen during the winter. In the spring, snow melts and the rivers carry much more water.

Continental landscapes

Continental landscapes are found in Europe, Asia and North America:

- In the **north**, winters are long and harsh, and summers are short and cold. The **taiga** (or coniferous forest) covers large regions. Coniferous trees can resist low temperatures, and are shaped like cones so the snow falls off them.
- **Grasslands** are found on plains in continental landscapes. High grass grows on **prairies** in regions with moderate rainfall. In drier areas, the **steppes** are covered by low grass.

The human impact

In the **taiga**, small groups of hunters and reindeer herders have lived for many centuries. More recently, a timber industry has developed, and roads have been built. However, the population is still very small.

Today, most **prairies** are humanized landscapes. Many of the grasslands have been replaced by agriculture and livestock grazing. Large cities have been built.

CONTINENTAL LANDSCAPES

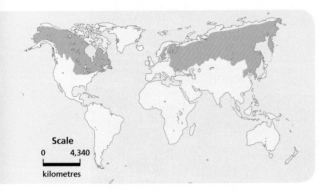

Scale
0   4,340
kilometres

THE CONTINENTAL CLIMATE

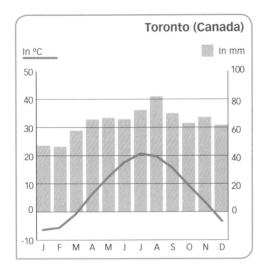

The taiga. The largest forests are found in Russia and Canada.

🛠️ WORK WITH THE MAP AND GRAPH

1 Study the map and the graph, and answer the questions.

a Where are continental landscapes found?

b Which are the coldest months in Toronto? What are the lowest temperatures?

A CONTINENTAL LANDSCAPE

🔑 DID YOU KNOW?

The Dukha

The Dukha are reindeer herders who live in the north of Mongolia. (Their Mongolian name is "Tsaatan", which means "reindeer herder".) They are nomads, who move around the taiga in search of pasture. But today their way of life is threatened. Only a few hundred people are left.

• Why do you think the way of life of this community is threatened? Look for more information.

A prairie in the United States.

🔑 ACTIVITIES

2 Where do most people live in continental landscapes? Why?

3 Why do you think continental landscapes are only found in the northern hemisphere?

The polar climate

There are two regions with a polar climate: the **Arctic** and **Antarctica**.

- The **temperatures** in polar climates are the coldest on Earth. In winter, they fall to between −20° C and −50° C. Temperatures are always below 10° C, so there is no real summer. It is night for six months a year.

- **Precipitation** is scarce, and falls as snow.

Polar landscapes

Landscapes are covered by ice and snow. The subsoil is frozen so plants cannot grow.

However, there is a short summer in the areas closest to the temperate zones. These areas have **tundra** landscapes of moss and lichen.

Human settlement

Human settlement is almost impossible in polar regions. But two native peoples, the Sami and the Inuit, live in parts of the Arctic region. There are a few scientific stations in Antarctica, where people stay and work.

👁 THINK ABOUT IT

You are going to work at a scientific station in Antarctica for one month. Which clothes and equipment would you take with you? What would you eat and drink?

ACTIVITIES

1 Use internet to find out about the Inuit and the Sami. Which modern countries do they live in?

A POLAR LANDSCAPE

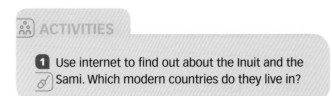

Scale
0   8,470
kilometres

THE POLAR CLIMATE

McMurdo Station (Antarctica)

In °C   In mm

J F M A M J J A S O N D

The mountain climate

The **mountain** climate (also known as the **alpine** climate) is found in mountain ranges such as the Himalayas in Asia, the Andes in South America and the Alps in Europe.

- **Temperatures** are very low in winter. It is cool in summer.

- There is heavy **precipitation** throughout the year. It often snows in winter.

- Temperatures and precipitation are connected to **altitude**. On the higher slopes of a mountain, temperatures fall and precipitation increases.

 ACTIVITIES

2 Find out what the "tree line" is, using internet. What grows below this line? Which vegetation is found above it?

Mountain landscapes

The vegetation on mountains is influenced by the following factors:

- **Altitude**. Vegetation varies because of changing temperatures and precipitation.

- **Orientation**. Some slopes are in the shade, while others receive more sunlight.

- **Wind**. Windy places have less vegetation.

Human settlement

In temperate zones, mountains are sparsely populated. People live in valleys, where the climate is milder. However, in hot climates people prefer to live in mountainous regions, which are cooler than the plains.

MOUNTAIN CLIMATE

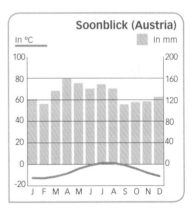

A MOUNTAIN LANDSCAPE

LEVELS OF VEGETATION

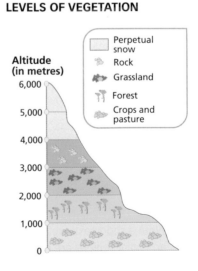

1 Copy and complete the table.

LANDSCAPE	WHERE?	CLIMATE	VEGETATION	HUMAN OCCUPATION
Rainforest	......	......	......	......
Savannah	......	......	......	......
Desert	......	......	......	......
Oceanic	......	......	......	......
Mediterranean	......	......	......	......
Continental	......	......	......	......
Polar	......	......	......	......
Mountain	......	......	......	......

2 Explain the difference between a natural landscape and a humanized landscape.

3 What is the difference between a hot desert and a cold desert? Where is each kind of desert found?

4 Describe the following types of vegetation. In which natural landscapes are they found?

- Taiga
- Moor
- Tundra
- Prairie
- Steppe

5 Write a short text explaining why rainforests, deserts and polar regions are not densely populated.

6 Analyse the climograph.

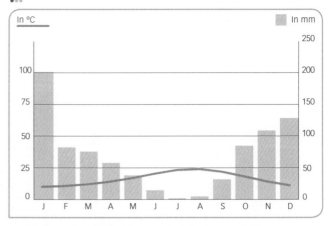

a What are temperatures like? And precipitation?

b What type of climate is shown?

c Which vegetation is characteristic of this climate?

7 Which type of landscape is shown in each photo? Explain your ideas.

8 Think about temperatures and precipitation:

a How do latitude, altitude and distance from the sea influence temperatures?

b How do they influence precipitation?

ENDANGERED SPECIES

An endangered species is a species that faces a high risk of becoming extinct. Many animal and plant species are threatened in this way. This is often because their natural habitat is disappearing.

Many thousands of species are on the IUCN Red List of Threatened Species, which lists endangered animals and plants. Endangered animals include the green sea turtle, the Asian elephant, the Goliath frog and the Iberian lynx.

Frigate bird

Giant panda

Tuna

Polar bear

Dragon tree

Bengal tiger

9 What do the letters "IUCN" mean? What is its Red List? Use internet to find out.

10 Identify three endangered animal species and three endangered plant species. Find out where they are found, and why they are becoming extinct.

11 In groups, share your information and prepare a report on endangered species. Include:

- An introduction on the importance of biodiversity, and threats to the environment.
- Examples of endangered species.
- Suggestions about how to deal with the problem.

TECHNIQUES. **Analyse changes in a landscape using aerial photos**

Why is aerial photography useful?

By comparing **aerial photos** of the same place at different periods of time, we can see how a landscape has changed.

The photos show all the transformations. We can see the growth of cities, changes in transport infrastructures, and other ways that the land is being used.

Moreover, aerial photography helps us to examine human impact on the natural environment.

For example, we can detect:

- The disappearance of woodland.

- The effects of fires on land use.

- The excessive expansion of coastal urban development.

How do we analyse the photos?

- **Locate the landscape.** Look at the place, and the date of each photo. Calculate the length of time between the two photos.

- **Identify the natural features.** Locate the mountains, plains, rivers, bays... Look at the area covered by natural vegetation in each photo.

- **Identify man-made features**: roads, railway lines, crops, factories and reservoirs.

- **Explain the changes.** Compare the features that are the same in both photos with those that have changed.

- **Draw your conclusions.** Has the landscape changed slightly or a great deal? What are the positive and negative aspects of the changes?

1 **Locate the landscape.**

a What type of place is shown in the photos?

b When do you think each photo was taken?

2 **Copy and complete the following tables.**

a Identify the natural features on both dates.

NATURAL FEATURES	
In 1970	**In 2010**
......	......

b Identify the man-made features on both dates.

MAN-MADE FEATURES	
In 1970	**In 2010**
......	......

3 **Explain the changes.**

a What were the main economic activities in 1970? How do you know?

b What were the main economic activities in 2010? How do you know?

c Which features are the same in both photos?

d What were the main changes in the period 1970-2010?

4 **Draw your conclusions.**

a What caused the changes that you have identified?

b What are the positive and negative aspects?

c Do you think the changes in this coastal region have caused greater water pollution? And air pollution?

6 The continents

The exploration of Antarctica

Antarctica was the last continent to be explored. For many centuries, geographers believed that there was a large continent – called Terra Australis – in the far south of the planet. But nobody was sure.

The British explorer James Cook crossed the Antarctic Circle in the 18th century. In 1820, Russian explorers were the first to see land. Since then, there have been many expeditions to Antarctica.

The race to the South Pole. In 1911, an expedition led by the Norwegian Roald Amundsen reached the South Pole. Only one month later, a British expedition led by Robert Scott also arrived there. But Scott and his team died on the return journey.

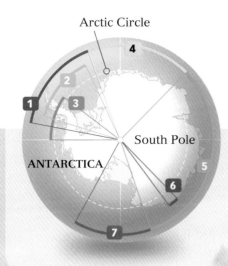

Arctic Circle

4 Norway

South Pole

ANTARCTICA

1. United Kingdom
2. Argentina
3. Chile
4. Norway
5. Australia
6. France
7. New Zealand

Whose continent?

Today, seven countries claim territory in Antarctica. But their claims do not have official international recognition.

? WORK WITH THE IMAGE

- What kind of landscapes can you see in these photos?
- Why do you think Antarctica was the last continent to be discovered?
- Find out more about the expeditions of Scott and Amundsen.

HOW DO WE KNOW?

There are a number of research stations in Antarctica run by different governments. Scientists collect data on geology, climate and biology.

- Look for 'Research station Antarctica' on internet. Find out about three stations, including one Spanish station.

- Summarise your findings in a short report. Explain where the stations are; if scientists stay there for the whole year; and what their scientific work involves.

Relief

Africa is the third largest continent. It has a surface area of over 30 million km².

- Africa has a high average altitude (750 m), and is fairly flat. It has many large **plateaus**. There are several **deserts** on the plateaus, including the Sahara and the Kalahari Deserts.

- There are **mountain ranges** on the edges of the continent, such as the Atlas Mountains in the north-west and the Drakensberg Mountains in the south.

- Very high volcanoes surround the **Great Rift Valley**. This is a huge geological fault in east Africa.

- Some **depressions**, such as the Congo and Niger river basins, are between the central plateaus.

- The **coasts** of Africa are mainly regular, and there are not many gulfs or capes. Narrow plains are found along the coasts. There are only a few **islands**: the largest is Madagascar.

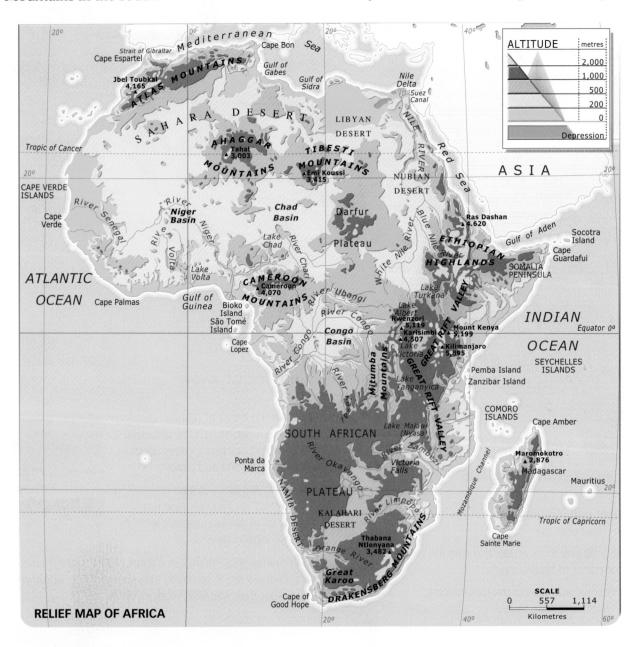

RELIEF MAP OF AFRICA

Rivers and lakes

We classify **rivers** according to the ocean or sea that they flow into:

- **Atlantic Ocean**. Long rivers, like the Niger, Congo and Orange, have an abundant flow.
- **Indian Ocean**. These rivers are shorter than the Atlantic rivers. They include the Zambezi and the Limpopo.
- **Mediterranean Sea**. The rivers are short, and their flow is generally scarce. However, the River Nile is the longest river in the world.

Africa has some very large **lakes**. The **Great Lakes** region, which includes Lakes Victoria, Tanganyika and Turkana, is in the Great Rift Valley. The largest lake is Lake Victoria.

Climate and landscapes

Most of Africa is between the two tropics so hot climates predominate:

- Tropical Africa has a **hot climate**. Temperatures are high all year round and precipitation is greatest near the equator. It has a range of equatorial, tropical and desert climates. There are rainforests, savannahs and deserts.
- A **temperate climate** is found in the north and south of the continent, where there are Mediterranean and oceanic landscapes.
- A **mountain climate** is found in the highest regions.

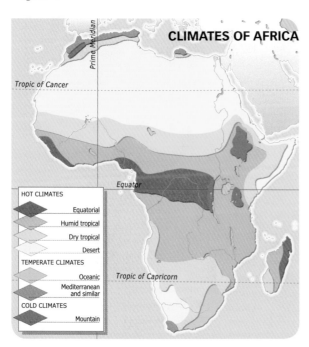

CLIMATES OF AFRICA

Prime Meridian

Tropic of Cancer

Equator

Tropic of Capricorn

HOT CLIMATES
- Equatorial
- Humid tropical
- Dry tropical
- Desert

TEMPERATE CLIMATES
- Oceanic
- Mediterranean and similar

COLD CLIMATES
- Mountain

WORK WITH THE MAP

1 What are the main types of relief on the African continent?

2 Study the text and the relief map of Africa and answer the questions:

 a Which oceans and seas surround Africa?

 b Where are the highest mountains in Africa?

 c What are the main deserts in Africa? Where are they?

 d What is the longest river in Africa?

3 Use a ruler to make a straight line between the Nile delta and the Cape of Good Hope. Which types of relief are along this line?

ACTIVITIES

4 Are all the following landscapes found in Africa? Discuss your ideas with a classmate.

- rainforest
- deciduous forest
- desert
- tundra
- savannah
- taiga

5 Copy and complete the following text. Then listen to the recording and check your answers.

Africa is the _____ largest continent. It is surrounded by the _____ Ocean to the west, the Mediterranean Sea to the _____, and the _____ Ocean to the east. There are many plateaus in Africa. Several _____, like the Sahara, are on these plateaus. The highest mountains are the _____ around the Great Rift Valley.

THINK ABOUT IT

Find the Nile River on this aerial photo. Why does a river carrying so much water flow through a desert?

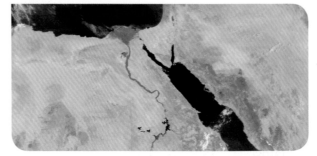

Where is Asia?

Asia is the largest continent, with a surface area of 44 million km². There are three oceans around its coasts: the Arctic, Pacific and Indian Oceans. It is separated from Europe by the Caucasus and Ural Mountains, the Ural River and the Caspian Sea. It is separated from Africa by the Red Sea. Nearly all of Asia is in the northern hemisphere.

Relief

The relief of Asia is extremely varied:

- Most of Asia's **mountain ranges** are in the centre and west of the continent. The Himalayas are the highest mountain range in the world. Mount Everest (8,850 m) is the world's highest mountain.

- **Plateaus** are found across the continent. Tibet, in the centre of Asia, is the highest plateau in the world. **Plains** cover much of the north, east and south of Asia. A vast plain crosses Siberia in the north. Large rivers form alluvial plains in the south and east of Asia.

- There are **depressions** in the west where three inland seas are found: the Caspian Sea, the Aral Sea and the Dead Sea.

- The **coast** of Asia is **irregular**, and has many gulfs and peninsulas. There are many **islands** in East Asia, including the archipelagos of Japan, the Philippines and Indonesia.

Rivers and lakes

Most Asian **rivers** are long. Their flow changes greatly during the year because of melting snow and monsoon rains:

- **Arctic Ocean**: the Obi, Yenisey and Lena are long rivers, which partly freeze in winter.

- **Indian Ocean**: the Indus and the Ganges descend from the Himalayas, and form large plains.

- **Pacific Ocean**: long rivers, including the Yangtze and the Huang He (Yellow River), form large plains.

Asia has some large **lakes**. Lake Baikal is the deepest lake in the world, while the Caspian Sea has the largest surface area.

Climates and landscapes

Asia has nearly all the climates and landscapes found on Earth:

- **Cold climates**. A **polar** climate is found in the far north. The subsoil is always frozen, so there is a **tundra** landscape. Mountainous regions like Tibet have a **mountain** climate.

- **Temperate climates**. A **continental** climate is found in the north, where the coniferous forests of the **taiga** cover large areas. The climate in eastern China is similar to the Mediterranean. Inland there are **cold deserts**, like the Gobi Desert.

- **Hot climates**. Equatorial, tropical and desert climates are found in the south of the continent.

CLIMATES OF ASIA

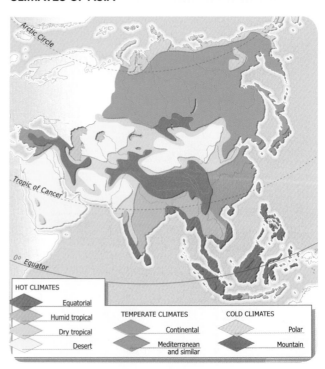

HOT CLIMATES		
Equatorial		
Humid tropical	TEMPERATE CLIMATES	COLD CLIMATES
Dry tropical	Continental	Polar
Desert	Mediterranean and similar	Mountain

RELIEF MAP OF ASIA

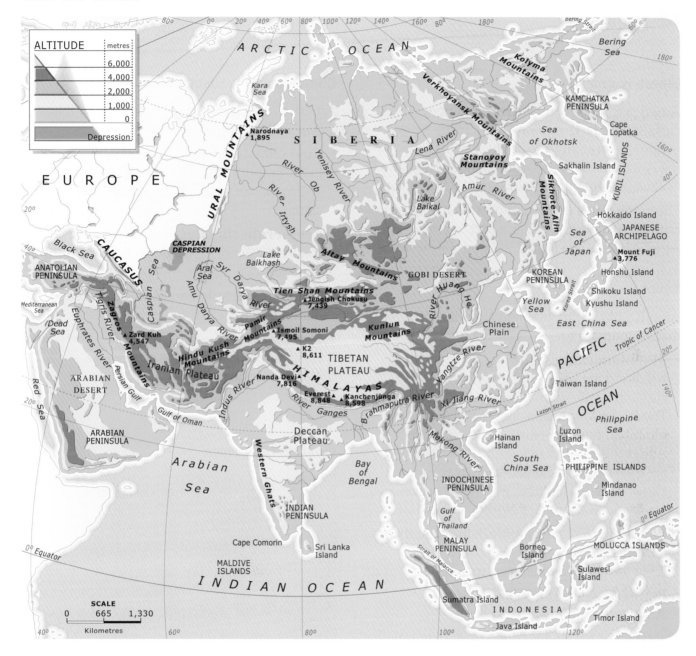

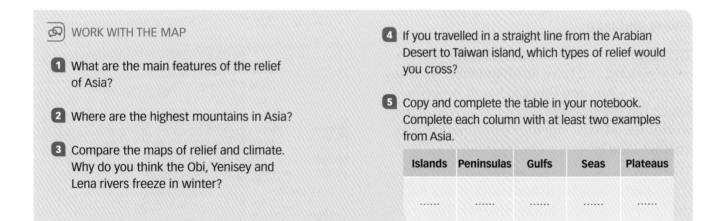

WORK WITH THE MAP

1 What are the main features of the relief of Asia?

2 Where are the highest mountains in Asia?

3 Compare the maps of relief and climate. Why do you think the Obi, Yenisey and Lena rivers freeze in winter?

4 If you travelled in a straight line from the Arabian Desert to Taiwan island, which types of relief would you cross?

5 Copy and complete the table in your notebook. Complete each column with at least two examples from Asia.

Islands	Peninsulas	Gulfs	Seas	Plateaus
....	....	....	....	....

Where is America?

America is the second largest continent with a surface area of 42 million km². It is the longest continent, stretching from the Arctic Circle to the Antarctic Circle. It is surrounded by three oceans: the Atlantic, Pacific and Arctic Oceans.

The continent is divided into two **sub-continents**, North America and South America. They are joined in Central America.

Relief

America has a high average altitude, and has many mountain ranges, plains and plateaus:

- **Mountain ranges**. The highest mountains belong to the young mountain ranges running north-south along the Pacific coast. The Rocky Mountains are the highest mountain range in North America, while the Andes are the highest in South America. Older, lower mountains, like the Appalachians, are found in the east of North America.

- **Plains**. The Great Plains are in the central part of North America. The basin of the Amazon River forms the largest plain in South America.

- **Plateaus**. The highest plateau is the *Altiplano* in Bolivia.

The **coast** of North America is irregular. It has peninsulas, like Florida, and gulfs and bays. The coast of South America is more regular.

Rivers and lakes

The **rivers** that flow into the **Atlantic Ocean** are very long and have an abundant flow. They include the Amazon River in South America, which has the greatest flow of any river in the world. The Mississippi in North America is another long river with many tributaries.

There are many large **lakes**, including the Great Lakes, which are between Canada and the United States. In South America, Lake Titicaca is the highest lake in the world.

Climates and landscapes

America stretches from pole to pole, so it has a very wide range of climates and landscapes:

- **Cold climates**. A **polar** climate is found in the far north and far south of the continent. The mountain ranges have a **mountain** climate.

- **Temperate climates**. Coniferous forests are found in the north, which has a **continental** climate.

  There are **oceanic** and **Mediterranean** climates at lower latitudes.

- **Hot climates**. Equatorial, tropical and desert climates are found in the southern areas of North America, Central America and South America.

CLIMATES OF AMERICA

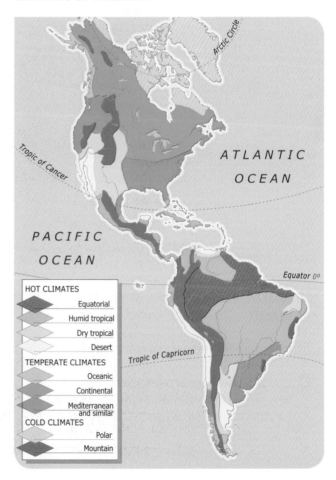

RELIEF MAP OF AMERICA

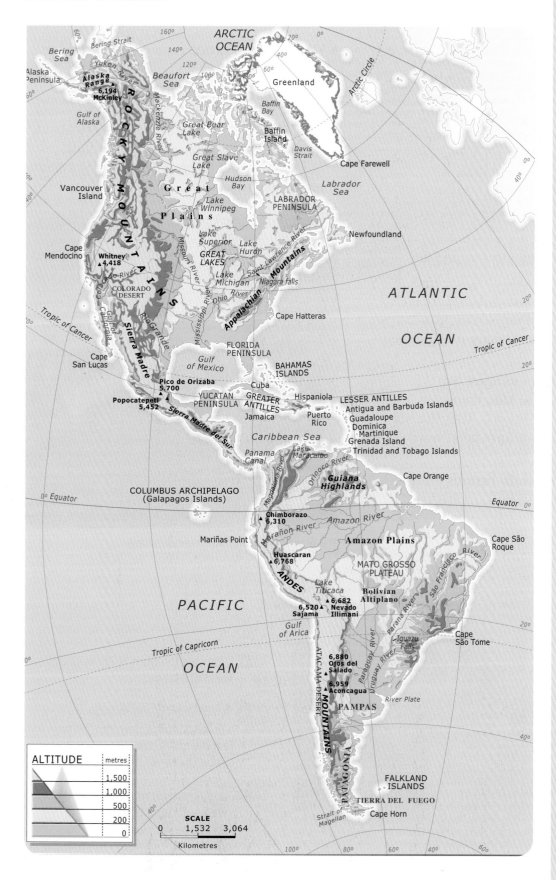

⟲ WORK WITH THE MAPS

1 What are the main physical features of America? How are they distributed across the continent?

2 Compare the map of climates to the relief map.

  a Which types of climate are found in America?

  b Why are there more hot climates in South America than North America?

  c Which types of climate are found in the following regions?
  • Greenland
  • Cuba
  • Gulf of California
  • Matto Grosso Plateau

3 Copy and complete the table with the names of American mountains, plains and plateaus.

Mountain ranges
......

Plains
......

Plateaus
......

4 If you travelled in a straight line from Baffin Island to Cape Horn, which types of relief would you cross?

97

Where is Europe?

Europe is a small continent with a surface area of 10.5 million km². It is surrounded by the Arctic Ocean, the Atlantic Ocean and the Mediterranean Sea. In the east, it is separated from Asia by the Caucasus and Ural Mountains, the Ural River and the Caspian Sea.

Relief

The relief of Europe is mainly flat, and its altitude is low.

- Great **plains** cover most of the centre and east of Europe, from France to Russia. Large rivers flow across these plains, making them very fertile.

- The **oldest mountain ranges**, like the Scandinavian and Ural Mountains, are in the north and east of Europe. They are not very high because they have been worn down by erosion.

- The **youngest mountain ranges**, such as the Alps, Pyrenees and Balkans are considerably higher.

- The **coast** of Europe is long and **irregular**, and has many bays and gulfs. There are large peninsulas, such as Scandinavia, Italy and the Iberian Peninsula.

- There are many big **islands** such as Iceland, Ireland, Great Britain, Corsica, Sardinia, Sicily, Crete and Cyprus. The Balearic Islands are an **archipelago**.

The Alps are a young, high mountain range.

CLIMATES OF EUROPE

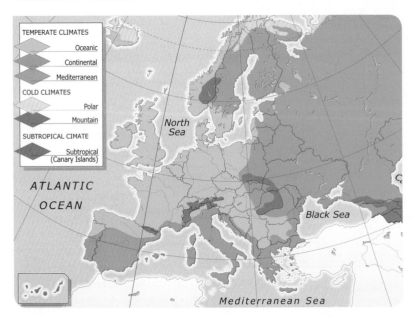

TEMPERATE CLIMATES
- Oceanic
- Continental
- Mediterranean

COLD CLIMATES
- Polar
- Mountain

SUBTROPICAL CIMATE
- Subtropical (Canary Islands)

ATLANTIC OCEAN

North Sea

Black Sea

Mediterranean Sea

WORK WITH THE MAP

1 What are the main features of the relief of Europe?

2 Which oceans and seas do European rivers flow into? What are the characteristics of each group of rivers?

3 Study the map of climates. Bring photos of three European landscapes to class. See if your classmates can match them to the right climate.

RELIEF MAP OF EUROPE

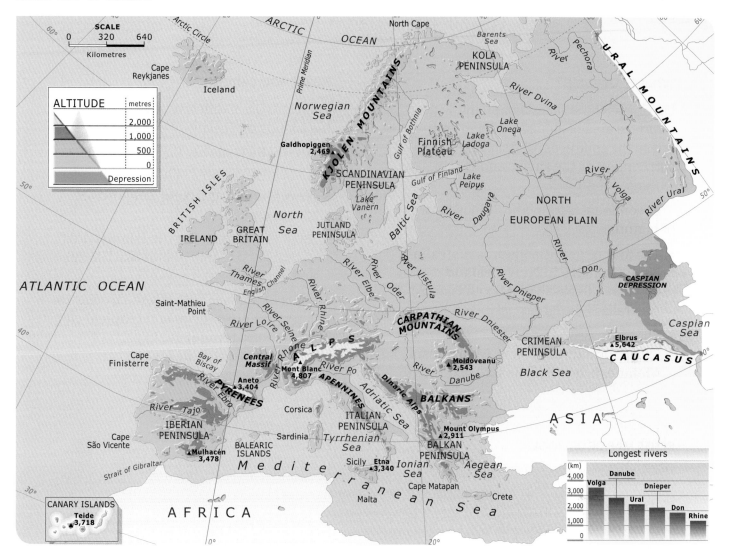

Rivers

Many rivers cross the continent and flow into the following oceans and seas:

- **Arctic Ocean**. The Pechora and Northern Dvina are long rivers with an abundant flow. They freeze in the winter.

- **Atlantic Ocean**. Long rivers like the Oder, Rhine and Tajo have an abundant flow all the year round.

- **Mediterranean Sea**. These rivers, which include the Rhône, Po and Ebro, have an irregular flow that is low in the summer.

- **Black Sea**. The Danube, Dnieper, Dniester and Don form an important communications network across central and eastern Europe.

- **Caspian Sea**. The Volga is the largest river in Europe.

Climates and landscapes

Most parts of Europe have temperate climates:

- An **oceanic** climate is characteristic of the Atlantic side of the continent, where deciduous forests and moors are found.

- Around the Mediterranean Sea, the southern regions have a **Mediterranean** climate.

- Eastern Europe and parts of central Europe, have a **continental** climate. Their natural landscapes include prairies and steppes.

There are also cold climates in Europe:

- A **polar** climate is found in the north of Scandinavia and Russia, where there are tundra and taiga landscapes.

- **Mountain** climates are characteristic of mountainous regions like the Alps.

What is Oceania?

Oceania is the smallest continent, with a surface area of almost 9 million km². It is to the south-east of Asia, and is surrounded by the Pacific and Indian Oceans.

This continent is formed by thousands of **islands**:

- The four largest islands are **Australia**, **New Guinea** and **New Zealand** (divided into North and South Islands). Australia is the largest island on Earth.

- There are also thousands of small islands, which form three groups: **Micronesia**, **Melanesia** and **Polynesia**.

Relief and climate

There are great differences between the islands of Oceania.

- **Australia** is mainly flat, but has a mountain range along its east coast.

- **New Guinea** and **New Zealand** are mountainous.

- Most of the small **Pacific islands** are flat, except for volcanic islands like Hawaii and Samoa.

Most of Oceania is between the tropics so it has warm **equatorial** and **tropical** climates. The climate is **temperate** in parts of Australia and New Zealand. A **desert** climate is found in inland Australia.

RELIEF MAP OF OCEANIA

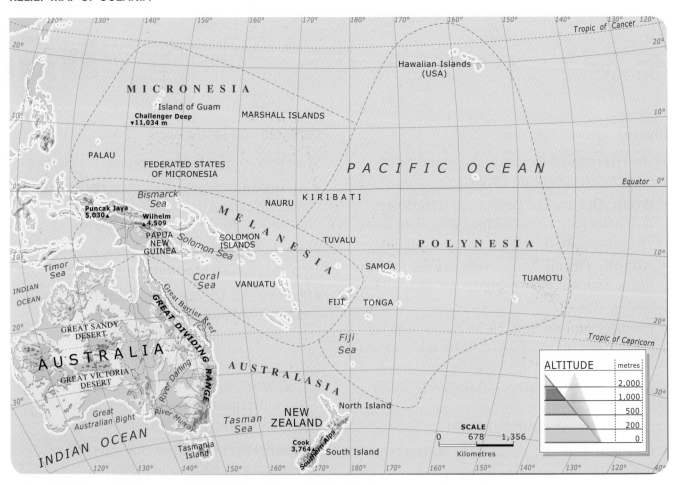

6 Antarctica

What is Antarctica?

Antarctica is in the southern hemisphere. It has a surface area of 14 million km², so it is larger than Europe. In winter, the water around Antarctica freezes and the continent doubles in size.

About 80% of the Earth's fresh water is in Antarctica, but it is frozen. About 98% of the land surface is covered by ice. Antarctica is the world's highest continent, with an average altitude of 2,000 m. But only the highest mountains rise above the ice.

Antarctica is nearly circular in form.

Climate and resources

Antarctica has the coldest climate in the world. Cold, icy winds blow across it. There are only a small number of plants, such as lichen, algae and mosses. A few species of animals, like penguins, seals and sea-lions, live around the coast.

Abundant **oil** and **mineral resources** are found beneath the surface. Many countries would like to have access to these resources. But international agreements regulate economic activity on the continent.

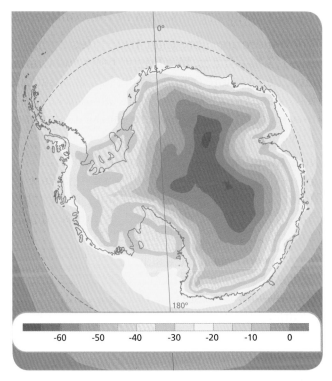

This map shows surface temperatures in Antarctica in winter.

 **ACTIVITIES**

1 Do you think many people live in Antarctica? Why?

2 Investigate the following questions. Then debate your ideas and findings with your classmates.

   a What are the natural resources of Antarctica? Is ice also a resource?

   b Why are governments interested in Antarctica? Do any treaties regulate their role on the continent?

   c Is it important to preserve the natural environment of Antarctica?

Only animals like penguins can survive in Antarctica.

The territorial organisation of the continents

Today, there are more than **190 states** in the world. Some states, like Egypt, India and China, have their remote origins in ancient civilisations that existed thousands of years ago. However, their modern **frontiers** were established in the 20th century.

New states are still being created in the 21st century. For example, in south-east Asia East Timor became an independent state in 2002. In Europe, Montenegro declared its independence from the former Yugoslavia in 2006.

Countries do not have a standard **size**. The Russian Federation is the largest in the world and has a greater land surface than the continent of Oceania. On the other hand, some states, like Monaco, the Vatican, Singapore and San Marino, consist of a single city.

WORK WITH THE MAP

1 On which continents are these countries located?

- San Marino
- Indonesia
- Greece
- Uganda
- Honduras
- Bangladesh
- New Zealand
- Chile
- Chad

2 Which countries have these cities as their capitals?

- Abuja
- Buenos Aires
- Kathmandu
- Amsterdam

3 Choose five states on each continent and make a table.

CONTINENT	COUNTRY	CAPITAL CITY
......	......	......

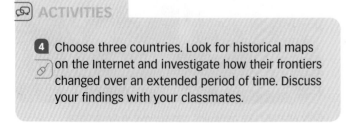

ACTIVITIES

4 Choose three countries. Look for historical maps on the Internet and investigate how their frontiers changed over an extended period of time. Discuss your findings with your classmates.

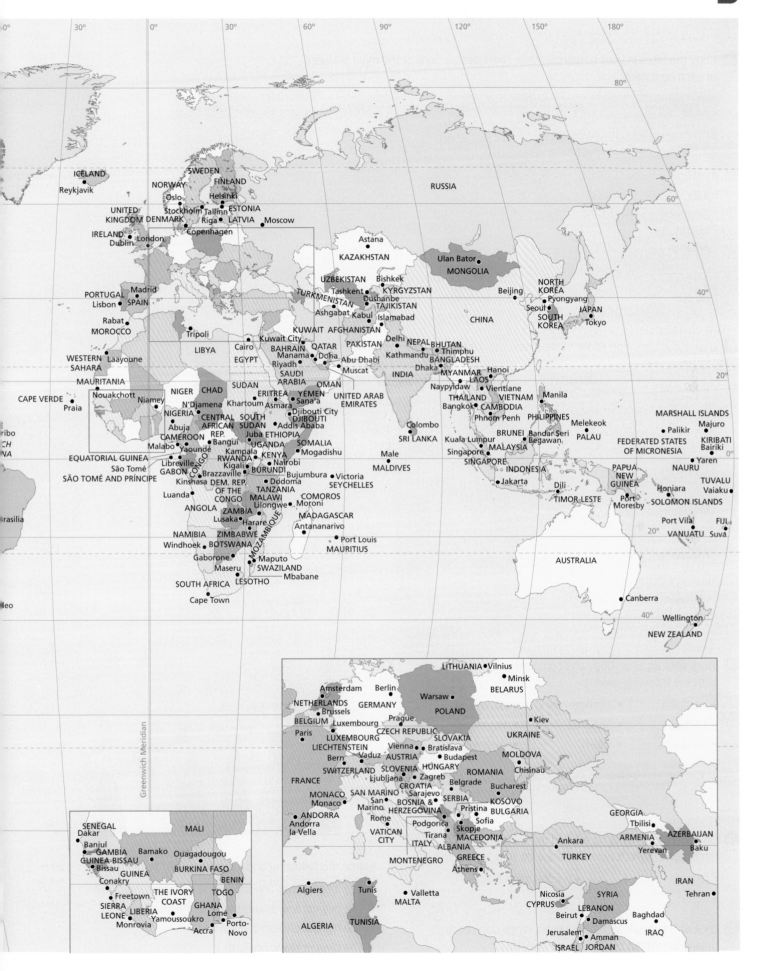

ICELAND
Reykjavik

SWEDEN
NORWAY FINLAND
Oslo Helsinki
UNITED Stockholm Tallinn ESTONIA
KINGDOM DENMARK Riga LATVIA Moscow
IRELAND Copenhagen
Dublin London

RUSSIA

PORTUGAL Madrid
Lisbon SPAIN
Rabat
MOROCCO
Tripoli
WESTERN Laayoune
SAHARA
MAURITANIA
CAPE VERDE Nouakchott
Praia Niamey
NIGER CHAD
N'Djamena Khartoum
NIGERIA
Abuja CENTRAL SOUTH
AFRICAN SUDAN
CAMEROON REP. Juba ETHIOPIA
Malabo Yaoundé Bangui
EQUATORIAL GUINEA
São Tomé Libreville
SÃO TOMÉ AND PRÍNCIPE GABON
Kinshasa DEM. REP.
OF THE
Luanda CONGO
ANGOLA ZAMBIA
Lusaka
NAMIBIA ZIMBABWE
Windhoek BOTSWANA
Gaborone Maputo
Maseru SWAZILAND
SOUTH AFRICA LESOTHO Mbabane
Cape Town

KAZAKHSTAN
Astana
Ulan Bator
MONGOLIA
UZBEKISTAN Bishkek
Tashkent KYRGYZSTAN Beijing
TURKMENISTAN Dushanbe NORTH
Ashgabat TAJIKISTAN KOREA
Kabul Islamabad Seoul Pyongyang
Cairo Kuwait City CHINA SOUTH JAPAN
LIBYA BAHRAIN QATAR PAKISTAN KOREA Tokyo
EGYPT Manama Doha Delhi NEPAL BHUTAN
Riyadh Abu Dhabi Kathmandu Thimphu
SAUDI Muscat BANGLADESH
ARABIA OMAN INDIA Dhaka MYANMAR Hanoi
SUDAN ERITREA YEMEN Naypyidaw LAOS
Asmara Sana'a UNITED ARAB Vientiane Manila
EMIRATES THAILAND VIETNAM
DJIBOUTI Bangkok CAMBODIA PHILIPPINES
Djibouti City Phnom Penh Melekeok
Addis Ababa SOMALIA Colombo BRUNEI Bandar Seri PALAU
UGANDA Mogadishu SRI LANKA Kuala Lumpur Begawan
Kampala KENYA Male MALAYSIA
RWANDA Nairobi Singapore
Kigali MALDIVES SINGAPORE INDONESIA
BURUNDI SEYCHELLES Jakarta
Brazzaville Bujumbura Victoria
CONGO Dodoma
TANZANIA
MALAWI COMOROS Dili
Lilongwe Moroni TIMOR-LESTE
MOZAMBIQUE MADAGASCAR
Harare Antananarivo
Port Louis
MAURITIUS
AUSTRALIA

MARSHALL ISLANDS
Majuro
Palikir
FEDERATED STATES KIRIBATI
OF MICRONESIA Bairiki
Yaren
NAURU
PAPUA TUVALU
NEW Honiara Vaiaku
GUINEA SOLOMON ISLANDS
Port
Moresby Port Vila
VANUATU FIJI Suva

Canberra
Wellington
NEW ZEALAND

80°
60°
40°
20°
0°
20°
40°

LITHUANIA Vilnius
Minsk
Amsterdam Berlin BELARUS
NETHERLANDS Warsaw
GERMANY POLAND
Brussels
BELGIUM Prague Kiev
Luxembourg
Paris CZECH REPUBLIC UKRAINE
LUXEMBOURG SLOVAKIA
LIECHTENSTEIN Vienna Bratislava MOLDOVA
Bern Vaduz AUSTRIA Budapest
SWITZERLAND SLOVENIA HUNGARY ROMANIA Chisinau
FRANCE Ljubljana Zagreb Belgrade Bucharest
MONACO SAN MARINO CROATIA
Monaco San Sarajevo SERBIA
Marino BOSNIA & KOSOVO GEORGIA
ANDORRA HERZEGOVINA Pristina BULGARIA Tbilisi
Andorra Rome Podgorica Sofia
la Vella VATICAN Tirana Skopje ARMENIA AZERBAIJAN
CITY ITALY MACEDONIA Ankara Yerevan Baku
MONTENEGRO ALBANIA TURKEY
GREECE
Athens IRAN
Algiers Tunis Valletta Nicosia SYRIA Tehran
MALTA CYPRUS LEBANON
ALGERIA TUNISIA Beirut Baghdad
Damascus
Jerusalem Amman IRAQ
ISRAEL JORDAN

SENEGAL
Dakar MALI
Banjul Bamako
GAMBIA Ouagadougou
GUINEA-BISSAU
Bissau BURKINA FASO
GUINEA BENIN
Conakry
Freetown THE IVORY TOGO
SIERRA COAST GHANA
LEONE LIBERIA Lomé
Yamoussoukro Porto-
Monrovia Accra Novo

Greenwich Meridian

ACTIVITY ROUND-UP

1 Copy the table in your notebook. Write short descriptions of the main features of each continent.

Continent	Relief	Coasts	Climates	Landscapes
Africa	......	......	......	......
Asia	......	......	......	......
America	......	......	......	......
Europe	......	......	......	......

2 Look for information about these rivers. Copy and complete the table in your notebook.

	Volga	Nile	Yangtze	Danube	Mississippi
Source	......	......	......	......	......
Length	......	......	......	......	......
Mouth	......	......	......	......	......
Tributaries	......	......	......	......	......
Continent	......	......	......	......	......

3 Work with an atlas. Copy and complete the table with the following islands:

- Australia
- Cyprus
- Bahamas
- Madagascar
- Sri Lanka
- Iceland
- Greenland
- Polynesia
- Galapagos

Island or archipelago	Ocean or sea	Continent
...	...	...

4 On which continents do we find the following landscapes? Which type of climate do they belong to?

- tundra
- desert
- tropical rainforest
- moors

5 Look at the graph. Which mountain range does each belong to? Which continents are they on?

6

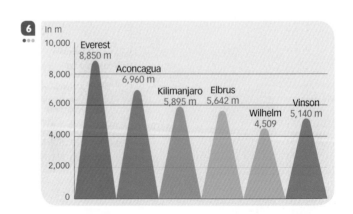

Name the following and say where they are found:

a The longest river and the river with the greatest flow.

b The biggest and deepest lakes in the world.

c The highest plateau in the world.

d The biggest island on Earth.

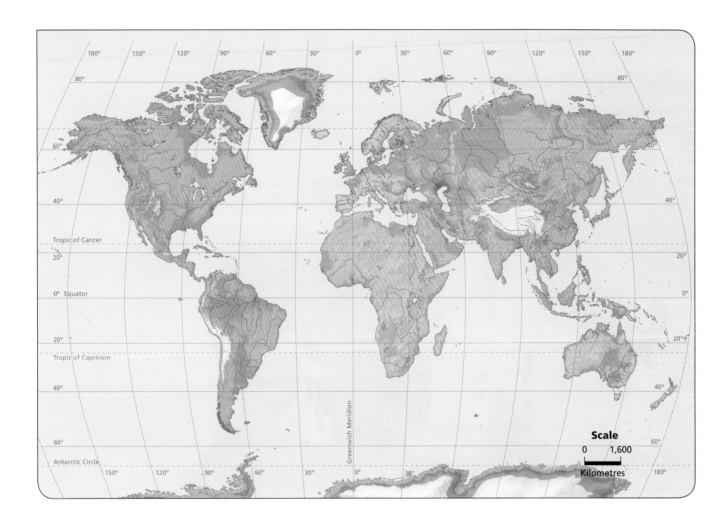

7 Find the following landforms on the map:

- The Himalayas
- Gulf of Mexico
- Anatolian Peninsula
- Great Dividing Range
- The Andes
- The Alps
- European Plain
- Ural Mountains
- New Zealand islands
- Mount Kilimanjaro
- Rocky Mountains
- Archipelago of Japan
- Greenland

8 Look at the map and describe the relief of Europe.

9 Look at the continent of America. Where are the highest mountain ranges and most plains found? Give examples.

10 Do Africa and Europe have regular or irregular coastlines? Give examples to explain your answer.

11 Where are most mountains found in Asia? Give the names of some of the highest mountains.

12 Compare Europe and Asia. Which continent has flatter relief?

13 Draw a diagram of the hot, temperate and cold climate zones of the world. Explain the temperatures and precipitation of each zone.

14 In six groups, make murals on the continents. Each group chooses a different continent.

a Before you begin, discuss what the main headings will be, for example: Climates; Landscapes; Mountains; Rivers and lakes...

b Think about what you wish to show. For example, you could include a map of climates and information on the longest river...

c Include a 'Did you know...?' section with some unusual facts.

d Illustrate it with visual material: photos of landscapes, attractive maps...

In your groups, present your murals to the rest of the class.

THINK LIKE A GEOGRAPHER. **Explaining frontiers**

Europe: are political frontiers influenced by relief?

Many relief features are shared by more than one country – for example, a mountain range
may cross several countries. But in the past, natural frontiers also reflected physical relief.
For example, the Roman Empire had a frontier along the Rhine and Danube Rivers.
Do similar natural frontiers still exist today?

Before you look at any maps, think about the national frontiers of Europe that you already know about.
Think, too, about the types of relief that may influence frontiers: mountains, rivers…

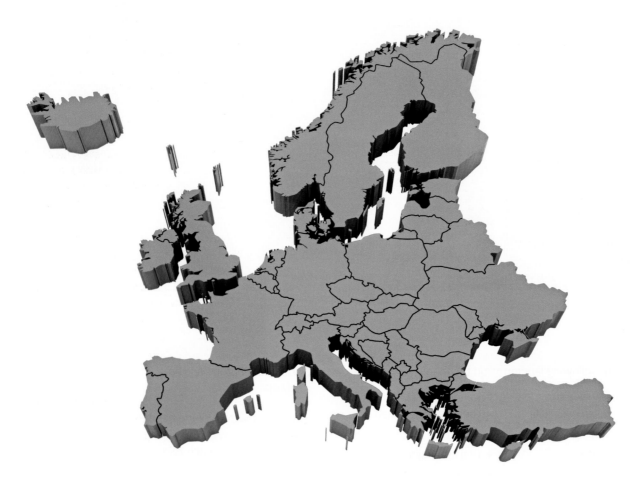

1 Look for relief and political maps of Europe and compare them. Then answer the following questions:

a Which mountain ranges create a natural frontier between Europe and Asia?

b Does the international boundary between France and Spain correspond to any relief feature? What about Sweden and Finland?

c How many countries are there on the Italian Peninsula? And the Scandinavian Peninsula?

d How many countries does the Rhine River flow through? Are there places where its course matches international frontiers?

2 Look for more information about the Carpathian Mountains and answer the following questions:

a In which countries are the Carpathian Mountains found?

b Do the mountains form a natural frontier between any of these countries?

c How high is Moldoveanu Peak? Which country is it in? Do any of this country's boundaries match natural frontiers?

3 In general, do you think relief features unify or divide European countries?
Discuss your ideas with your classmates.

THINK LIKE A GEOGRAPHER. **A classic novel**

Around the World in 80 Days, by Jules Verne

Jules Verne wrote a novel about the adventures of Phileas Fogg and his servant. Together they travelled round the world in 80 days. Why did they do it? To win a bet!

In the following scene (from Chapter 3) a group of friends discuss a bank robbery. They ask themselves where the bank robber is now.

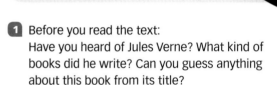

1 Before you read the text:
Have you heard of Jules Verne? What kind of books did he write? Can you guess anything about this book from its title?

2 Look quickly at the text. Which means of transport
are mentioned? Are they still used today?

3 Now read the text more carefully and answer the questions:

a When does this story take place?

b What is the bet?

c What do they mean when they say "The world has got smaller"?

d Look for the cities that are mentioned in an atlas.
Which continents are they on?

e What do you think happens next in the novel?

f How do you think the novel ends?

4 In groups, use Google Earth to make a virtual trip: "Around the world in --- minutes."

a Which means of transport will you use? Are they the same as in the 19th century?

b Find out about interesting places to visit. Include cities on at least four continents.

c Discuss all the things (clothes, equipment…) that you need to take with you. Remember to check what the climate is like in each place.

d Use Google Earth to make your virtual journey. "Visit" all the places that you have chosen. Time how long you take.

"Has the world grown smaller?" Stuart said. "Certainly," Fogg said. "The world has grown smaller, because a man can now go round it ten times more quickly than a hundred years ago. And that is why the search for the thief is likely to succeed."
"But that is also why the thief may escape."
"You have a strange way of proving that the world has grown smaller", Stuart said. "Just because you can go round it in three months…"
"In eighty days," Phileas Fogg interrupted.
"That is true, gentlemen," another friend added. "Only eighty days, now that they have opened the section between Rothal and Allahabad on the Great Indian Peninsula Railway. Here is the estimate made by the Daily Telegraph:
From London to Suez via Mont Cenis and Brindisi, by railway and steamboat 7
From Suez to Bombay, by steamboat 13
From Bombay to Calcutta, by railway.......................... 3
From Calcutta to Hong Kong, by steamboat 13
From Hong Kong to Yokohama (Japan), by steamboat 6
From Yokohama to San Francisco, by steamboat 22
From San Francisco to New York, by railway 7
From New York to London, by steamboat and railway 9
TOTAL 80
"Yes, in eighty days!" Stuart exclaimed. "But there may be bad weather. Ships could be destroyed in shipwrecks. There could be railway accidents."
"Everything is included in the calculation," Phileas Fogg replied.
"In theory, you are right," Stuart said, "but in practice…"
"In practice, too, Mr Stuart."
"I'd like to see you do it in eighty days."
"It depends on you. Shall we go?"
"No, thank you! I bet four thousand pounds that such a journey is impossible."
"On the contrary, it is quite possible," Mr Fogg replied.
"Well, make it, then!"
"The journey round the world in eighty days?"
"Yes."
"I should like nothing better."
"When?"
"At once!"

Source: Jules Verne,
Around the World in 80 Days, 1873 (adapted)

The physical relief of Spain

FIND OUT ABOUT:

- The relief of Spain
- The rivers and lakes of Spain
- The climates and landscapes of Spain

KNOW HOW TO:

- Investigate natural environments

The Strait of Gibraltar. This narrow strait separates the Iberian Peninsula from Africa. It connects the Mediterranean Sea to the Atlantic Ocean. At its narrowest, it is only 14 km wide.

Spain, seen from space

The **European Space Agency** is dedicated to space exploration. Twenty European countries are members. The agency was created in 1975, and its headquarters are in Paris. Its other centres include the European Space Astronomy Centre in Villanueva de la Cañada (Madrid).

Canary Islands

Iberian Peninsula

The Pyrenees. This mountain range is more than 400 km long. It stretches from the Cantabrian Sea to the Mediterranean Sea.

It is a natural frontier between Spain and France.

Balearic Islands

Ceuta

Melilla

HOW DO WE KNOW?

Remote sensing is the collection of data about the Earth's surface from satellites. Computers are then used to create satellite images.

- Can a satellite image provide information about the shape and relief of Spain?

- Do political frontiers appear on satellite images? Why?

? WORK WITH THE IMAGE

- Study the satellite image. Where is Spain in relation to the rest of Europe? And Africa?

- Where are the Balearic Islands and the Canary Islands? On which continent are Ceuta and Melilla found?

- What is a natural frontier? Does Spain have any natural frontiers?

The territorial organisation of Spain

DID YOU KNOW?

How big is a Spanish municipality?

Some Spanish municipalities, like Cáceres and Lorca, have a surface area of more than 1,500 km². Others are very small – Emperador (Valencia) has a surface area of only 0.03 km², although it is densely populated. The municipality of Madrid has a population of over 3,200,000 inhabitants. But just ten people live in Villarroya, in La Rioja!

WORK WITH THE MAPS

1 Use the maps to explain the territorial organisation of Spain.

Municipalities and provinces

Spanish territory is organised into municipalities, provinces, and Autonomous Communities and Cities. Each entity has its own institutions.

- A **municipality** is the basic unit of territorial organisation. It consists of one or several population centres, and the surrounding area that it administers. There are more than 8,100 municipalities in Spain; some are much larger than others.

- A **municipal council** (or **ayuntamiento**) governs each municipality. It consists of a mayor and an assembly of councillors, who are elected in local elections every four years. The council controls basic services, like street lighting and the supply of drinking water.

- A **province** is a group of municipalities. Spain has 50 provinces. They are governed by a **Provincial Deputation**, which consists of a president and a number of provincial deputies, who are appointed by the municipalities. Its role is to organise and coordinate the work of the municipalities. Spain's islands have their own form of administration: **Cabildos** in the Canary Islands, and **Consejos** in the Balearic Islands.

ACTIVITIES

2 How many municipalities, provinces, Autonomous Communities and Autonomous Cities are there in Spain?

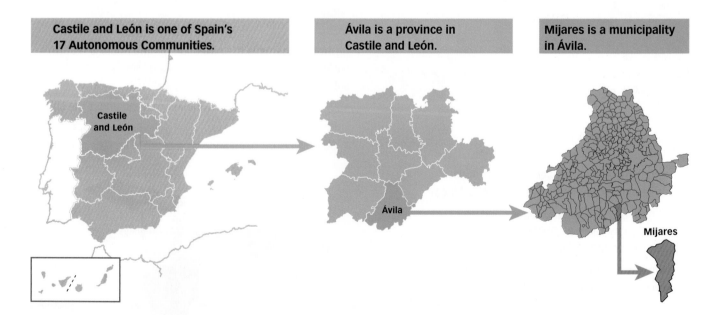

Castile and León is one of Spain's 17 Autonomous Communities.

Ávila is a province in Castile and León.

Mijares is a municipality in Ávila.

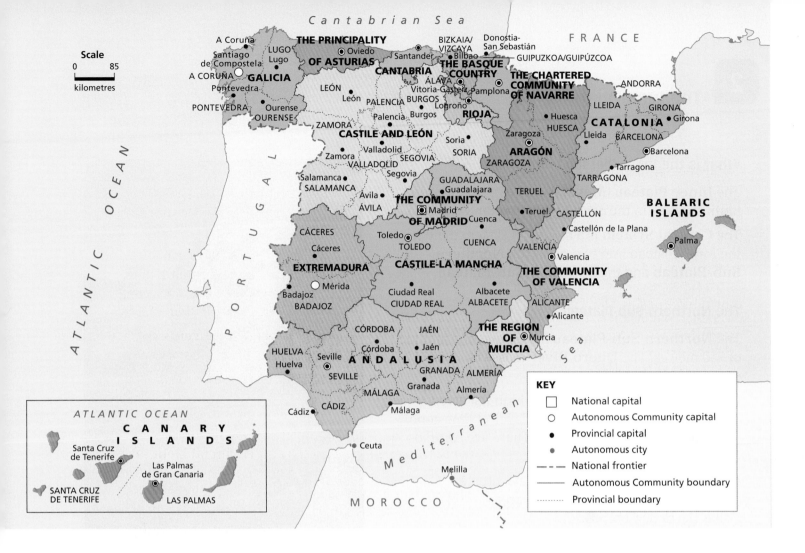

Autonomous Communities

An **Autonomous Community** is formed of one or more provinces. It has a range of powers, including the right to pass laws.

Autonomous Communities were established between 1978 and 1995. Today, Spain has 17 Autonomous Communities and two Autonomous Cities (Ceuta and Melilla).

The **Statute of Autonomy** is the key law regulating self-government in each Autonomous Community. It establishes official institutions, and sets out their authority in areas like health, education and transport. The Statute defines the main features of each Autonomous Community: its territorial frontiers, capital, flag, and official language or languages.

ACTIVITIES

3 Investigate your own Autonomous Community. Include the following information:

- When was your Autonomous Community founded?
- What are its main institutions?
- Who is its President?

Prepare an illustrated fact file.

WORK WITH THE MAPS

4 Which Autonomous Community has the most provinces? What are they called?

5 Which Communities have a single province?

6 What are Spain's two Autonomous Cities?

7 Is the capital of a Community always a provincial capital?

8 Which Communities share a frontier with your Autonomous Community?

What is the Inner Plateau?

The **Inner Plateau** (**Meseta**) is an extremely large, highland area in the centre of the Iberian Peninsula.

The **Central System** is a mountain system dividing the Inner Plateau into two parts: the **Northern Sub-Plateau** and the **Southern Sub-Plateau**.

The Northern Sub-Plateau

The **Northern Sub-Plateau** has an average altitude of 750 metres. The **Duero River** crosses it in an east-west direction.

- *Páramos* (moors) are found in high flat areas. The land has eroded, leaving a layer of limestone where little vegetation grows. There are *páramos* in the east of the Duero basin.

- At a lower altitude, the rivers have created fertile **clay** agricultural land, in areas like Tierra de Campos.

The Southern Sub-Plateau

The **Southern Sub-Plateau** has an average altitude of 650 metres.

- The **Montes de Toledo** mountain range separates the Tajo river system in the north from the Guadiana river system in the south.

- There are *páramos* and clay agricultural plains in the **Tajo basin**.

- The plain of La Mancha occupies much of the **Guadiana basin**.

Moorland near Chinchón (Madrid).

ACTIVITIES

1 What is the Inner Plateau? Which mountain systems cross it?

2 Would it be easier to build a north-south road across the Northern Sub-Plateau or the Southern Sub-Plateau? Why?

The Guadarrama Mountain Range is part of the Central System.

RELIEF MAP OF SPAIN

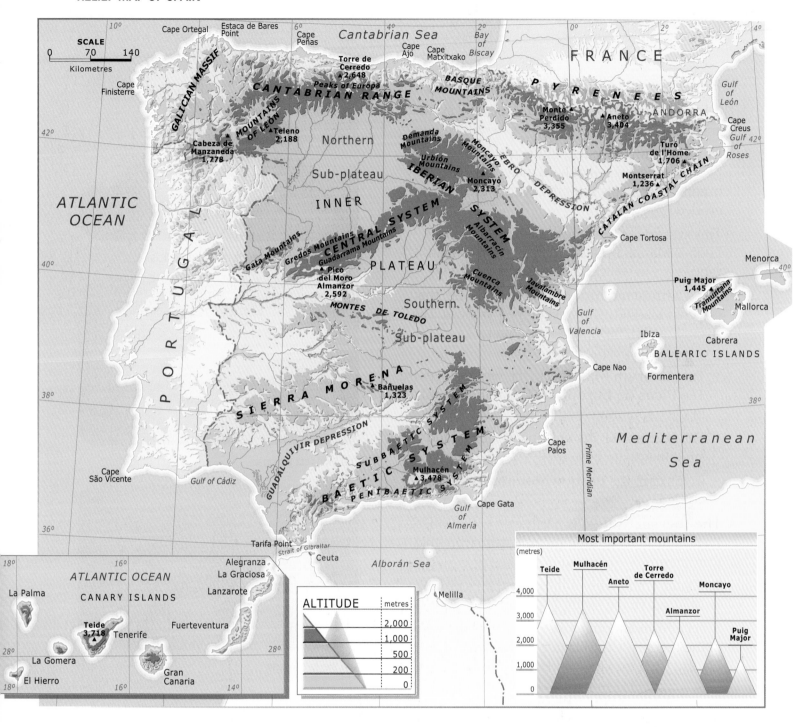

Mountain ranges

- The **Central System** is formed by a number of mountain ranges: Gata, in the west; Gredos and Guadarrama, in the centre; Somosierra, Ayllón and Pela in the east.

- The **Montes de Toledo** mountain range on the Southern Sub-Plateau is at a lower altitude than the Central System.

🔗 WORK WITH THE MAP

3 With a partner, locate the following relief features on the map.

- Northern Sub-Plateau
- Montes de Toledo
- Guadarrama Mountains
- Iberian System
- Sierra Morena
- Central System

4 Locate three high mountain peaks.

Mountain ranges surrounding the Inner Plateau

The Inner Plateau is surrounded by several systems of mountain ranges:

- **The Galician Massif**, in the north-west of the peninsula, is formed of hard materials, like granite. Its relief is smooth because the rocks are eroded.

  This system is sometimes called the 'Galician-Leonés Massif' because some of its mountain ranges are in Galicia, and others are in León.

- **The Cantabrian Mountains** stretch from the Galician Massif to the west of the Pyrenees. The rivers flowing through the mountains have created many deep narrow valleys.

  - The **Asturian Massif** is in the west and centre. The **Picos de Europa** are the highest points in the Cantabrian Mountains.

  - The **Santander Mountains** are lower and smoother than those of the Asturian Massif.

  - In the east, the **Basque Mountains** are very eroded.

- **The Iberian System** is north-east of the Inner Plateau. It separates the Inner Plateau from the Ebro basin.

  Its highest mountain ranges, like the Picos de Urbión, are in the north.

- **Sierra Morena** runs east-west across the south of the Iberian Peninsula. It separates the Inner Plateau from the Guadalquivir basin.

Granite rocks in Penedos de Traba (Galicia).

The Picos de Europa.

The Sierra Morena.

 **ACTIVITIES**

1. Copy and complete the table in your notebook.

Mountain ranges in Spain	
On the *Meseta*:	......
Surrounding the *Meseta*	......
Away from the *Meseta*	......

2. Look for the name and altitude of the highest peak in each of the following mountain ranges.
   - The Galician Massif
   - The Cantabrian Mountains
   - The Iberian System

3. The mountain ranges surrounding the Inner Plateau are a barrier that separates it from the influence of the sea. What are the consequences?

Relief away from the Inner Plateau

Some relief features of the Iberian Peninsula
are not connected to the Inner Plateau.
They include several high mountain ranges,
and the Guadalquivir and Ebro river basins.

- **The Pyrenees**. In the north of the Iberian
  Peninsula, the Pyrenees stretch for
  nearly 500 km from the Bay of Biscay to
  Cape Creus in the Mediterranean Sea.
  They form a natural frontier between Spain
  and France.

  They consist of young, steep mountains.
  The Central Pyrenees have the highest peaks,
  like Aneto (3,404 m).

- **The Catalan Coastal Range**. In the north-east,
  this consists of a system of mountain ranges
  that run parallel to the Mediterranean coast.

- **The Baetic System**. In the south-east,
  this stretches from the Gulf of Cádiz
  to Cape Nao:

  - The **Penibaetic System** runs parallel
    to the coast. The highest mountain
    on the Iberian Peninsula, Mulhacén
    (3,480 m) is in the Sierra Nevada.

  - The **Sub-Baetic System** is north
    of the Baetic System, and is at a
    lower altitude.

River basins

The Ebro and Guadalquivir Rivers form
very large triangular **depressions**.

- The **Ebro river basin** is in the north-east
  of the Iberian Peninsula. The Ebro River
  flows through this large valley in a
  west-east direction.

  It lies between the Pyrenees in the north,
  the Iberian System in the south, and
  the Catalan Coastal Range in the east.

  This depression was formed at the
  same time as the Pyrenees Mountains.

- The **Guadalquivir river basin** is
  in the south-east of the Iberian Peninsula.
  The Guadalquivir River flows through
  the valley from east to west.
  There is **marshland** near
  the river mouth.

Mulhacén.

The Guadalquivir River.

 **ACTIVITIES**

4 Is the land in the Ebro and Guadalquivir
   river basins good for agriculture? Why?

5 Label a blank map of the Iberian
   Peninsula with the main mountain
   ranges, and the Ebro and Guadalquivir
   river basins.

The coastline of the peninsula

The peninsula has a very long coastline:

- The **Cantabrian** coast is a straight coastline with many cliffs, and only a few beaches.

- The **Mediterranean** coastline is very varied.

  - The coast of **Andalucía** is straight. It has cliffs in some regions, and flat plains in others.

  - The coast of **Murcia** and **Valencia** has long beaches and coastal lagoons, like the Albufera.

  - Along the **Catalan** coast, there are cliffs and small bays. The **Ebro Delta** is a large alluvial plain with coastal lagoons and marshland.

- On the **Atlantic** coastline:

  - The coast of **Galicia** is very irregular. It has many *rías*, or coastal inlets.

  - The coast of **Andalucía** is very low, and has long, sandy beaches.

The coastline in Cantabria.

The Albufera in Valencia.

 ACTIVITIES

1 What are the different types of coastline on the Mediterranean coast? And the Atlantic coast?

2 Does the erosive action of the sea influence the characteristics of the coastline? How?

 DID YOU KNOW?

The Ebro Delta

The Ebro River flows into the Mediterranean Sea at Deltebre (Tarragona). At its river mouth, there is a very large delta, of more than 300 km^2. It has great ecological value.

About a fourth of the delta was declared a National Park in 1983. The rest is agricultural land or for urban use. A lot of rice is grown there.

- Look for the Ebro Delta on this aerial photo. Can you see the agricultural land? What proportion of the delta does it cover?

The Balearic Islands

The **Balearic Islands** are an archipelago in the Mediterranean Sea. There are five main islands: **Mallorca**, **Menorca**, **Ibiza**, **Formentera** and **Cabrera**.

Their relief is mainly flat, except for the Sierra de Tramontana mountain range in Mallorca.

The Canary Islands

The Canary Islands are an archipelago in the Atlantic Ocean, off the coast of Africa.

There are seven main islands: **Tenerife**, **La Palma**, **La Gomera**, **El Hierro**, **Gran Canaria**, **Fuerteventura** and **Lanzarote**.

The islands are of volcanic origin. Lanzarote and Fuerteventura are the oldest islands, and have flat, eroded relief. The other islands have steeper, higher relief.

Mount Teide (3,718 m) on Tenerife is the highest mountain in Spain.

The Sierra de Tramontana, Mallorca.

Lanzarote, in the Canary Islands.

 ACTIVITIES

3 Look in internet for photos of different kinds of volcanic relief on the Canary Islands. Explain them to your classmates.

 DID YOU KNOW?

Volcanoes on the Canary Islands

The Canary Islands emerged from the ocean floor as a result of volcanic activity. Today, there are many types of volcanic landscapes, including craters, cones and lava fields.

There have been several volcanic eruptions on the Canary Islands. In 2011-2012, there was an underwater eruption near the island of El Hierro and some of the population was evacuated. Mount Teide is one of the biggest volcanoes in the world, measured from its base.

The volcano of Fuencaliente (La Palma).

Rivers

The rivers of Spain flow into three oceans or seas. The ridge dividing each area is called a **watershed**.

- **The Cantabrian Sea**. The Cantabrian Mountains are near the coast, so rivers flow short distances down their steep slopes. It rains all the year round, so the rivers have an abundant, regular flow.

  The **Nervión**, **Nalón** and **Navia Rivers** are among the rivers that flow into the Cantabrian Sea.

- **Atlantic Ocean**. These long rivers have their sources in high regions far from the coast. Precipitation is heavy in the mountains, where the rivers have their tributaries. So their flow is abundant, and they end in large estuaries.

  From north to south, the main Atlantic rivers are the **Miño**, **Duero**, **Tajo**, **Guadiana** and **Guadalquivir**.

- **Mediterranean Sea**. Most rivers are short and have a scarce, irregular flow, like the **Turia**, **Júcar** and **Segura**.

  However, the **Ebro River** has the largest flow of all Spanish rivers. Many of its tributaries begin in the Pyrenees, where there is heavy rainfall.

The upper course of the Nervión River.

The Duero River.

ACTIVITIES

1. Investigate the geography and ecology of one Spanish river. Prepare an illustrated report:
   a Look for basic information about the river: its length, tributaries, the cities it flows through, etc.
   b Find out about the ecology of the river. Are there any environmental problems?

2. Which ocean or sea do the rivers in your Autonomous Community flow into? Find out more about one river in your Autonomous Community.

The Júcar River.

RIVERS, LAKES AND RESERVOIRS IN SPAIN

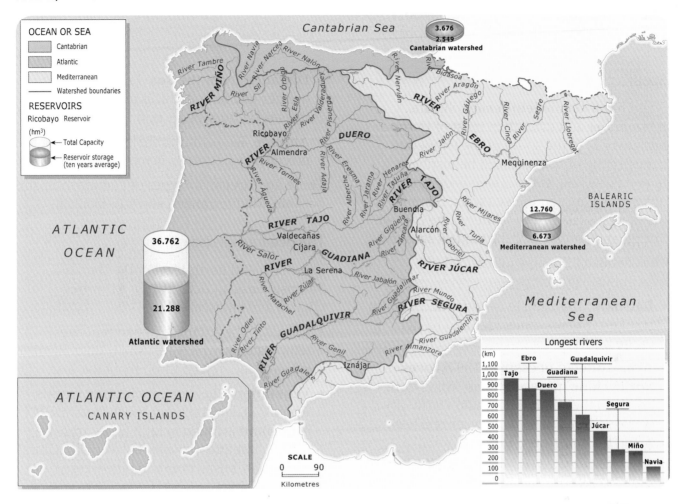

OCEAN OR SEA
- Cantabrian
- Atlantic
- Mediterranean
- Watershed boundaries

RESERVOIRS
Ricobayo Reservoir
(hm³)
← Total Capacity
← Reservoir storage (ten years average)

Cantabrian Sea

3.676 / 2.549
Cantabrian watershed

River Tambre
River Navia
River Narcea
River Nalón
River Órbigo
RIVER MIÑO
River Sil
River Esla
River Pisuerga
River Valderaduey
River Bidasoa
River Nervión
River Aragón
RIVER
River Gállego
EBRO
River Cinca
River Segre
River Liobregat

Ricobayo
DUERO
RIVER
Almendra
River Tormes
River Águeda
River Adaja
River Eresma
River Alberche
River Tajuña
River Jalón
Mequinenza

ATLANTIC OCEAN

RIVER TAJO
Buendía
River Henares
River Jarama
RIVER TAJO
Valdecañas
Cijara
River Salor
RIVER
La Serena
GUADIANA
River Jabalón
River Gigüela
River Zancara
Alarcón
River Mijares
River Turia
River Cabriel
RIVER JÚCAR
River Guadalimar
River Mundo
RIVER SEGURA

BALEARIC ISLANDS

12.760 / 6.673
Mediterranean watershed

36.762 / 21.288
Atlantic watershed

RIVER GUADALQUIVIR
River Odiel
River Tinto
River Zújar
River Matachel
River Genil
River Guadalete
Iznájar
River Guadiamar
River Almanzora
River Guadalentín

Mediterranean Sea

ATLANTIC OCEAN
CANARY ISLANDS

SCALE
0 — 90
Kilometres

Longest rivers

(km)
1,100 — Ebro — Guadalquivir
1,000 — Tajo — Guadiana
900 — Duero
800
700 — Segura
600
500 — Júcar
400
300 — Miño
200
100 — Navia
0

DID YOU KNOW?

Lakes and reservoirs

Some **lakes** formed in the craters of volcanoes, like Campo de Calatrava (Ciudad Real). Other lakes were caused by the erosion of glaciers.

Spain has more than 1,200 **reservoirs**. They are very useful because they control flooding, create hydraulic energy and supply water for industrial and agricultural use. They also provide us with much of our drinking water. But their construction has had an environmental and human cost. Some villages were flooded when new reservoirs were built.

WORK WITH THE MAP

3 Which rivers flow into the Cantabrian Sea, the Atlantic Ocean and the Mediterranean Sea? What are the main characteristics of each group of rivers?

4 What are the tributaries of the Duero and Tajo rivers?

ACTIVITIES

5 Which is the longest river in Spain? Does it also have the greatest flow?

6 Is there a reservoir in your region? Find out more about it.

Spain's climate

Spain has a mainly **temperate** climate. It is warmer and drier than most of Europe because it is in the south of the temperate climate zone of the northern hemisphere. In most of Spain, there is a considerable difference between the **seasons**. Summer is the hottest season, and winter is the coldest. Spring and autumn are the wettest seasons.

The climate of Spain is influenced by a number of factors:

- **Latitude**. The climate is hotter and drier in southern Spain, and colder and wetter in the north.

- **Atmospheric pressure**. The **Azores anticyclone** moves to Spain from North Africa in the summer, causing warm, dry weather. In winter, cold dry air reaches Spain from northern Europe.

- **Distance from the sea**. Precipitation is greater and temperatures are milder near the sea because or air humidity.

- **Altitude**. Temperatures are lower, and precipitation is greater, in mountainous regions.

There are three main types of climate in Spain: oceanic, Mediterranean and sub-tropical.

The oceanic landscape

The north and north-west of the Iberian Peninsula has an **oceanic** (or **Atlantic**) climate and landscape.

- **Climate**. The **Atlantic Ocean** regulates temperatures, which are usually mild. Rainfall is heavy and regular throughout the year.

- **Vegetation**. There are **deciduous woods**, where oak, chestnut and beech trees grow. **Moorland** is found in high areas. In some regions, **meadows** have replaced the natural vegetation, eucalyptus and pine trees.

SPAIN'S CLIMATE

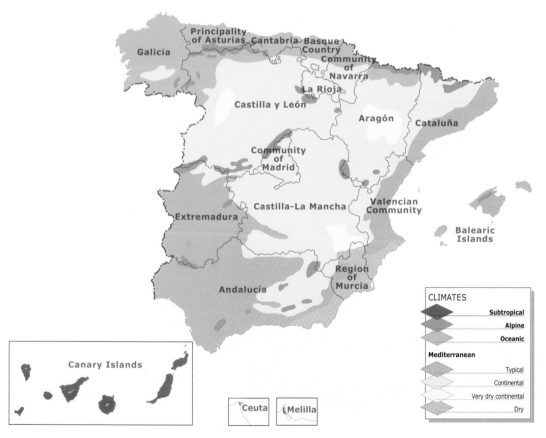

The Mediterranean landscape

A Mediterranean climate and landscape is found in the east, south and centre of the Iberian Peninsula, as well as on the Balearic Islands.

- **Climate**. Precipitation is mainly scarce and irregular (less than 800 mm.). In **coastal regions**, temperatures are mild because of the proximity of the sea. On the **Inner Plateau**, the mountain ranges are a barrier against the influence of the sea. Consequently, summers are extremely hot and winters are very cold.

- **Vegetation**. In **Mediterranean forests**, evergreen trees like the holm oak, cork oak and Mediterranean pine grow. In many regions, shrubs like rosemary, thyme and lavender have replaced the forests. In coastal regions, fruits and vegetables are grown.

The subtropical landscape

A subtropical climate is found in the Canary Islands, which are close to the Tropic of Cancer.

- **Climate**. Temperatures are mild all the year round, and precipitation is scarce, especially in the eastern islands.

- **Vegetation** includes date palms, pine trees, drago trees, and laurisilva vegetation.

An oceanic landscape.

An inland Mediterranean landscape.

Subtropical vegetation in Gomera (the Canary Islands).

 **ACTIVITIES**

1. Bring photos of Spanish landscapes into the classroom. In groups, ask your classmates to identify them as oceanic, Mediterranean or subtropical landscapes.

2. Look on internet for information about your Autonomous Community. Complete a fact file with the following information:

My Autonomous Community	
Relief:	......
Climate:	......
Rivers and lakes:	......
Vegetation:	......

1 Copy and complete the diagram.

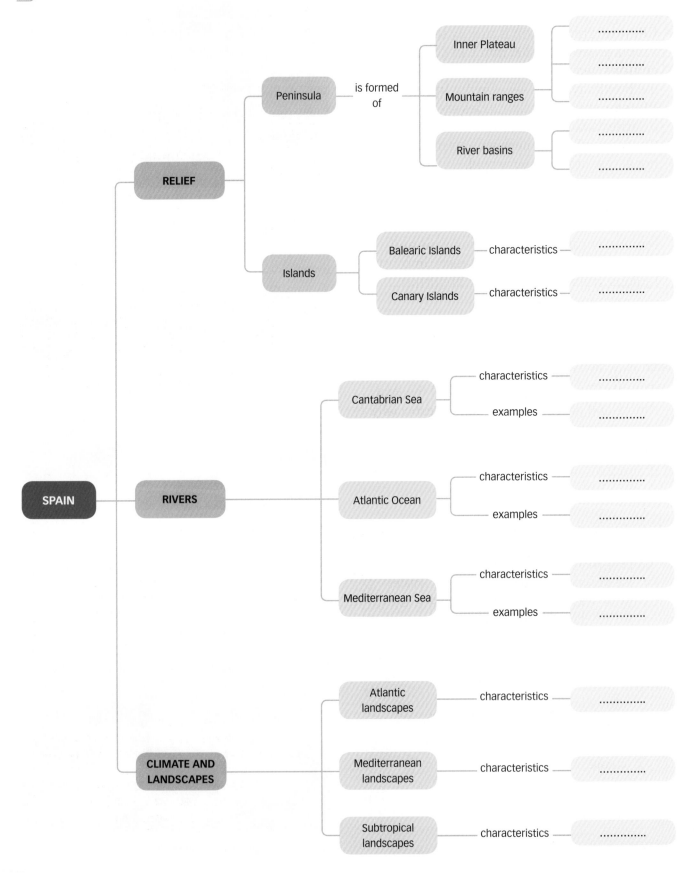

2 Are the following sentences true or false? Listen to the recording and check your answers.

a The Inner Plateau is a large, flat area in the south-west of the Iberian Peninsula.

b The Cantabrian Mountains are near the coast, so rivers only flow short distances.

c The Ebro River has the largest flow of all Spanish rivers.

d The Balearic Islands are an archipelago consisting of three main islands.

e In north-west Spain, the Atlantic Ocean regulates temperatures, which are usually mild.

f Evergreen trees like the holm oak and cork oak grow in Mediterranean forests.

3 Copy and complete a blank map of Spain with the following features:

- **Oceans and seas:** the Cantabrian Sea, the Atlantic Ocean, the Mediterranean Sea.
- **Landforms:** the Central System, Cantabrian Mountains, Iberian Mountain Range, Sierra Morena, Pyrenees, the Catalan Coastal chain, Baetic Mountains, the Ebro river basin, the Guadalquivir river basin, Mount Teide.
- **Rivers:** Miño, Nalón, Ebro, Duero, Tajo, Guadiana, Guadalquivir, Júcar, Segura.

4 Draw a map of your own Autonomous Community. Label it with the main relief features.

5 What type of landscape is shown in the photo? Which man-made features does it have?

ENVIRONMENTAL CONSERVATION: NATURE RESERVES

Doñana.

Spain's natural environment is regulated by the Natural Heritage and Biodiversity Act. Many of Spain's finest nature reserves have been declared national parks, like the wetlands at Tablas de Daimiel, near Ciudad Real. However, there are still many threats to these natural environments. For example, in 2013, ecologists protested against plans to build a gas pipeline through the national park in Doñana.

- Why do you think a gas pipeline might be a threat to a nature reserve?

6 Organise a debate.

With your classmates, identify one nature reserve in your region. Investigate and make notes on its ecological, economic and cultural importance. Then organise a debate with your classmates about whether it should be declared a national park.

PRACTICAL KNOWLEDGE. **Muniellos, natural landscape and cultural heritage**

The Nature Reserve of Muniellos is in a mountainous region in Asturias. It has one of the most important oak forests in Europe.

In 2000, Muniellos was declared a biosphere reserve by UNESCO. In 2003, the reserve was extended, and the Natural Park of Fuentes del Narcea, Degaña and Ibias was created. There are plans to create an even bigger nature reserve.

Fauna includes the brown bear, wild boar, wolf and wood grouse (*urogallo*).

About 6,000 people live in Muniellos, which has an exceptional cultural heritage. A number of buildings show us how people used to live there. For example, there were *pallozas*, which were stone houses with thatched roofs. There were *cortinos*, which were stone walls that protected beehives from the bears.

Cortino. This was a circular stone wall, 2 metres high.

1 Find Muniellos on a map.
   a Which mountain range is it in?
   b How do you explain the survival of its traditional way of life?

2 What type of landscape is found in Muniellos? What are its main characteristics?

3 Why does an area like Muniellos need legal protection? What would happen to Muniellos if it was not protected?

4 Only 20 people are allowed to visit this area each day. What do you think about this measure?

A *palloza*.

THINK LIKE A GEOGRAPHER. **Investigate Spain's natural environments**

Spain has four main types of natural environment: oceanic, Mediterranean, subtropical and mountain. With a partner, study the four maps on this page, and establish where each natural environment is found.

OCEANIC NATURAL ENVIRONMENTS

MEDITERRANEAN NATURAL ENVIRONMENTS

SUBTROPICAL NATURAL ENVIRONMENTS

MOUNTAIN NATURAL ENVIRONMENTS

1 In groups, look for information about one of these natural environments.

2 Complete a table similar to the one opposite.

3 Look for attractive photos on internet, and prepare a computer presentation of the natural environment that you have chosen.

Natural environment	
Relief	......
Climate	......
Rivers and lakes	......
Vegetation	......

8 Prehistory

Gran Dolina. Archaeologists found the fossil remains of *Homo antecessor*, who lived here 800,000 years ago.

Railway trench

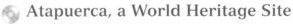

Atapuerca, a World Heritage Site

In the late 19th century, workers at Atapuerca, near Burgos, were making a trench to build a railway line when they discovered a remarkable archaeological site.

Atapuerca became a key site for our understanding of Prehistory. Its many remains showed that early humans lived in Western Europe about a million years ago. Archaeologists even found the remains of a previously unknown species: *Homo Antecessor*.

In 2000, UNESCO declared Atapuerca a World Heritage Site.

Sima de los Huesos (Bone Pit). The remains of thirty individuals were found here. One skull, called Miguelón, is exceptionally well preserved. The remains of a pelvis, called Elvis, indicate that some early humans were as tall as us, but stronger.

But only one tool was found here, and there were no animal remains. Was this place a sanctuary?

Sima del Elefante (Elephant Pit). Tools and animal bones show how early humans obtained food.

Archaeologists found pieces of a human jawbone about 1.2 million years old.

HOW DO WE KNOW?

At an **archaeological excavation**:

1. The surface is divided into squares.

2. Each archaeologist removes a layer of earth. A record is kept in notes, photographs and drawings.

3. Findings are carefully recorded. It is important to know exactly where the different objects were found.

4. They are sent to a scientific laboratory. They are analysed, and their date is established.

• What information can we get from the pieces of a single jawbone? And a pelvis?

? WORK WITH THE IMAGE

• Why do you think Atapuerca is such an important archaeological site?

• Why was *Sima de los Huesos* possibly a sanctuary?

• Look on internet for the website of the 'Fundación Atapuerca'. Find out more about Atapuerca.

1 What is Prehistory?

Prehistory

We use the term **Prehistory** to refer to the period before writing was invented. It began with the evolution of the early ancestors of humans in Africa about 5 million years ago. It only ended about 5,000 years ago when writing was invented.

We have no written evidence to study Prehistory. Instead, **archaeologists** interpret the remains that they find in archaeological excavations.

The periods of Prehistory

We divide Prehistory into three periods:

- The **Palaeolithic Age** began with the appearance of early humans, about 5 million years ago. They lived from hunting animals and gathering food.

- The **Neolithic Age** began with the invention of agriculture about 10,000 years ago. Human beings settled in villages. They grew crops and raised animals.

- The **Metal Age** began about 7,000 years ago. Human beings used metal to make objects.

THE PERIODS OF PREHISTORY

PALAEOLITHIC | NEOLITHIC | METAL AGE

5 million years ago | 10,000 years ago | 7,000 years ago | 5,000 years ago

Human evolution

Human beings today are the result of a long process of evolution called **hominization**. Our ancestors gradually acquired the characteristics that make us different from the other primates:

- They became **bipedal**, which means they could walk upright on two feet. As a result, they could use their hands freely. They could see further.

- They could turn their **thumbs** back on their other fingers. Consequently, their hands could hold objects and make tools.

- The **brains** of early humans grew in size and complexity. They began to think creatively, and they used **language** to communicate.

What were hominids?

For millions of years, species of **hominids** (primates with some human characteristics) appeared and became extinct. Many of these species were not the direct ancestors of modern human beings.

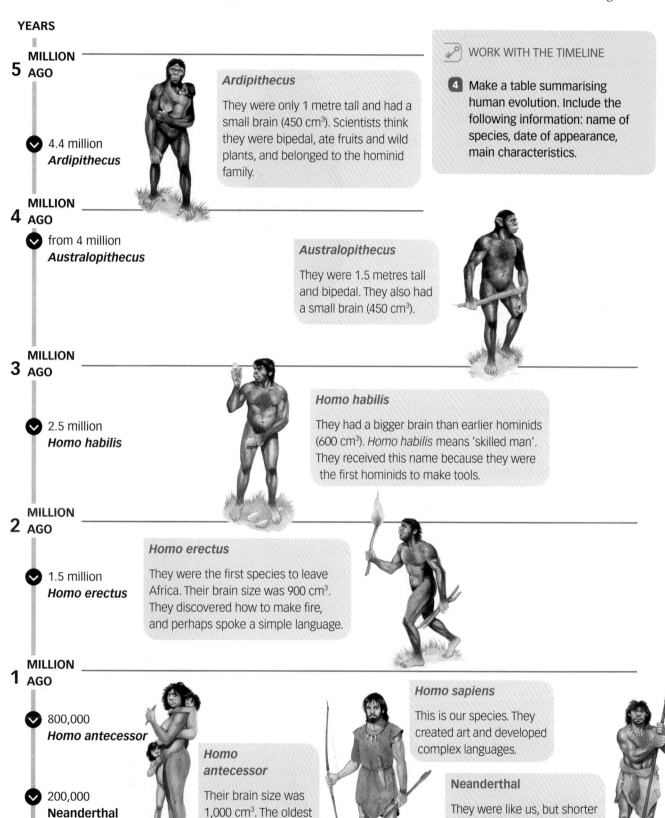

YEARS

5 MILLION AGO

4.4 million
Ardipithecus

Ardipithecus

They were only 1 metre tall and had a small brain (450 cm³). Scientists think they were bipedal, ate fruits and wild plants, and belonged to the hominid family.

4 MILLION AGO

from 4 million
Australopithecus

Australopithecus

They were 1.5 metres tall and bipedal. They also had a small brain (450 cm³).

3 MILLION AGO

2.5 million
Homo habilis

Homo habilis

They had a bigger brain than earlier hominids (600 cm³). *Homo habilis* means 'skilled man'. They received this name because they were the first hominids to make tools.

2 MILLION AGO

1.5 million
Homo erectus

Homo erectus

They were the first species to leave Africa. Their brain size was 900 cm³. They discovered how to make fire, and perhaps spoke a simple language.

1 MILLION AGO

800,000
Homo antecessor

200,000
Neanderthal

195,000
Homo sapiens

Homo antecessor

Their brain size was 1,000 cm³. The oldest remains were found at Atapuerca, Burgos.

Homo sapiens

This is our species. They created art and developed complex languages.

Neanderthal

They were like us, but shorter and stronger. They had quite big brains (1,500 cm³). They buried their dead.

WORK WITH THE TIMELINE

4 Make a table summarising human evolution. Include the following information: name of species, date of appearance, main characteristics.

What was the Palaeolithic Age?

The **Palaeolithic Age** is the first and longest period in Prehistory. It extends from the emergence of early hominids about 5 million years ago, to the invention of agriculture about 10,000 years ago.

What did people eat?

Early humans were **hunter-gatherers**: they lived from hunting animals, fishing and gathering food.

- They **hunted** all kinds of animals, including mammoths, bears, deer and bison. They ate the meat of the animals, and made clothes from their skins.

- They **gathered** wild plants and fruit.

A flint hand axe. This tool was used to cut meat and carve wood.

How did people live?

People were **nomads**: they followed the animals that they hunted, and looked for places where they could find food and water.

They stayed in **rock shelters** and **caves**. They sometimes made **huts** from branches, leaves and animal skins. They made **tools** from stone, bone and wood.

Fire was a key discovery. About half a million years ago, humans learned how to use fire when it was caused naturally by lightning. Later, they learned how to make fire. They used it to heat their shelters, cook food and drive wild animals away.

They lived together in **tribes** of twenty to forty people. Several tribes formed a **clan**.

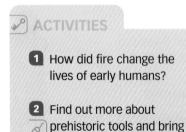 ACTIVITIES

1. How did fire change the lives of early humans?

2. Find out more about prehistoric tools and bring a photo into class. Explain it to your classmates.

WORK WITH THE IMAGE

3. Describe the daily life of a Palaeolithic tribe. Do you think women and men did the same tasks?

cave

cave paintings

makin[g] fire

gathering fruit

leather skins

hunting

hut

eating roots

treating leather

making tools

fishing

Palaeolithic beliefs and art

They were buried with valuable objects.

A late Palaeolithic burial.

 WORK WITH THE PHOTO

1 What does this burial tell us about late Palaeolithic attitudes to death?

Venus of Willendorf. This famous statuette is only 11 cm high. It was created over 20,000 years ago.

What did people believe?

Early human beings were afraid of **natural forces** like thunder and lightning. They believed that spirits could help or harm them, when they were hunting, ill or pregnant. They practised **rituals** to ask the spirits for assistance.

Burials indicate that early humans had respect for those who had died. Archaeological excavations have shown that the Neanderthals buried their dead 150,000 years ago.

Art

About 40,000 years ago, human beings began to decorate caves with art work. **Cave paintings** show that early human beings were talented artists. The most famous Palaeolithic paintings were found in caves in **Altamira** in northern Spain, and **Lascaux** in south-west France.

- Cave art often represented **animals**, such as deer, bison, horses and mammoths.

- It was **realistic**. It was given volume by the surface relief of the cave.

- It was **polychrome**, which means that several colours were used. Minerals were mixed with eggs and oil to make colours. Animal hair was sometimes used to make brushes.

- It probably had a **religious** purpose, and asked for success in hunting.

Small stone statues of women, called **Venus statuettes**, were another art form. They were made from stone, ivory or bones. They were highly exaggerated, and were probably fertility symbols.

 DID YOU KNOW?

The cave art of northern Spain

The Palaeolithic cave paintings of Altamira were discovered in the late 19th century. They were so extraordinary that many people did not believe that they had been painted thousands of years before. Other cave paintings were discovered in southern France, and other parts of northern Spain (like Tito Bustillo cave in Asturias). UNESCO declared Altamira a World Heritage Site in 1985. According to UNESCO, "the caves are masterpieces of creative genius and humanity's earliest accomplished art."

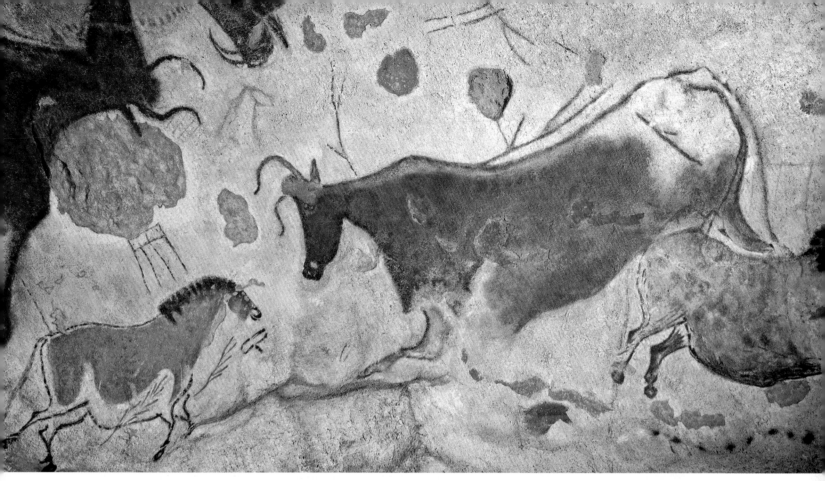

Cave paintings in Lascaux (France).

painting by hand

fire provides light

mixing colours

Cave painting.

ACTIVITIES

2 What evidence helps us to understand the beliefs of Palaeolithic men and women?

3 Investigate Palaeolithic cave art.

a Look on Internet for representations of animals from two of the following caves:

- Tito Bustillo
- El Pindal
- Santimamiñe
- Ekain
- El Pendo
- Altamira

b In groups, discuss your photos with your classmates:

- Which animals are shown? Do these animals still exist today?
- Are the animals in groups? Are they moving? Do you think they are being hunted?
- What is the purpose of the painting?

c Which is the finest painting? Find out if other groups made a similar choice.

Neolithic sickle

Grinding stone

Polished stone axe

Pottery vessel

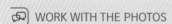 WORK WITH THE PHOTOS

1 With a partner, discuss how each of the objects shown in the photos was probably used.

ACTIVITIES

2 What were the main changes in the Neolithic period? What term is used to describe these changes?

3 Why did people become sedentary?

4

The Neolithic Revolution

What was the Neolithic Revolution?

The Neolithic period began about 10,000 years ago. There were so many important social and economic changes that we call this period the **Neolithic Revolution**.

The beginning of agriculture and livestock farming

People learned how to cultivate plants and raise livestock. This process began in the Middle East, but it soon spread to other regions.

- **Agriculture** probably started when people saw that plants grew after seeds fell to the ground. The earliest cultivated crops were grown in different parts of the world:

  - **Wheat** was grown in the Middle East and Europe.

  - **Rice** was grown in Asia.

  - **Corn** and **potatoes** were grown in America.

- **Domestication of animals**. It was easier to keep animals in an enclosed area than to move around to hunt them.

  The first **domesticated animals** were goats, sheep, oxen, horses and dogs.

A social revolution

Why was the development of agriculture and livestock farming so important? It meant that people had a regular supply of food, and didn't have to go from one place to another to find something to eat.

As a result, their lives changed completely:

- Many people became **sedentary**, and lived in settlements. Their villages had fences or walls to protect them against other human beings and wild animals. They built **storehouses** to store grain, and **animal pens** where they kept livestock.

- People often settled near **rivers**. The rivers provided a regular supply of water for agriculture, as well as for human consumption.

- Work became **specialised**. Some people worked in agriculture, and others raised livestock. There were artisans who made textiles and pottery.

Technical changes

'Neolithic' means 'New Stone', but in fact there were many types of technical changes:

- Neolithic people used **polished stone** to make agricultural instruments like scythes for cutting grass, and grinding stones for crushing grains.
- They invented the **loom**. They used wool and threads from animals to make **textiles**.
- They invented **pottery**. They made clay vessels to store cereals, and used bowls for cooking and eating.

Neolithic beliefs and art

In the Neolithic period, people believed in **natural forces**, like the Sun and the stars, because they thought they helped their crops to grow. They had **fertility cults**, and buried clay **fertility goddesses** in the earth to favour good harvests.

They buried the dead with their personal objects in a special cemetery called a **necropolis**.

Neolithic **cave paintings** were more schematic than in the Palaeolithic period. They were often done in a single colour. They used lines and circles to represent animals and humans.

A Neolithic fertility goddess from Crete.

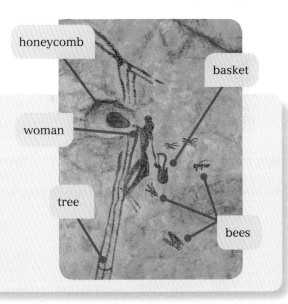

honeycomb

basket

woman

tree

bees

 DID YOU KNOW?

What is Levantine art?

The Neolithic period began later on the Iberian Peninsula than in the Middle East. The first settlements were created about 7,000 years ago. Cave art, known as Levantine painting, was created in eastern Spain.

People are often represented in Levantine art. In this cave painting from La Araña (Valencia), a woman is shown climbing up a tree to collect honey.

 WORK WITH THE IMAGE

4 Answer the questions.

a Describe the scene.

b Did people hunt individually, or in groups?

c Is this painting similar to Palaeolithic art?

Cave painting from La Valltorta (Castellón).

Early metallurgy. 1 They beat the cold metal with a hammer. 2 They heat the metal in a forge and then beat it. 3 They heat the metal until it forms hot liquid, and then pour it into a mould.

ACTIVITIES

2 Match the columns:

Iron •   • It was a mixture of metals.

Copper •   • It was the strongest metal.

Bronze •   • It was the first metal to be used.

THINK ABOUT IT

The Palaeolithic ('Old Stone') Age, Neolithic ('New Stone') Age and Metal Age are all named after the materials that were used to make tools and weapons.

• Why do you think these names are used?

The use of metals

Metallurgy was invented about 7,000 years ago. Metals were used to make tools, weapons and jewellery.

The use of **metals** gives this period its name: the **Metal Age**.

• **Copper** was the first metal to be used.

• **Bronze** was made later by melting copper and tin together. Bronze was harder than copper.

• **Iron** later replaced bronze, because it was more resistant.

Other inventions

About 5,500 years ago, three extremely important inventions were made:

• The **wheel** greatly improved transport.

• The **sail** used wind energy so ships became bigger and faster.

• The **plough** made it easier and quicker to work the land.

Social change

There were many **changes** in the Metal Age:

• Some metals were not found everywhere so **trade** developed with the regions where metals were found.

• With the wealth that trade produced, small settlements grew into important **cities**.

  They had shops and workshops as well as houses, and were protected by city walls.

• Greater wealth led to the development of larger, more complex societies.

  There were new types of specialised **occupations**, such as warrior, merchant and priest. Wealth was not equally distributed, and there were **social divisions**.

Megalithic monuments

At the end of the Neolithic period and during the Metal Age, large monuments were built with blocks of stone. They were called **megaliths** and had the following characteristics:

- **Menhirs** were single, vertical stones. They were probably used to worship the Sun.

- **Dolmens** were more complex constructions. Vertical stones formed walls which were covered by horizontal blocks. They were used for burials.

- **Stone circles** were formed of standing stones. They had a religious purpose.

The Metal Age on the Iberian Peninsula

Metallurgy was first developed on the Iberian Peninsula about 5,000 years ago. There were a number of important sites:

- **Los Millares** culture developed during the Copper Age. It takes its name from a walled settlement in Almería.

- **Argar** culture developed during the Bronze Age. The people made bronze weapons and lived in walled settlements.

- **Megalithic monuments** were built on the Iberian Peninsula and the Balearic Islands.

Stonehenge stone circle, England.

Dolmen of Santa Elena (Biescas).

'El Cabezudo' menhir (Valdeolea).

WORK WITH THE MAP

3 Look at the map key. What does the orange colour indicate?

4 Find two Palaeolithic sites, two Neolithic sites and two sites from the Metal Age.

5 Write short descriptions of the location of Palaeolithic, Neolithic and Metal Age sites:
There were several (Palaeolithic) sites in (northern) Spain. There were also...

PREHISTORIC SITES ON THE IBERIAN PENINSULA

Cantabrian Sea

Peñatú
Tito Bustillo
Altamira   La Hoya
Trasmañó   Huidobro   Basarán
Sacaojos
Manganeses   Atapuerca   Buñuel   Banyoles
de la Polvorosa   Oteruelos   El Cogul   Abric Agut
Las Cogotas   Los Casares   *Mediterranean Sea*
Las Batuecas   Cova Fosca
Ciempozuelos
Ibahernando   Alcúdia
Cova Negra   Parpalló
Cova de l'Or
Cova de la Sarsa   Barranc Blanc
Castellón Alto   Orce
El Algar
ATLANTIC OCEAN   Los Millares
Gibraltar

Palaeolithic
Neolithic
Metal Age
Megalithic monuments

ACTIVITY ROUND-UP

1 Copy and complete the table.

PREHISTORY			
CHARACTERISTICS	**PALAEOLITHIC**	**NEOLITHIC**	**METAL AGE**
PERIOD	-------	-------	-------
WHERE DID THEY LIVE?	-------	-------	-------
WHAT DID THEY EAT?	-------	Food from agriculture and livestock farming.	-------
TOOLS	-------	-------	-------
DISCOVERIES AND INVENTIONS	-------	-------	-------
BELIEFS AND ART	-------	-------	Megalithic monuments, like menhirs and dolmens.

2 Which invention or discovery indicates the end of Prehistory?

3 How many periods will you include in a timeline of Prehistory? Draw the timeline, using a different colour for each period.

5 million years ago   5,000 years ago

4 There were several species of hominids in Prehistory. Put the following species in chronological order, beginning with the oldest:

- Australopithecus
- Homo habilis
- Homo sapiens
- Ardipithecus
- Homo erectus

5 Copy and complete the text in your notebook. Use the recording to check your answers

In the Neolithic period, people began to live in settlements: they became _____ instead of nomadic. Their settlements were often near _____, which provided them with water for agriculture.

There were many inventions in this period. They used _____ to make textiles. They invented _____: they made clay vessels to store cereals.

Neolithic people believed in the Sun and the stars. They had _____ cults, which favoured good harvests. They buried the dead in a _____.

6 Put the following discoveries or inventions in chronological order. Begin with the oldest:

> The invention of pottery
> The discovery of fire
> The invention of the wheel

- Which periods of Prehistory do they belong to?
- When were the loom, the sailing boat and the plough invented?

7 Look at these two cave paintings and say if they belong to the Palaeolithic or Neolithic periods. Explain your answers.

A

B

8 Imagine that you lived in the Palaeolithic period. Decide where you live, who forms part of your band, what you eat, and which clothes you wear. Then write a diary about one week in your life.

9 Why were the following discoveries or innovations exceptionally important?

- Fire
- Agriculture

10 Write short explanations of the following terms, giving examples.

- The Neolithic Revolution
- Hominization

11 Compare the following terms.

- Nomadic and sedentary lifestyles

12 What is shown in this photo? What was it used for? Which other megalithic monuments have been preserved?

ICE AGES

For extremely long periods, the climate of the Earth was much colder than it is today. Ice covered large regions in Europe, Asia and America. Many humans had to survive in extreme conditions until the last Ice Age ended about 10-12,000 years ago.

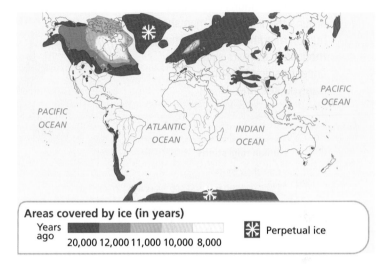

Areas covered by ice (in years)

Years ago 20,000 12,000 11,000 10,000 8,000

✳ Perpetual ice

13 Study the map, and investigate the Ice Age on internet. (Use the terms 'Ice Age Glacial Period' or 'Ice Age Prehistory'.)

a What are ice ages?

b Have there been many ice ages?

c What are the periods between ice ages called?

d Which types of fauna were found in cold regions during an ice age?

e According to the map on this page, which regions were covered by ice during the last ice age?

f Are we living in an ice age today?

THE LEGACY OF PREHISTORY

Prehistory is the longest period in all human history. It was a period of great achievements:

- Hominids evolved into creative human beings with the capacity to think. They learned how to express complex ideas using language.
- They created extraordinary artwork.
- They learned how to use fire.
- They made and used tools and weapons.

- They made important inventions like the loom, pottery, the wheel, the sail and the plough.
- They developed agriculture and livestock farming.

14 In groups, discuss the legacy of Prehistory:

- Are the achievements listed in chronological order?
  - Is anything important missing?
  - Which three developments in Prehistory were most important for later human history?

THINK LIKE AN HISTORIAN. **Analyse maps and archaeological objects**

Human migrations

The earliest hominids only lived in some parts of Africa. Yet today, human populations are spread around the world. This map shows human migrations over the many thousands of years since our ancestors first left Africa. Can you interpret it?

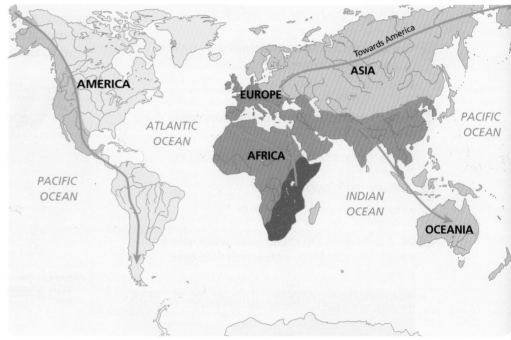

Human migrations

→ Likely routes

■ 5,000,000 to 1,500,000 years ago
■ 1,500,000 to 100,000 years ago
□ 100,000 to 10,000 years ago
□ 10,000 years ago

1 Which continents did humans live on?

- 2 million years ago
- 200,000 years ago
- 10,000 years ago

2 Which human species probably left Africa? (Look at the dates on the map and the chronology in this unit.)

3 Which species populated America?

4 Why do you think early humans emigrated from one region to another?

5 Look for more information on internet about how humans crossed from Asia to America about 20,000 years ago.

An archaeological excavation

Imagine that you are an archaeologist. You have excavated a prehistoric tomb and you have found the objects shown in the photos.

6 Answer the questions:

- Identify the objects: what were they used for?
- What are they made of?
- Which period is the tomb from?
- What was the occupation and status of the dead man?
- How do you know?

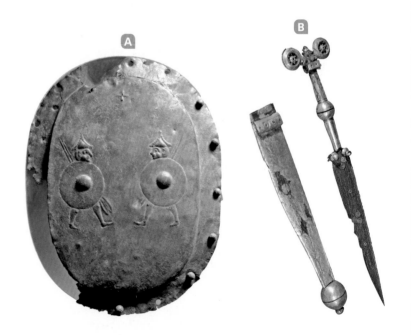

A   B

🏛 PRACTICAL KNOWLEDGE. **Conservation of cave art**

🌀 Altamira and Lascaux

The Altamira caves in northern Spain and the Lascaux caves in south-west France contain some of the most extraordinary art ever created. After visiting the Lascaux caves, the great artist Pablo Picasso declared: "We have invented nothing." For many thousands of years, cave art was perfectly preserved underground. But when thousands of visitors visited the caves every month, it created a huge problem of conservation.

The Lascaux cave was opened in 1948, but the humidity caused by the breathing of the visitors damaged the paintings. The cave was closed to the public in 1963. A replica Lascaux II was opened in 1983, so that visitors could admire the art without destroying the original. In Altamira, there were similar problems. The Altamira cave was closed to the public in 1977, but a replica was opened in 2001. In 2014, small groups were allowed to enter the caves again.

Visitors can now look at a reproduction of almost 200 square metres of the polychrome roof of the cave. In fact, they can see some paintings which are too high to be visible in the original cave.

1 Read the text and say if the following sentences are true or false. Correct the false sentences.

a The Altamira caves are in northern Spain, and the Lascaux caves are in north-east France.

b Pablo Picasso thought that Palaeolithic art was very bad because the artists had not discovered anything.

c The caves were damaged by water leaking into the ground.

d A replica of the Lascaux cave was opened in 1983.

e Visitors to the replica of Altamira can now see paintings that are hidden in the original cave.

2 Look for more information about Altamira and Lascaux and answer the questions:

a When were the caves discovered?

b How old are the cave paintings? Are they the oldest surviving cave art?

c What does the expression 'Sistine Chapel of Palaeolithic Art' mean? How is it used?

3 You have been asked to prepare a report about whether the public can visit the original Altamira cave. Your report should include the following information:

• Where are the caves? How were they discovered?

• Why are the caves so important?

• What are the advantages of opening the caves?

• What are the disadvantages?

4 In groups, debate your reports about access to the caves. Decide who will be represented: for example, an archaeologist, representatives of the Ministry of Culture and the Regional Government, a local hotel owner...

Choose your roles, and discuss the issues. You may decide that the caves should be closed, completely open, or visited by a limited number of people each month.

9 Ancient Mesopotamia and Egypt

FIND OUT ABOUT:

- The invention of writing
- The main characteristics of river civilisations
- Government, society and the economy in Mesopotamia and Egypt
- Culture and art in Mesopotamia and Egypt

KNOW HOW TO:

- Interpret a social pyramid
- Analyse early works of art
- Discuss archaeological conservation and our cultural heritage

Pyramid of Khufu. This pyramid was built by 50,000 people. Two million blocks of stone were used.

Mediterranean Sea
Alexandria
Pyramids of Giza — Cairo
River Nile
Luxor
EGYPT
Aswan — Red Sea
N
200 km

🌍 **Pyramid of Khufu, one of the Seven Wonders of the Ancient World**

About 5,000 years ago, the Pharaoh Khufu ('Cheops' in Greek) built a huge pyramid on the plain of Giza.

The **Pyramid of Khufu**, known as the Great Pyramid of Giza, is 147 metres high and 230 metres wide. It is the biggest pyramid ever built – five cathedrals would fit inside it.

Khufu's son Khafra and his nephew Menkaura also built pyramids in Giza.

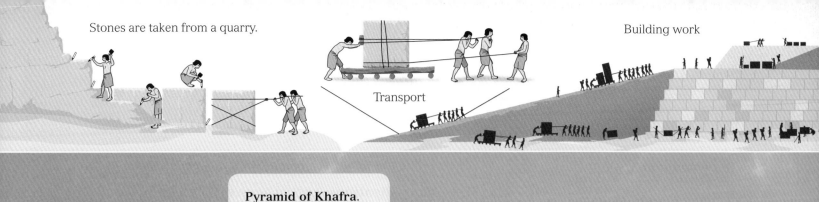

Stones are taken from a quarry.

Transport

Building work

Pyramid of Khafra. This was built on high ground, so it looks almost as high as the Pyramid of Khufu.

Pyramid of Menkaura. It is the smallest of the three pyramids. It is 60 metres high and 100 metres wide.

HOW DO WE KNOW?

Art and architecture are important sources for historians. They show us how people lived.

- Think about the resources required to build a pyramid. What type of person was buried there?

- Why did pyramids have secret passages?

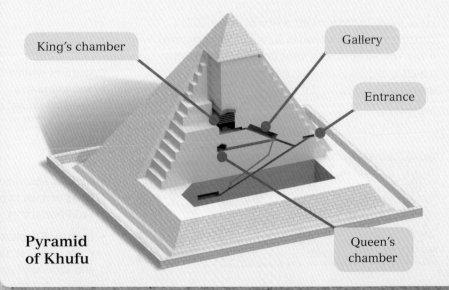

King's chamber

Gallery

Entrance

Queen's chamber

Pyramid of Khufu

? WORK WITH THE IMAGE

- Why do you think the pyramids of Giza were built near the River Nile?

- Which is the oldest pyramid? And the largest?

- What function did they have?

- How was a pyramid built?

- Look on internet for information about the Seven Wonders of the Ancient World. Write a list.

THINK ABOUT IT

What is a civilisation?

Early civilisations were large states (or groups of cities) that had urban life and writing, and shared similar customs and beliefs. Unlike the nomadic bands that existed in Prehistory, they were led by great rulers: emperors, kings or pharaohs. There were important differences between social groups.

- How do we use the term 'civilisation' in the world today? Give an example.

Where did the earliest civilisations appear?

The first **civilisations**, known as **river civilisations**, appeared in **Mesopotamia**, **Egypt**, **India** and **China**. In these regions, the flooding of great rivers fertilised the land and produced abundant harvests. As a result, there was enough food for large populations.

The earliest civilisations developed in the following river valleys:

- The **Tigris** and **Euphrates** in Mesopotamia.
- The **Nile** in Egypt.
- The **Indus** in Pakistan and India.
- The **Huang He** (Yellow) and **Yangtze** (Blue) Rivers in China.

The importance of writing

Writing was first used in Mesopotamia in about 3500 BC. It was a decisive development. In a small village, people could remember essential information. But in a growing city, writing was the only way to keep a record of taxes, trade and population.

Writing is used to separate History from Prehistory. Historians study the past in a different way when they can use written sources.

 DID YOU KNOW?

Cuneiform

In the fourth millennium BC, a type of writing called **cuneiform** was developed in Sumer, in Mesopotamia. It was written by making signs on a clay tablet with a reed. Later, it was called cuneiform because the patterns looked as if they were made by a wedge (*cuneus* in Latin).

Cuneiform writing. A reed was used to make marks on wet clay. The clay was left to dry in the Sun.

- Look for illustrations and information about other types of ancient writing by the Chinese, Egyptians and Phoenicians.
- Look for 'Egyptian Hieroglyphs Name' on internet. Write your first name in Egyptian hieroglyphs, and show it to your classmates.

RIVER CIVILISATIONS

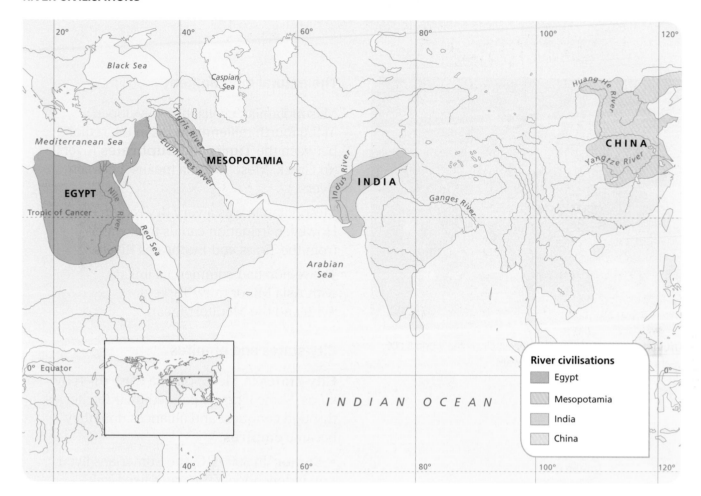

The characteristics of river civilisations

River civilisations were large-scale, complex societies. They shared the following characteristics:

- **Political power**. They had very powerful rulers. The king led the **army**, made laws, and was also a religious leader.

  He was assisted by **state officials**.

- **Social hierarchy**. There was a small minority of privileged people, who were often members of the king's family.

  But most people were very poor.

- **Large-scale building works**. Irrigation canals carried water from the rivers to the fields where crops were grown.

  The kings built impressive palaces, temples and tombs.

ACTIVITIES

1. What development marks the end of Prehistory? Why?

2. Which characteristics were shared by the early civilisations?

3. Why did river civilisations emerge near great rivers?

4. What do you think state officials did? Why were they important?

WORK WITH THE MAP

5. List the river civilisations, from east to west.

6. Which rivers were near each civilisation?

7. Which parallel was closest to the river civilisations? Were they in hot or cold zones?

Uruk in Sumer. This was the biggest city in the world 5,000 years ago. It was surrounded by walls.

The natural environment

Mesopotamian civilisation developed in the fourth millennium BC in the region between the **Tigris** and **Euphrates** Rivers. (In Greek, Mesopotamia means 'between rivers'.)

Mesopotamia was a very dry region. However, irrigation canals took water from the Tigris and Euphrates Rivers.

The region had commercial links with Asia Minor (now Turkey), Syria and the Mediterranean.

City-states and empires

City-states in Mesopotamia were ruled by kings. Some kings expanded their territories through conquest and alliances until they became **empires**.

- **Sumer**. In 3000 BC, the Sumerians lived in independent city-states like Uruk and Ur.

- **Akkadian Empire**. In 2300 BC, King Sargon conquered the Sumerian city-states. He founded the Akkadian empire.

- **Babylonian Empire**. After 1800 BC, the rulers of the city-state of Babylon established the first Babylonian Empire.

- **Assyrian Empire**. After 1350 BC, the Assyrians created a series of empires. In the seventh century BC, the Assyrian Empire stretched from the Mediterranean to the Persian Gulf.

- **Neo-Babylonian Empire.** In the late seventh century, a new Babylonian Empire was founded. Nebuchadnezzar II was its most famous ruler.

In the sixth century BC, the **Persians** conquered the region, and Mesopotamian civilisation came to an end.

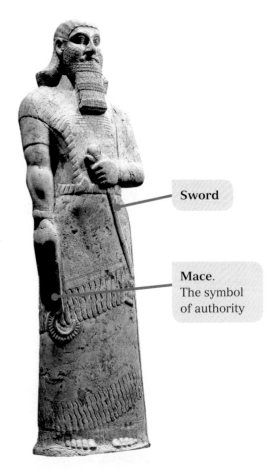

Sword

Mace. The symbol of authority

Ashurbanipal. This Assyrian ruler conquered many territories in the seventh century BC.

MESOPOTAMIA

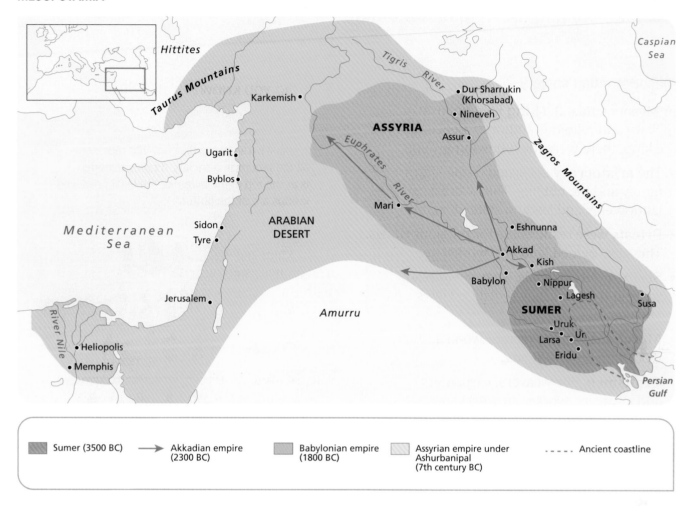

▨ Sumer (3500 BC)	→ Akkadian empire (2300 BC)	▨ Babylonian empire (1800 BC)	▨ Assyrian empire under Ashurbanipal (7th century BC)	----- Ancient coastline

MESOPOTAMIAN HISTORY

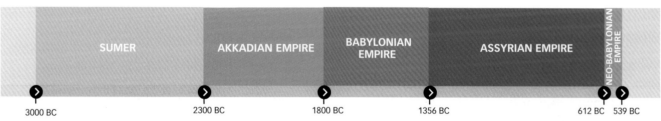

SUMER — AKKADIAN EMPIRE — BABYLONIAN EMPIRE — ASSYRIAN EMPIRE — NEO-BABYLONIAN EMPIRE

3000 BC 2300 BC 1800 BC 1356 BC 612 BC 539 BC

🔗 WORK WITH THE MAP AND THE TIMELINE

1 Which cities were near the Euphrates River? Which cities were near the Tigris River?

2 Which Mesopotamian empire ruled the largest territory?

3 Was the ancient coastline the same as it is today?

4 Look at a modern political map. Which present-day countries are now found in Mesopotamia?

🔑 ACTIVITIES

5 What is the meaning of the word 'Mesopotamia'?

6 When did Mesopotamian civilisation begin? How long did it last?

7 What were the main stages of Mesopotamian history?

8 Look on internet for an important event in each stage of Mesopotamian history. Locate it on the timeline.

Mesopotamian society

In Mesopotamia, the **king** held political, military and religious authority. Beneath the king, there were the following groups:

- The **aristocracy** consisted of the king's family and the nobility. They were landowners and leading state officials.

- **Priests** were responsible for religious rituals. They also owned land and workshops.

- **Scribes** were officials. They could read, write and count. They registered laws and commercial transactions.

- **Merchants** traded metals, wood and wool with other regions.

- **Craftsmen**, like weavers, carpenters and jewellers, worked in workshops.

- **Peasants** rented land around the city belonging to the king or the church. In exchange, the peasants gave them part of the harvest. They grew barley, wheat and beans.

- **Slaves** had no rights, and worked for the state, the church and wealthy people.

Women in Mesopotamia

Women were under the authority of men: first, their fathers, and later their husbands. But they had some rights. Women could buy and sell goods, own property and have jobs.

Women's lives reflected their wealth and social position. Poor women lived in harsh conditions. But an aristocratic woman could become a high priestess, who supervised the work of hundreds of people in a temple.

THINK ABOUT IT

- Imagine that you are a Mesopotamian scribe, and you live in Uruk. Describe your daily life at the king's service.

DID YOU KNOW?

A social pyramid

A social pyramid is a diagram that represents all the groups in a society. A ruling minority is at the top of the pyramid. The least privileged groups are at the bottom.

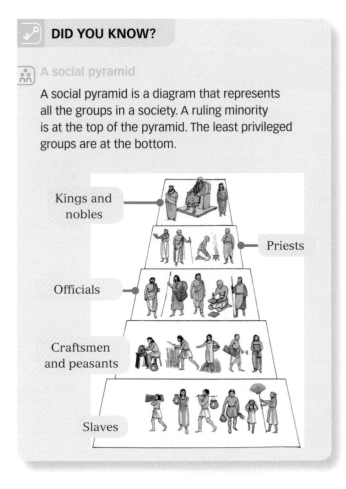

Kings and nobles

Priests

Officials

Craftsmen and peasants

Slaves

WORK WITH THE DIAGRAM

1 Study the diagram and answer the questions.

a Which groups were at the top of the pyramid?

b Where were merchants on this pyramid?

c Which groups do you think most people belonged to?

ACTIVITIES

2 Which social groups had the most power and wealth in Mesopotamia? What were the other social groups?

3 In Mesopotamia people had power and prestige if they knew how to read and write. Is it the same today? Why?

Religion in Mesopotamia

The Mesopotamians were **polytheistic**: they believed in many gods. Anu was the god of heaven, Enlil was the god of wind, and Ishtar was the goddess of war and love. Their gods had emotions just like human beings, but they were immortal.

Temples were the places where the gods lived on Earth. Some temples were built on stepped pyramids called **ziggurats**.

Mesopotamian art

The Mesopotamians made important innovations in both architecture and sculpture:

- **Architecture**. The Mesopotamians built magnificent palaces, like Dur-Sharrukin. They invented the **arch** and the **vault**. Mud bricks and stone were used for construction.

- **Sculpture**. They made stone **statues** of kings, gods and animals. They also depicted imaginary creatures, like bulls with human heads. **Reliefs** showed political and religious scenes.

The Suns represent the gods.

The king is wearing a helmet with horns.

Stele of Naram-Sin. This decorated monument shows a victory of the Akkadians.

Sanctuary of the Moon God Nanna

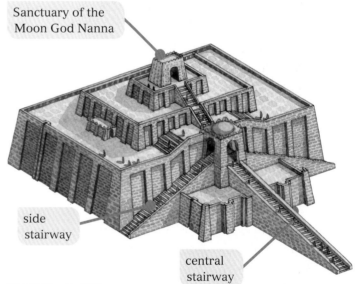

side stairway

central stairway

The Ziggurat of Ur.

 THINK ABOUT IT

The Code of Hammurabi

The Code of Hammurabi was one of the oldest codes of law in the world. It was written on a stone monument in Babylon in about 1800 BC. It was based on the idea: "an eye for an eye, a tooth for a tooth". This meant that your punishment was similar to your crime.

- Under this law, what would your punishment be if you broke your friend's smartphone?

- What is your opinion of this law?

 DID YOU KNOW?

Mesopotamian inventions

The Mesopotamians invented writing, and recorded the earliest literature, like the 'Epic of Gilgamesh'. They were the pioneers of mathematics, astronomy and the measurement of time. (They divided time into units of 60 parts.) They also invented the sailing boat and the wheel.

- How important were these inventions in later history?

Egypt, gift of the Nile

Each year floods descended the River Nile as a result of rainfall in the mountains of north-east Africa. Between June and October, water covered the Nile river valley.

In November, the water level fell, and mud made the soil fertile. The peasants planted seeds. They harvested their crops between March and June.

The Egyptians built dams to control the flow of the river. Irrigation canals carried water to the surrounding land.

The Nile was so important to the Egyptians that they worshipped it as a god. In the fifth century BC, a Greek historian Herodotus wrote that Egypt was the 'gift of the Nile'.

The importance of the River Nile

Ancient Egypt is one of the most important civilisations in human history. It developed along the **River Nile** in north-east Africa more than 5,000 years ago.

Most Egyptians lived near the River Nile, which flows from south to north. They called the river valley the '**black land**' because it was covered by dark fertile mud from the river. The dry deserts were called the '**red lands**'.

The River Nile was vital for Egyptian civilisation. It provided water for human needs and agriculture. It was also the main route of communications.

The history of Egypt

In the fourth millennium BC, independent kingdoms appeared in **Lower Egypt** (near the Nile delta), and **Upper Egypt** (further south). In 3100 BC, King **Menes** united these kingdoms and became the first **pharaoh**, or ruler, of Egypt.

The main periods of ancient Egyptian history were:

- The **Old Kingdom** (3100-2050 BC). The Egyptian state was created, and the pharaoh became a powerful, divine figure. The pharaohs Khufu, Khafra and Menkaura built huge **pyramids** in Giza. The capital was at Memphis.

- The **Middle Kingdom** (2050-1580 BC). The power of the pharaohs increased. New territories were conquered in the south. The capital was moved to Thebes.

- The **New Kingdom** (1580-31 BC). Thutmose I, Amenhotep III, Akhenaten, and Ramesses II were famous pharaohs. Large palaces and temples were built. Libya and Syria were conquered.

From 1100 BC, there were several **foreign invasions**. Egypt was conquered by the Assyrians, Persians, Greeks and Romans.

 WORK WITH THE ILLUSTRATIONS

1 Look at the pictures of the River Nile. Which period of the year is shown in each illustration?

ANCIENT EGYPT

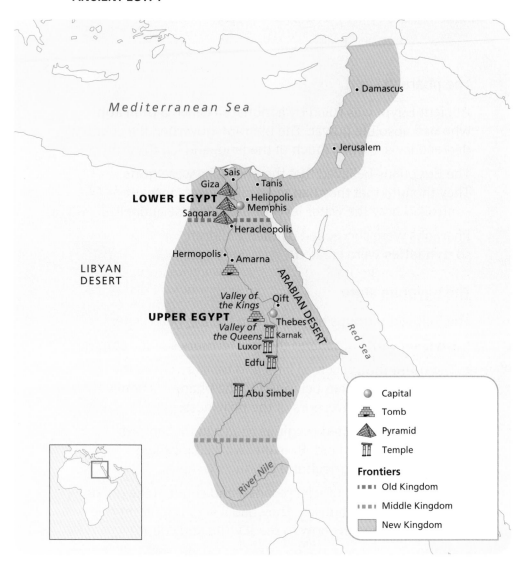

WORK WITH THE MAP AND THE TIMELINE

2 Study the map, the timeline and the text. Answer the questions.

a What were the frontiers of Egypt in the north, south, east and west?

b Which region was Lower Egypt? And Upper Egypt?

c Which of the three Kingdoms lasted for the longest time?

d The Nile flowed from south to north. Which places did it flow past?

e Where in Egypt were the pyramids built?

f Which city was the capital of the Old Kingdom? Which city later became the capital?

g In which period did Egypt have the largest territory?

h Did the history of Ancient Egypt take place Before Christ (BC)?

THE HISTORY OF EGYPT

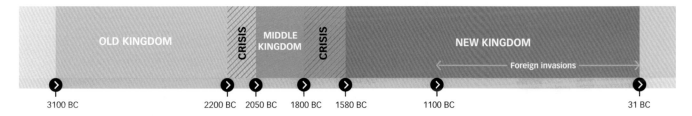

ACTIVITIES

3 What were the 'red' and 'black' lands? Where did most people live? Why?

4 Match the columns:

Old Kingdom • • The capital was moved to Thebes.

Middle Kingdom • • Libya and Syria were conquered.

New Kingdom • • Huge pyramids were built in Giza.

5 How long did Ancient Egypt last? What were the dates when it began and ended?

6 Is the phrase 'Egypt, the gift of the Nile' a good way to describe Ancient Egypt? Can you think of an alternative?

The **vulture** was the symbol of Upper Egypt.

The **snake** was the symbol of Lower Egypt.

The **Nemes** (striped head clothing) symbolised the power given by the gods.

A **ceremonial beard** showed the pharaoh's divinity.

The **crook** symbolised authority.

The **whip** showed the pharaoh's role as a guide.

A pharaoh.

The pharaoh

Ancient Egypt was ruled by a monarch called a **pharaoh**, who had absolute power. The pharaoh governed the country, decreed laws, owned much of the land, and led the army.

The Egyptians believed that the pharaohs were **gods**. They thought that they had magical powers, and controlled how the water level of the Nile rose and fell.

Pharaohs were succeeded by their children, so **dynasties** were created.

The Egyptian state

The following groups helped to run the Egyptian state:

- **Civil servants** organised the vast territories of the empire.
- The **noblemen** received land and treasures from the pharaoh. They often belonged to the pharaoh's family. They were the governors of the provinces.
- The **priests** directed religious rituals in the temples. They also owned land. Peasants worked for them and gave them agricultural products as taxes.
- The **scribes** kept official records, and counted the goods in the royal warehouses. They had a very important role because they knew how to read, write and count.
- **Soldiers** protected the frontiers. In return, they received land, gold and slaves from the pharaoh.

Papyrus

A scribe.

ACTIVITIES

1. What powers did the pharaohs have? How were they seen by other Egyptians?

2. What were the functions of noblemen, priests, scribes and soldiers?

3. Investigate life in Ancient Egypt.

   a Form groups of three students. Find good websites about ancient Egypt, and compare them. Record the links.

   b Choose one of the following subjects:
   - Who were the Egyptian gods?
   - Women pharaohs: Hatshepsut and Cleopatra
   - A famous tomb: Tutankhamun.

   c With your classmates, prepare a computer presentation or an illustrated poster on your chosen subject.

What was society like?

- Most people were poor **peasants** who lived in mud brick houses along the Nile. They worked on the lands belonging to the pharaoh, the priests or the noblemen. When the land was flooded, they helped to build the pharaoh's monuments.

- **Craftsmen** made sculptures, pottery, textiles and **papyrus** (a kind of paper).

- **Merchants** exchanged products because they didn't have money. They brought wood, minerals and perfumes from other regions.

- **Servants** were free people who worked for a salary.

- **Slaves** were often prisoners of war and had no rights. They worked in domestic service, the mines, and building work.

The role of women

Egyptian **women** had some rights, and enjoyed more freedom than in most early civilisations. For example, they could inherit and own property, and get divorced.

Most Egyptian women did housework, or worked as peasants or servants. It was unusual for women to hold official posts. However, a few women, like Hatshepsut and Cleopatra, were female pharaohs.

> **WORK WITH THE ILLUSTRATIONS**
>
> **4** Discuss the illustration with a partner.
> a Who do you think the people are?
> b What are they doing?
> c In what ways are they using the River Nile?

A peasant's house · Irrigation · Temple · Construction of a pyramid · Pyramids · Stone quarry · River Nile · Port · Market · Papyrus · A nobleman's house · Artisan's house

Religion and art in Egypt

A sarcophagus.

A polytheistic religion

The Egyptians were **polytheistic**: they believed in many gods. The most important god was the **Sun**, who was called Ra, Amun or Atum. Other important gods were Isis, Osiris and Horus. The Egyptians also worshipped:

- Some **animals**: the crocodile and the cat.
- Natural forces: the **River Nile**.
- People: the **pharaoh**.

The Egyptians believed that religion maintained the order of the universe. For example, religious rituals made sure that the River Nile flooded each year. Each god had a temple, where priests made offerings to its statue. On the god's feast day, the statue was taken out in procession.

Attitudes to death

Egyptians believed that people had a life after death if their bodies were preserved. Consequently, the dead body of an important person was dried to make a **mummy**. This was placed in a **sarcophagus**.

The tomb of a wealthy person contained everything they needed in the afterlife. They were buried with food, jewellery, and statues of the servants who would work for them.

The biggest tombs were the **pyramids** for the pharaohs.

Temples

The most important **temples**, such as the one at Karnak, had an avenue of sphinxes leading to the entrance. There were great halls and a sanctuary inside the building. The image of the god was kept in the sanctuary. Tall columns were engraved with representations of flowers or gods.

Egyptian art

Artists were the pharaoh's officials, and worked in teams. They were considered **craftsmen**.

- Most Egyptian art had a **religious** meaning. Temples and tombs were decorated.
- Other works of art had a **political** meaning. Large statues showed the power of the pharaohs.

The pharaoh Ramesses II.

Painting

Painting changed very little in 3,000 years, and artists followed strict rules. In Egyptian art:

- Figures are represented in a **hierarchical** order: the largest figures are the most important.

- Figures are painted **without perspective**.

- Objects are seen from **the front**. The human body is shown from the front, but the head, arms and legs are seen **in profile**.

- Important people are **idealised**. They are always young and beautiful.

- Human figures are **static**. The aim is to show stability and continuity.

WORK WITH THE IMAGE

1 Answer the questions.

a Why are Nakht and his wife much larger than the other people?

b Which typical features of Egyptian art can you see?

c Why was an agricultural scene painted in a tomb?

d According to this painting, did women and men do similar jobs?

2 With a partner, use the key to check the meaning of each scene. Then cover the explanations and ask each other questions.

Tomb of Nakht, a scribe and astronomer. 1 Nakht and his wife (the largest figures) are making a religious offering. 2 Two men are sacrificing an ox. A third man is offering the fat to Nakht. 3 They are planting the crops. 4 They are clearing the land. 5 They are ploughing the land. 6 They are harvesting the wheat. 7 They are collecting the harvest. 8 Women are collecting flax. 9 They are separating the grains. 10 They are counting the grain. An official is watching them. 11 Nakht is shown looking at the provisions. 12 A hieroglyph with the name of the god Amun.

ACTIVITY ROUND-UP

1 Copy and complete the table.

	MESOPOTAMIA	EGYPT
Territory	Between the Tigris and Euphrates rivers.	-------
Main stages in its history	-------	-------
Political organisation	-------	-------
Society	-------	-------
Religion and beliefs	-------	-------
Art	-------	-------

2 Where did the earliest civilisations develop? Which rivers were they near? Write the names of the rivers and civilisations on a blank map of the world.

3 What was the natural environment of Mesopotamia?

4 Copy the timeline of Mesopotamian history in your notebook. Add the periods.

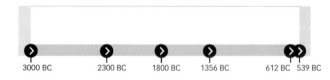

3000 BC   2300 BC   1800 BC   1356 BC   612 BC 539 BC

5 Copy the timeline of Egyptian history in your notebook. Add the Kingdoms.

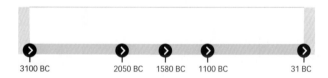

3100 BC   2050 BC   1580 BC   1100 BC   31 BC

- Find out when the following pharaohs ruled. Write their names in the right place on the timeline:
  Akhenaten, Khufu (Cheops), Thutmose III, Ramesses II, Menkaura, Mentuhotep II.

6 Are the following sentences true or false? Correct the false ones in your notebook. Then listen to the recording and check your answers.

a Writing was first used in Mesopotamia in about 3500 BC.

b Mesopotamian civilisation developed between the Tigris and Indus Rivers.

c The Mesopotamians believed in many gods.

d Upper Egypt was in the south, and Lower Egypt was in the north.

e The Egyptians called the Nile valley the 'black land' because there were dark rocks in the river.

f Only priests knew how to read and write in Ancient Egypt.

g The Egyptians believed that the pharaohs were gods.

7 Complete a map of Ancient Egypt with the following features:

- Upper Egypt
- Lower Egypt
- The River Nile
- Memphis and Thebes
- Deserts and seas

8 Write a short explanation of the authority of pharaohs. Include:

- Their political and military authority.
- Their religious role. (What did people think about them?)
- The monuments they built.

9 Explain the following terms:

- ziggurat • scribe • dynasty • pyramid

10 How are the people represented in this Egyptian painting?

11 Copy and complete the social pyramid of Ancient Egypt.

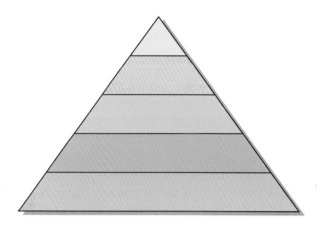

12 Complete a similar diagram showing the society of Mesopotamia.

13 Think about the previous unit on Prehistory. What were the differences between Neolithic settlements and early civilisations? Complete the table.

	Neolithic settlement	River civilisation
Political organisation	--------	-------
Social organisation	--------	-------

THE LEGACY OF MESOPOTAMIA AND EGYPT

Mesopotamia and Egypt left an important legacy to later civilisations:

- **Writing**. The earliest known writing was in Sumer.
- **Calendar**. The Mesopotamians invented a calendar. The year was divided into twelve months of 28 days. There was an extra month every three years.
- **The plough**. The Egyptians had wooden ploughs, which were pulled by oxen.
- **Architecture**. The arch and vault were invented in Mesopotamia. Impressive monuments like the pyramids were built in Egypt.
- **Mythology**. The gods and myths of Mesopotamia and Egypt have influenced other civilisations.

14 What type of construction is shown in the photo? What do we mean today when we say that a building project is of 'pharaonic proportions'?

15 The Mesopotamians invented the arch and vault. Do we still use them today? How?

16 What is a hieroglyph? Find out about hieroglyphic writing.

Which other types of writing were used by the early civilisations?

17 What is a myth? Why do you think myths were created? Look for information about Isis and Osiris on internet. Write a short account.

THINK LIKE AN HISTORIAN. **Analyse ancient art**

• Before you read the text, study the photos. What do they show? How are the scenes presented?

The Standard of Ur

The Standard of Ur was found in a royal tomb in the Sumerian city of Ur. It is made of wood covered in shells, red marble and precious stones. These exotic materials were traded across long distances. It is shaped like a box, and is narrower at the top.

It is not clear exactly what the Standard was used for. It was probably not a military standard that was carried in battles. Perhaps it was a musical instrument or a box for precious objects. It is decorated on both sides with scenes in three horizontal strips that show peace and war in the Sumerian city. It is a valuable source of information about life in Mesopotamia.

1 Study the Standard of Ur and answer the questions:

a Why do you think the king looks much bigger than the other figures?

b How are the defeated enemies represented? How are they dressed?

c What can we learn about Mesopotamian society from the Standard of Ur?

2 Look for a reproduction of the medieval Bayeux tapestry, and a modern comic strip. Are they similar to the Standard of Ur? Is this a good way to show a scene?

3 With a partner, think which people and scenes you would include in A Standard of (Your Region).

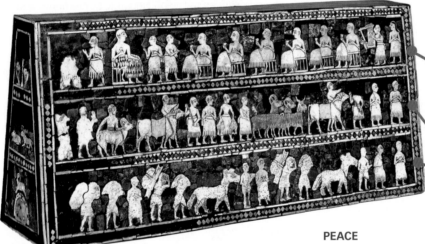

Top strip. The king (the largest figure) celebrates a banquet with the nobles and priests.

Middle and lower strips. People offer tribute in agricultural produce, sheep, goats, oxen and fish.

PEACE

Top strip. The king and the nobles receive the prisoners.

Middle strip. Soldiers take the defeated enemies to the king.

Lower strip. Warriors in chariots defeat the enemy.

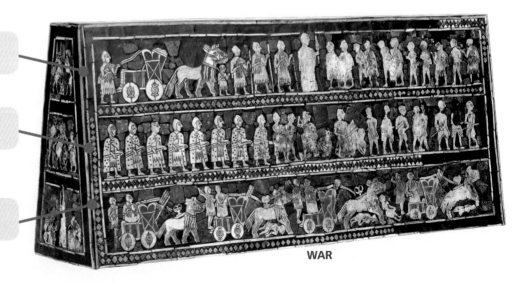

WAR

CULTURAL HERITAGE. **The conservation of ancient monuments**

The temple of Abu Simbel

The temple of Abu Simbel in southern Egypt was built in the 13th century BC, during the reign of Ramesses II. It was orientated in such a way that the Sun illuminated the statues of the gods twice a year.

In the 20th century, there was a project to build a dam on the Nile River. This would create a huge reservoir, flooding the temple of Abu Simbel and other ancient monuments.

The original location of the temple of Abu Simbel.

The present-day location of the temple of Abu Simbel.

Between 1964 and 1968, the temple was taken apart and reconstructed on higher ground near the original site. The project was promoted by UNESCO. Archaeologists from more than twenty countries participated in it.

The temple was taken down and rebuilt.

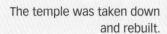

1 Answer the questions.

 a Who built the temple of Abu Simbel?

 b When was it built?

 c Look at the human figures in the photos. How tall are the statues compared to human beings?

 d Where was the temple first built? Why do you think that location was chosen?

 e Where is the temple today?

 f When was it moved? Why?

 g What consequences did this event have for Egypt's cultural heritage?

2 Think about this case. Discuss your ideas with your classmates.

 a Was this the right way to deal with this problem?

 b Were there any alternative solutions?

 c Was it right to spend so much money?

3 Look for information about the Temple of Debod on internet and prepare a project.

 • Include a photo of the temple.

 • Where was it built originally? When?

 • How did it come to Spain?

 • In which city is it found?

10 | Ancient Greece

FIND OUT ABOUT:

- Where Greek civilisation developed
- The stages of Greek history
- Athens and Sparta
- Hellenism
- Society and the economy
- Greek beliefs, culture and art

KNOW HOW TO:

- Classify information using tables and timelines
- Discuss Greek democracy
- Analyse Greek sculptures

The Sanctuary at Olympus

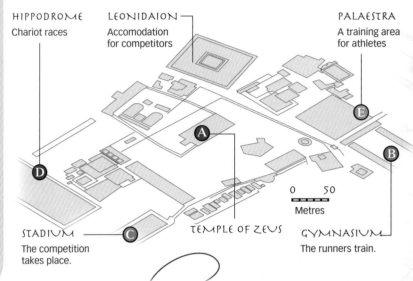

HIPPODROME
Chariot races

LEONIDAION
Accomodation for competitors

PALAESTRA
A training area for athletes

Ⓐ Ⓑ Ⓓ Ⓔ

0   50
Metres

STADIUM
The competition takes place.

Ⓒ

TEMPLE OF ZEUS

GYMNASIUM
The runners train.

Main competitions

DISCUS THROWING

CHARIOT RACES

WRESTLING AND BOXING

RUNNING

JAVELIN THROWING

LONG JUMP

PROGRAMME

– First day:
⊝ Procession and religious ceremonies

– Days 2-6:
⊝ Chariot races
⊝ Javelin and discus throwing
⊝ Long jump
⊝ Running
⊝ Pentathlon (jumping, running, discuss throwing, javelin and wrestling)
⊝ Wrestling and boxing

– Final day
⊝ Prize giving and banquet

💿 The first Olympic Games

The Greeks held competitions to honour the gods. The most famous sports competitions were the Olympic Games, which were held every four years in honour of the god Zeus. They were celebrated for the first time in Olympia in 776 BC.

The games lasted for seven days. Athletes and spectators came from everywhere in the Greek-speaking world.

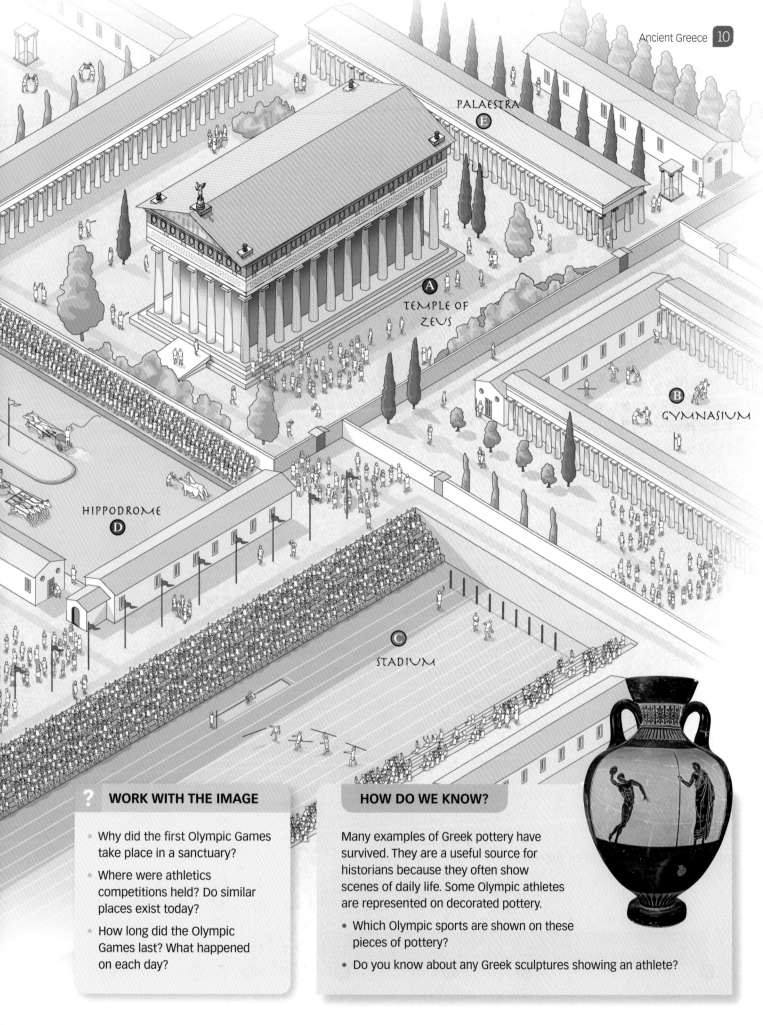

PALAESTRA
E

A
TEMPLE OF
ZEUS

B
GYMNASIUM

HIPPODROME
D

C
STADIUM

? WORK WITH THE IMAGE

- Why did the first Olympic Games take place in a sanctuary?

- Where were athletics competitions held? Do similar places exist today?

- How long did the Olympic Games last? What happened on each day?

HOW DO WE KNOW?

Many examples of Greek pottery have survived. They are a useful source for historians because they often show scenes of daily life. Some Olympic athletes are represented on decorated pottery.

- Which Olympic sports are shown on these pieces of pottery?

- Do you know about any Greek sculptures showing an athlete?

1 The origins of Greek civilisation

The natural environment

The Greek-speaking world was originally called **Hellas**. It was spread across a wide area:

- In the south of the **Balkan Peninsula**.
- On **islands** in the eastern **Mediterranean**.
- On the coast of **Asia Minor** (now Turkey).

Physical relief explains why Ancient Greece was not a single, unified country:

- **Mountains** divided mainland Greece into small valleys.
- **Islands** were separated from each other by the sea.
- Each valley or island was like a small country.

Most land was dry and rocky, and there was little agriculture. The Greeks got a lot of their food from the **Mediterranean Sea**. They were expert sailors, and crossed the sea for trade.

Each Greek territory had its own government and laws. However, the Greeks shared the same **culture**. They all spoke **Greek**, and believed in the same gods.

Periods of Greek history

Ancient Greek history is divided into the following periods:

- The **Archaic** period: 9th – 6th centuries BC
- The **Classical** period: 5th century BC – mid-4th century BC.
- The **Hellenistic** period: mid-4th century BC – 1st century BC.

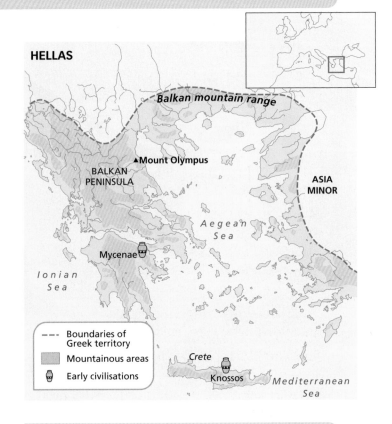

HELLAS

WORK WITH THE MAP

1. Compare the map to a modern map of the Mediterranean region. Which modern countries formed part of Hellas?

2. Which seas surrounded Greek territory?

ACTIVITIES

3. What influence did the natural environment have on Greek history?

4. Why do you think Ancient Greece did not become a single country?

TIMELINE OF ANCIENT GREEK HISTORY

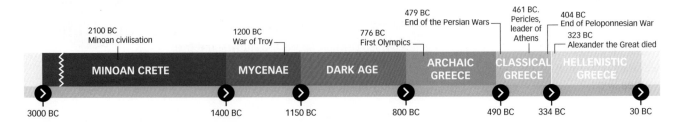

Pre-Hellenic civilisations

Minoan Crete and Mycenae were important civilisations in the eastern Mediterranean. These **pre-Hellenic civilisations** existed before Ancient Greece appeared:

- **Minoan Crete**. Minoan civilisation developed in **Crete** during the Bronze Age. Crete had an important role in trade across the eastern Mediterranean.

  Crete was ruled by powerful kings, including the legendary **King Minos**. **Knossos** was its most important city.

- **Mycenae** was another Bronze Age civilisation. In about 1400 BC, a northern people called the Achaeans settled in the Balkans and built walled cities.

  Mycenaean society was dominated by **warriors**, who were ruled by a king.

- **The Dark Age**. Mycenaean civilisation disappeared in about 1150 BC. We do not know much about the period between the 11th and 9th centuries BC.

ACTIVITIES

5 Investigate the legend of the Minotaur. How was it connected to Minoan Crete?

Mycenae.

The palace in Knossos, Crete. The palace was restored in the 1920s, but the original buildings were probably similar.

DID YOU KNOW?

The War of Troy

According to legend, the kings of Mycenae fought a war against the city of Troy in Asia Minor. Many centuries later, Homer created *The Iliad*, a long narrative poem about one episode in the war. In the 19th and 20th centuries, archaeologists carried out excavations to discover the original site of Troy.

The archaeological site of Troy.

Use internet to find out about the following people. How are they related?

- Homer
- Achilles
- Heinrich Schliemann
- Helen

2 Archaic Greece

⟨🔲⟩ WORK WITH THE MAP

1 With a partner, find Athens and Sparta on the map. Locate other important *poleis*.

2 Were most *poleis* near the coast or in the mountains? Explain your answer.

3 Was most of the Greek-speaking world mountainous or flat?

The *polis*

From the 8th century, the Greeks lived in **city-states**. A city-state, or **polis**, was a region with its own government, laws and army. (The plural of *polis* is *poleis*.) Athens, Sparta, Corinth and Thebes were the most famous *poleis*. But there were also many smaller city-states.

- A rich, privileged minority was an **aristocracy**. (*Aristoi* meant 'the best'.) **Sparta** was the most famous example of aristocratic government.

- **Democracy** replaced aristocracy in some *poleis*. Citizens met regularly in assemblies to make decisions and elect their representatives. They created councils which chose the subjects to be discussed at assemblies. **Athens** was the most famous example of democratic government.

THE MAIN GREEK CITY-STATES

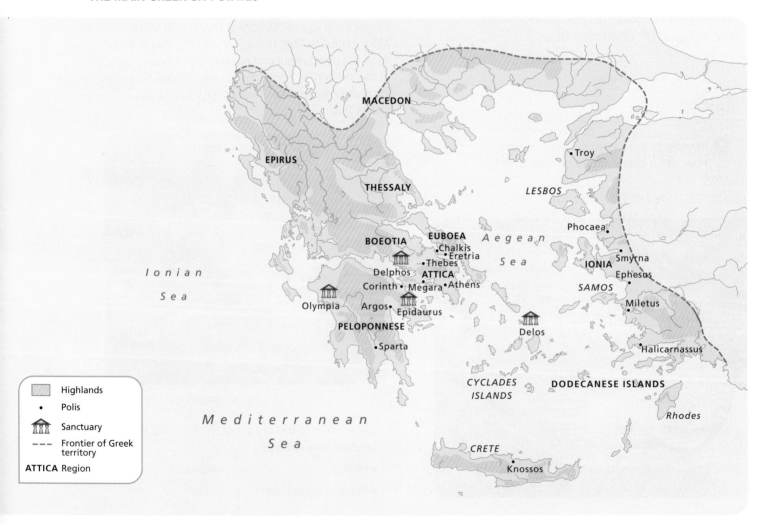

Legend:
- Highlands
- • Polis
- 🏛 Sanctuary
- --- Frontier of Greek territory
- **ATTICA** Region

GREEK OVERSEAS EXPANSION

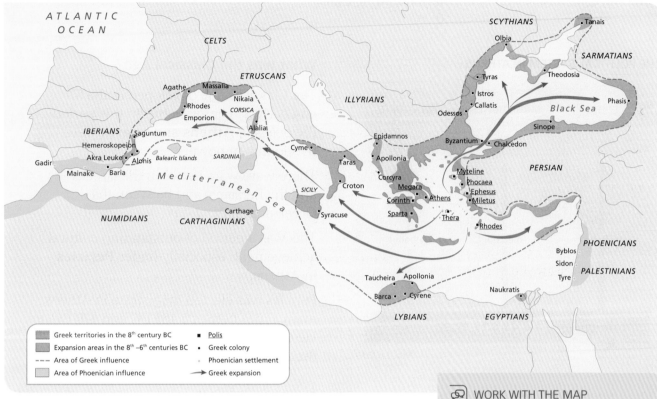

Legend:
- ■ Greek territories in the 8th century BC — ■ Polis
- Expansion areas in the 8th–6th centuries BC — • Greek colony
- --- Area of Greek influence — • Phoenician settlement
- Area of Phoenician influence — → Greek expansion

What were colonies?

Between the 8th and 6th centuries BC, the Greeks established **colonies** (settlements in other regions). There were two causes:

- **Overpopulation**. Population increased in Greece. There was not enough food for everyone.

- **The economy**. Colonies were created to promote trade, agriculture, and mining for precious metals.

Colonies were independent from their founding *polis*. However, they had the same beliefs, traditions and organisation.

Greek expansion

There were two stages in Greek overseas expansion:

- Between 750 BC and 650 BC, the Greeks settled in the **west**, on the islands and coasts of the Ionian Sea; Libya in northern Africa; Sicily, southern Italy and southern France; and on the east coast of the Iberian Peninsula.

- Between 650 BC and 550 BC, colonies were founded in the **east**, around the Black Sea.

As a result of overseas expansion, the Greeks came into contact with **other peoples** like the Phoenicians, Etruscans and Egyptians. Colonisation spread Greek influence beyond the original frontiers of Greek civilisation.

WORK WITH THE MAP AND THE TEXT

4 Name three colonies founded in the first stage of Greek overseas expansion (750-650 BC). Name three colonies founded in the second stage (650-550 BC).

5 Write the ship's log of a sailor travelling from Athens to Akra Leuke: the places he visits, the things he sees, the people he meets…

ACTIVITIES

6 Explain the following terms:
- aristocracy • *polis* • colony

7 What were the causes and consequences of Greek overseas expansion?

8 What were the differences between a Greek *polis* and a colony? What were the similarities?

THE POLITICAL SYSTEM IN ATHENS

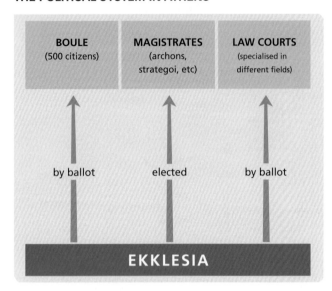

What was the Classical Age?

The Classical Age developed in the 5th and early 4th centuries BC. In this period, the *poleis* of **Athens** and **Sparta** were the dominant powers.

There were wars between the Greeks and the Persians, and between the Greek *poleis*.

This was a period of outstanding cultural achievement, especially under **Pericles** in Athens.

Pericles was elected magistrate in Athens many times between 461 BC and 429 BC. He directed political life, and rebuilt the **Acropolis**.

Democracy in Athens

From the 7th century BC, lawmakers like **Solon** introduced political reforms in Athens.

Athens became a **democracy,** which means 'rule by the people'. However, only **citizens** (Athenian men) participated in political life.

Women, slaves and *metics* (foreigners) were not citizens.

There were the following institutions:

- The *Ekklesia,* or assembly. All the citizens met to vote laws, decide foreign policy, and elect magistrates.

- The *Boule,* or council, was made up of 500 citizens, who were chosen by ballot. They prepared the debates in the assembly.

- Athenian leaders were **magistrates**. The *archons* were the chief magistrates, and the *strategoi* led the army.

- Each year, members of the **law courts** were chosen by ballot.

ACTIVITIES

1. Who could participate in political life in Athens? Which groups did not have a political role?

2. Answer the following questions about the institutions of Athens and Sparta:

   a What type of government did each *polis* have?

   b What were the most important official positions?

   c What were the names of the councils, and who were their members?

   d Did the assemblies in Athens and Sparta have similar powers?

3. Write a short text comparing the political systems of Athens and Sparta. Think about the language you will need:

   In Athens, the assembly had greater powers than in Sparta. / However, in Sparta...

THE ACROPOLIS OF ATHENS

Parthenon

Erechtheum

Statue of
Athena

Propylaea

Temple of
Athena Nike

Oligarchy in Sparta

Sparta was the great rival of Athens. Spartans spent most of their time preparing for warfare. Prisoners of war worked the land. Sparta was an **oligarchy**, which means 'rule by the few':

Sparta had the following institutions:

- Two **kings** held military and religious authority.

- The *Gerousia* was a council formed by prestigious, older citizens. They drew up laws and were responsible for justice.

- The *ephors* were five magistrates, who carried out the decisions of the *Gerousia*.

- The **assembly** or *Apella* consisted of all free men over 30 years old. It only had limited powers. Its main role was to choose the *ephors* and the members of the *Gerousia*.

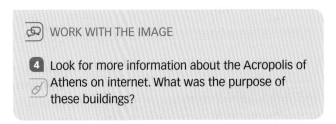

WORK WITH THE IMAGE

4 Look for more information about the Acropolis of Athens on internet. What was the purpose of these buildings?

THE POLITICAL SYSTEM IN SPARTA

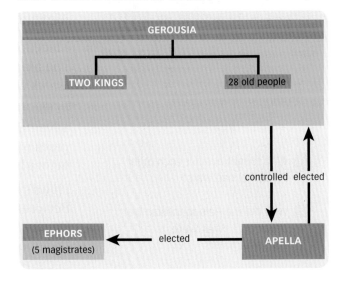

GEROUSIA

TWO KINGS   28 old people

controlled   elected

EPHORS
(5 magistrates)   ← elected   APELLA

Hoplites were Greek soldiers who used spears and shields.

The Persian Wars (499-479 BC)

In the 6th century BC, the *Persians* conquered many of the *poleis* in Asia Minor and the eastern Mediterranean. In 499 BC, these cities rebelled against the Persians, and other *poleis* supported them. This was the beginning of the **Persian Wars** (499-479 BC).

- The **First Persian War** ended when the Greek soldiers, or **hoplites**, defeated the Persians at the Battle of Marathon in 490 BC.

- King Xerxes I of Persia began the **Second Persian War** in 480 BC. He invaded Greece, but was defeated at the **Battle of Salamis** in 480 BC.

After the Greeks resisted the Persian invasion, Athens became the richest and most influential *polis*.

The Peloponnesian War (431-404 BC)

Under the leadership of Athens, many *poleis* formed a union called the **Delian League** in 477 BC. Its aim was to defend the city-states against future Persian attacks.

The economic, political and cultural domination of Athens threatened other *poleis*, such as Sparta. Some *poleis* supported Sparta in the **Peloponnesian League**, which opposed the Delian league of Athens and its allies.

The two sides fought against each other in the **Peloponnesian War**, which broke out in 431 BC. In 404 BC, Sparta won the war and became the leading *polis*. But after many years of warfare, the Greek city-states were much weaker than before.

Alexander the Great

Macedon was a mountainous kingdom, north of Greece. The Macedonians were strongly influenced by Greek culture.

In the mid-4th century BC, King **Philip II of Macedon** took advantage of the weakness of the Greek *poleis*, after many years of disputes. Philip conquered nearly all the *poleis* before he was assassinated in 336 BC.

Philip's son **Alexander the Great** continued his conquests. Between 334 and 323 BC Alexander defeated the Persian Empire. He ruled territories from Greece in the west to the Danube in the north, Egypt in the south, and western India in the east.

THE EMPIRE OF ALEXANDER THE GREAT

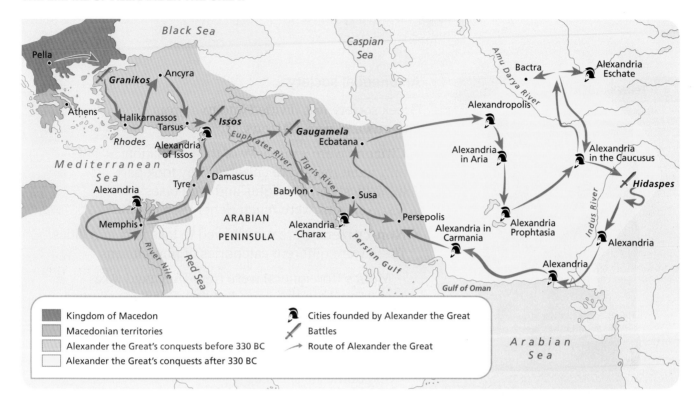

Hellenism

Alexander founded many cities in the conquered territories. One of these cities, **Alexandria** in Egypt, became the leading centre of Greek learning. Greek culture spread through many regions, but was also influenced by eastern ideas. This fusion was called **Hellenism**.

Alexander the Great died in 323 BC, before he had organised his empire effectively. His generals divided up the empire into separate kingdoms. Egypt, Syria and Macedon were notable **Hellenistic monarchies**.

WORK WITH THE MAP

5 Which modern countries belonged to Alexander the Great's empire?

6 Describe the route that Alexander's army followed.

7 Why do you think so many cities were called Alexandria?

ACTIVITIES

3 Find out who Alexander the Great's teacher was. What did Alexander learn from him?

4 Look on internet to find out what the Macedonian phalanx was? Find an illustration.

Alexander the Great.

THINK ABOUT IT

A wife

My wife did not know anything when she arrived at my house. She was only fifteen years old when I married her. Before that, she was controlled strictly so that she saw and heard as little as possible. She was taught to ask as few questions as possible. I told her to stay in the house all the day, and send the servants out to get things.

Xenophon, text adapted from *Oeconomicus*

- What does this text tell us about the position of women in Ancient Greek society?
- How is life for women today different from Ancient Greece?

ACTIVITIES

1 What were the differences between a citizen and a non-citizen?

2 Which groups made up Greek society? What were the characteristics of each group?

An unequal society

Greek society was divided into two groups: **citizens** and **non-citizens**.

- **Citizens** were a minority of the population: only adult men were citizens. They took part in politics, had full rights and paid taxes. Some citizens were much richer than others.

- **Non-citizens** were not allowed to take part in politics. There were different categories of non-citizens:

  – *Metics* (foreigners) were free. They paid taxes and fought in the army, but they were not allowed to own land. They worked in trade and crafts.

  – **Slaves** were not free. They were prisoners of war, or their children. They worked in agriculture and domestic service.

  – **Women** were free or slaves. They had no political rights, and did not go to public shows. They were under the authority of a man, who was either their father or their husband. Rich women ran their homes. Poor women looked after the children of rich families, worked as peasants, and sold food in the markets.

Economic activities

There were different types of economic activity:

- **Agriculture**. The land was poor in many regions. The main products were **vines**, **wheat** and **olives**. Many farms were small.

- **Long distance trade**. Wealthy merchants traded across the Mediterranean. They sold Greek products, and imported food, wood and copper.

  They used silver coins called **drachmas**.

- **Local commerce**. Peasants went to the cities to sell their crops. Craftsmen sold their products in their workshops. There were also small shops. They often exchanged products.

- **Crafts**. The Greeks made excellent **pottery**, which they exported to other regions. They also manufactured **textiles** and **leather**.

Daily life in Ancient Greece

- **Food.** The Greeks ate cereals, cheese, eggs, fruit and vegetables. Their food also included olive oil, goat's milk and fish. Meat was only eaten by wealthy families on special occasions.

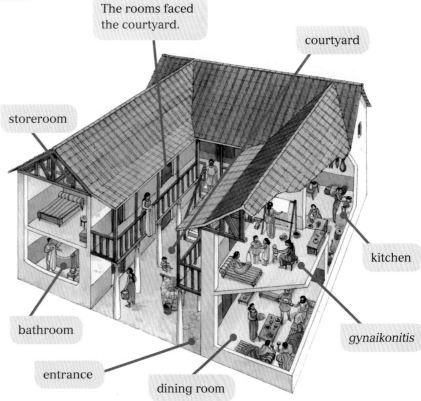

They lay down to eat at a banquet.

Musicians and dancers provided entertainment.

A banquet. This was a special meal for guests.

mantle

sunshade

tunic

tunic

tunic

sandal

- **Clothing.** Both women and men wore long **tunics**. In winter, they wore a **mantle** over one shoulder.

  They usually wore leather sandals on their feet.

- **Houses.** Wealthy families lived in houses with one or two levels. There was a space reserved for women called the **gynaikonitis**.

  Poor people lived in small houses made of wood, bricks or mud brick.

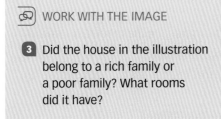

WORK WITH THE IMAGE

3 Did the house in the illustration belong to a rich family or a poor family? What rooms did it have?

The rooms faced the courtyard.

courtyard

storeroom

kitchen

bathroom

gynaikonitis

entrance

dining room

THE MAIN GODS AND GODDESSES

Hades
(Underworld)

Zeus
King of gods
(Sky and thunder)

Hera
(Family)

Demeter
(Agriculture)

Hestia
(Home)

Poseidon
(Sea)

Hephaestus
(Fire)

Ares
(War)

Athena
(Wisdom)

Apollo
(Beauty)

Artemis
(Hunting)

Hermes
(Commerce)

Dionysus
(Wine)

Aphrodite
(Love)

Gods and heroes

The Greeks were **polytheistic**. Each city-state had a god that gave it special protection. For example, Athena was the patron of Athens.

- The **gods** were immortal, but looked human. Like humans, they loved and fought with each other. The leader of the gods was **Zeus**, who lived on **Mount Olympus**, along with other gods and goddesses.

- **Heroes** were born from the union of a god and a human being. Legendary heroes like **Achilles** and **Heracles** were extremely powerful, but they were not immortal. Many cities had **foundation myths**, which explained how they were founded by a great hero. Important families claimed descent from a hero.

- Greek **myths** were colourful stories about all these gods and heroes. They featured fantastic creatures like the **Cyclops** (one-eyed monsters), and the **centaurs** (horses with a human head, chest and arms).

Religious cults

As the gods had the same needs as human beings, the Greeks believed that they had to give them food and wealth. The **temples** were the homes of the gods, and priests and priestesses were their servants.

The Greeks also believed that the gods could help or harm human beings. Before beginning any important action, it was important to consult the opinion of the gods. **Oracles** were messages from the gods, and were usually interpreted by a priest or priestess. The shrine at Delphi was the most important place where the gods were consulted. Even rulers used to go there, to find out what the gods thought.

ACTIVITIES

1 Investigate a legend and prepare a computer presentation.

a Choose one of the following subjects:
- Ulysses • Orpheus and Eurydice • The Labours of Heracles

b Find out when the legend was first known.

c Make notes on the story so that you can tell it in your own words.

d Look for illustrations.

e Find out how the legend was represented in later times.

Greek theatre

Drama originated in religious celebrations to the god Dionysus. The golden age of theatre started in Athens after it was rebuilt following the Persian Wars.

Tragedies, **comedies** and **satyr** plays (parodies) were presented in outdoor theatres. Two or three main actors performed, along with a supporting chorus. Male actors wore masks, and played both male and female roles.

Aeschylus, **Sophocles** and **Euripides** were the greatest writers of tragedies. **Aristophanes** was the finest writer of comedies. The playwrights presented their plays in a public competition called the **Dionysia**, where they were awarded first, second or third prize.

Philosophy and science

The civilisations of Mesopotamia and Egypt used myths to explain the world. The Greeks, too, had many myths. But they were the first to use **reason** and **logic** to explain the universe. They were the founders of philosophy and science.

In the 5th and 4th centuries BC, the leading Greek philosophers lived in **Athens**. After the 4th century BC, **Alexandria** (in Egypt) was a key centre of science and learning.

The three greatest Greek philosophers were **Socrates**, **Plato** and **Aristotle**. There were important scientists, such as **Pythagoras** and **Archimedes**. **Herodotus** and **Thucydides** were the first historians.

Ruins of the Theatre of Delphi, Greece.

 ACTIVITIES

2 Look for information about scientists and philosophers on internet.

a Copy and complete the table in your workbook.

b Listen and check your answers.

c With a partner, ask and answer questions about ancient Greek scientists and philosophers: *When did (Socrates) live? Who demonstrated that the Earth is round?*

NAME	CENTURY	FIELD	ACHIEVEMENTS
Pythagoras	6th BC	Mathematics	Invented -------
Herodotus	-------	-------	'The Father of History'
Socrates	-------	Philosophy	The founder of ethics and moral philosophy
Plato	5th-4th BC	-------	Said that people followed reason in search of truth and beauty.
Hippocrates	-------	Medicine	Developed scientific medicine.
Aristotle	-------	Philosophy	Wrote on all fields of human knowledge.
Aristarchus	3rd BC	Astronomy	-------
Archimedes	3rd BC	Physics and mathematics	-------
Eratosthenes	-------	Geography	Demonstrated that the Earth is round.

Plan of a Greek temple

🔗 WORK WITH THE IMAGE

1 Study the plan and the text. Identify the parts of the temple.

7 Architecture

Temples

Greek **temples** were usually built in white marble. However, they were originally painted in bright colours, which gradually disappeared.

Greek temples were rectangular. The Greeks did not use arches and vaults, and flat roofs were supported on columns:

- The ***pronaos*** was the entrance porch to the temple.
- The ***naos*** was the main hall, where the statue of the god was kept.
- The ***opisthodomos*** was a back room where offerings were left.

The three orders

The Greeks were concerned about proportion, beauty and harmony. Their architects followed strict rules, called **orders**, which determined the style of a building.

The three orders were **Doric**, **Ionic** and **Corinthian**.

Doric column

Ionic column

Corinthian column

Doric temple in Paestum, Italy.

Ionic temple of Athena Nike, Athens.

Corinthian columns in the temple of Olympian Zeus, Athens.

The Parthenon

The **Parthenon** was built in Athens in the 5th century BC. It replaced an earlier temple that was destroyed during the Persian invasion in 480 BC.

The Parthenon was located on the acropolis, which was the fortified area above the city. It was built in honour of the goddess Athena, who was the patron of the city. Inside the temple, there was a huge statue of Athena by the sculptor Phidias.

The Parthenon.

The outside walls were decorated with reliefs of the **Panathenaic procession**. This was celebrated in Athens every year in honour of Athena.

The statue of the goddess **Athena** was made of gold and ivory. Athena's helmet was decorated with winged horses and a sphinx. She held a small figure representing victory.

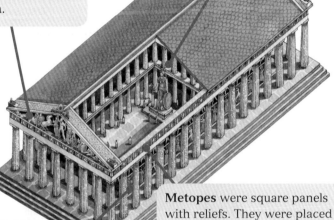

The **pediments** of the Parthenon were decorated with sculptures, which narrated legends about Athena.

Metopes were square panels with reliefs. They were placed around the entire building. The sculptures showed battles between giants, centaurs and other mythical creatures.

WORK WITH THE IMAGE

2 Answer the questions.

a Which Greek order did the columns in the Parthenon belong to?

b Find photos of the Capitol in Washington DC, and the 'Palacio de las Cortes' in Madrid. Compare them to the Parthenon and other Greek temples. Why were later architects influenced by the Greeks?

ACTIVITIES

3 What was the *agora*? Investigate on internet and find a photo. Are there similar places in towns and cities today?

Panathenaic procession.

One of the metopes of the Parthenon.

Sculpture

Sculpture

Greek sculptures and reliefs usually represented **gods** and **heroes**, and were made for temples.

- Sculptors tried to represent **human beauty**. They believed that a sculpture should show the ideal proportions of the human body.

- They worked in **marble** and **bronze**. They then painted their sculptures in bright colours.

- Most Greek bronze sculptures have disappeared. However, we know what they looked like because the Romans made marble copies.

Greek sculpture evolved over a long period of time:

- In the **Archaic** period, sculpture was static and rigid.

- In the **Classical** period, it became more realistic and represented ideal beauty.

- In the **Hellenistic** period, it was expressive and dynamic.

The Parthenon frieze. This marble sculpture adorned the Parthenon. It was created in the 5th century BC under the direction of the sculptor Phidias.

The Archaic period

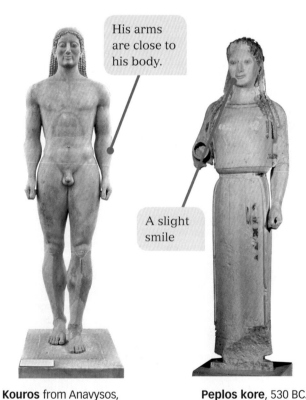

His arms are close to his body.

A slight smile

Kouros from Anavysos, 540-510 BC. A *kouros* was a standing sculpture showing a warrior or athlete.

Peplos kore, 530 BC. A *kore* was a standing female figure. This *kore* was perhaps a goddess.

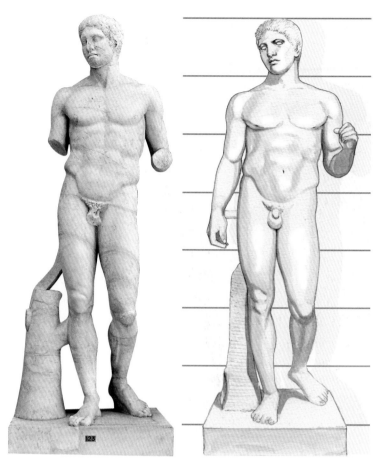

Canon of Polykleitos. In the 5th century BC, the sculptor Polykleitos established a canon (or rule) for human beauty. The height of a human body should be seven times its head.

ACTIVITIES

1 Match the periods with the artistic characteristics.

Archaic period •   • Dynamic, expressive, and emotional

Classical period •   • Shows very little movement

Hellenistic period •   • Represents balance and ideal beauty

2 Look on internet for information about the Elgin Marbles:

- What are they?
- Why is their current location controversial?
- Should works of art be returned to their country of origin? Think of reasons for and against.

Discuss your ideas with your classmates.

The Classical period

This shows a discus thrower. We can see the movement in his body.

Diskobolus, by Myron, 450 BC

There is no tension in his face.

The Hellenistic period

A priest tries to free his sons from snakes sent by a god.

Twisted figures

Laocoön and His Sons, 1st century BC

1 Copy and complete the diagram.

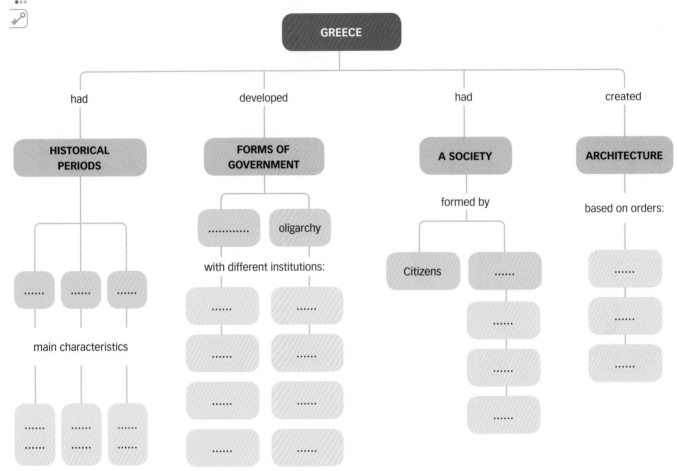

2 Copy the timeline in your notebook.
Complete it with the periods of Ancient Greek history.

3000 BC   30 BC

3 Which period of Greek history do the following belong to?
Add them to the timeline from the previous activity.

- Alexander the Great
- The Peloponnesian War
- The first colonies
- The reconstruction of the Parthenon
- The foundation of Alexandria
- The emergence of the *poleis*

4 Label a blank map of the eastern Mediterranean
with the following features:

- Greece and Macedon
- Athens, Sparta, Corinth and Mycenae
- Asia Minor, the Balkan Peninsula and the seas
surrounding Greece

5 Explain the following terms:

- Democracy
- Oligarchy
- Colony
- Hellenism

6 Who were the following people?
Why were they important?

- Alexander the Great
- Pericles
- Socrates
- Aristotle

7 What were the main differences between
the systems of government in Sparta
and Athens?

8 Look on internet for a photo showing
Greek economic activity.

- For example, look for an ancient coin,
decorated pottery, or a container (amphora),
used to transport goods.
- Show the object to your classmates,
and explain how it was used.

9 Copy and complete the following text. Check your answers with the recording.

The city-state, or _____, appeared in the Greek-speaking world in the eighth century BC. Each city-state had its laws and army, and its own system of government. Some states, like _____, had aristocratic government. Other states, like _____, were democracies: citizens met regularly in assemblies and elected their representatives. Athens and Sparta led alliances against each other during the _____ _____, which began in 431 BC. This war ended with the victory of _____ in 404 BC. After the war, the city-states were much weaker. They were conquered by King Philip II of _____ in the 4th century BC. King Philip's son, _____ __ _____, became famous for the vast empire he created.

10 Explain the social pyramid of Ancient Greece.

- What were the main social groups?
- What were their characteristics?

11 Are the following columns Doric, Ionic or Corinthian? Explain your answer.

12 Look for a film about Ancient Greece on internet.
- Watch for a few minutes and make notes about how accurate you think it is.

13 Compare Greece and Egypt.

a In what ways was Greek religion similar to Egyptian religion? In what ways was it different?

b What were the main characteristics of Egyptian sculpture? In which period was Greek sculpture similar? Explain your answer.

THE LEGACY OF GREECE

Greek culture is the basis of Western civilisation. Its influence can be seen in many areas:

- **Democracy** began in Athens.
- **Literature**. The Greeks created poetry and drama.
- **Science**. The Greeks developed science and mathematics (Pythagoras), history (Herodotus), geography (Eratosthenes), physics (Archimedes) and medicine (Hippocrates).
- **Art**. Greek architecture and sculpture had great influence on Western art.
- **Philosophy**. Socrates, Plato and Aristotle were the founders of Western philosophy.
- **Sport**. The Greeks invented the Olympic Games.
- **Language**. We use many Greek words like 'policy', 'geometry', 'history' and 'philosophy'.
- **Currency**. The Greeks were the first to use coins as money.

14 How did the Greeks use money? Is it used in the same way today?

15 Find out the origin and meaning of the following terms. Are they still used today?

- Hippocratic Oath
- Pythagorean Theorem

16 What are the main government institutions in our democratic system? Are they similar to those of Ancient Athens?

17 Which of these were Olympic sports in Ancient Greece?

THINK LIKE AN HISTORIAN. **Classify information**

Create a chronological table

It is useful to create tables and timelines to classify historical information.
This helps us to understand events in their historical context. It is also an excellent way to revise our knowledge of a period.

Create a chronological table of Greek civilisation in your notebook. Before you begin, think about how much space you will need for each section.

- Complete the column on the left with the names and dates of the periods.
  (Are you going to refer to centuries, or use exact dates like 490 BC and 334 BC?)

- Look through the unit, and put information under each heading.

- Look for additional information in encyclopaedias or on internet. For example, find out more about Pericles, or when Sophocles was born, wrote his greatest plays, and died.

- Use your table to ask and answer questions in groups.

Period	Main events	Government	Society and culture
Archaic period (9th – 6th century BC)			776 BC: Olympic Games
_____ period (_____ – _____)	499-480 BC: Persian Wars	461- 429 BC: Pericles was the leading figure in Athens.	
_____ period (_____ – 1st century BC)			300 BC: Library of Alexandria was founded.

Identify Greek pottery

The Greeks used many kinds of pottery in their daily lives. These were very different according to their use, decoration and size.

Read the descriptions and match them to the photos:

- **Kylix**. A very flat drinking cup with two handles.

- **Amphora**. A tall container with two handles that was used to store and transport liquids.

- **Krater**. A large, open vase that was used to mix wine and water.

- **Oenochoe**. A wine jug with one handle.

A

B

C

D

CIVIC EDUCATION. **Democracy in Athens**

At first, only the aristocracy had political rights in Athens. But in about 600 BC, Solon (known as the 'Law-Giver') created a constitution that gave rights to male property owners. In the late 6th century BC, another leader Cleisthenes established a democratic constitution in Athens. Under Ephialtes and then Pericles in the mid-5th century BC, poorer Athenians participated more fully in Athenian political life.

Athens had a direct democracy, so all citizens helped to make decisions. Today, we have a representative democracy – we elect representatives who make decisions for us.

Only adult male citizens participated in Athenian government. Women, foreigners and slaves had no political rights. Today all women and men have political rights in democratic societies.

HOW WERE LAWS APPROVED IN ATHENS?

1. Proposal. The citizens proposed new laws. The *Boule* (council) selected some of the proposals.

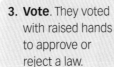

2. Debate. The citizens expressed their opinions in the *Ekklesia* (assembly).

3. Vote. They voted with raised hands to approve or reject a law.

1 The Greek philosopher Aristotle said that 'man is by nature a political animal'. What did he mean?

2 With a partner, check the meaning of the following terms. Why do you think they have a Greek origin?

• monarchy   • tyranny   • aristocracy
• oligarchy   • democracy

3 Make a list of the main characteristics of Athenian democracy. Is it right to call Athens a democracy when women, foreigners and slaves did not have political rights?

4 Today we live in a representative democracy. Imagine that we had a direct democracy like the Greeks – for example, we all decided laws and political decisions by voting on internet.

What advantages and disadvantages would this system have? Discuss your ideas with your classmates.

DID YOU KNOW?

What was ostracism?

Citizens voted to decide which leading politician should go into exile for ten years. This practice was called **ostracism** because they scratched the leaders' names on pottery (called *ostraka* in Greek). Critics of Athenian democracy said that ostracism was unfair.

• Find out what 'ostracism' means today? Has its meaning changed?

Athenian *ostraka*.

11 Ancient Rome

Who were the legionaries?

The Roman army was formed of legions. Each legion was divided into smaller units called centuries, with 80 men.

The professional soldiers, or legionaries, were subject to strict discipline. They marched very long distances, carrying all their heavy equipment.

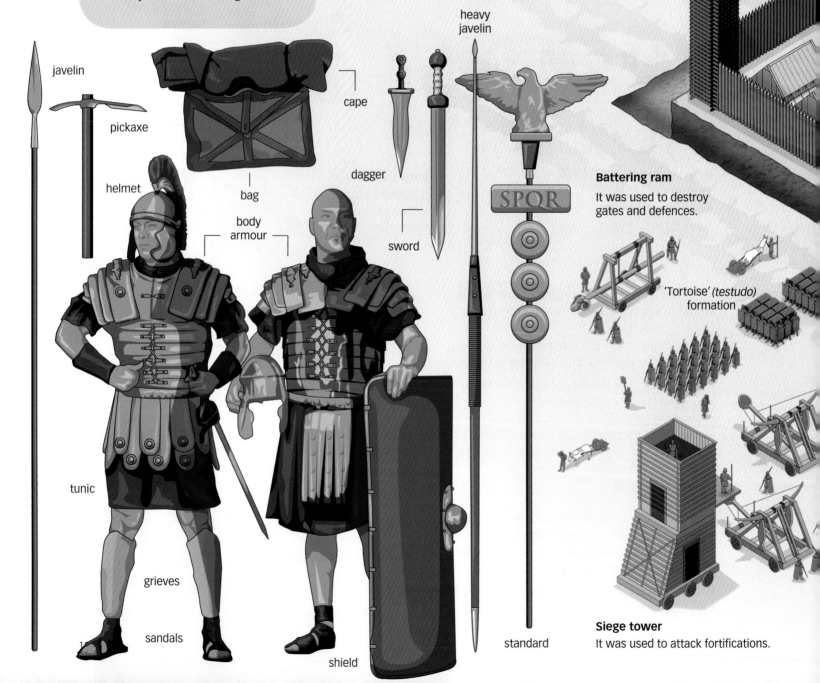

javelin

pickaxe

helmet

tunic

grieves

sandals

cape

bag

body armour

dagger

sword

heavy javelin

SPQR

standard

shield

Battering ram
It was used to destroy gates and defences.

'Tortoise' (testudo) formation

Siege tower
It was used to attack fortifications.

A ROMAN LEGION

1 Legion = **10** Cohorts = **4,800** men

Contubernium
8 men

Manipulus
2 Centuries

Cohort
6 Centuries

Century
80 men
10 *contubernia*

A Roman camp

The legionaries built a military camp when they reached their destination. Some camps were permanent, and became important cities.

Forum
HEADQUARTERS

main axes

tents of
the officers

Catapult
It was used to throw huge rocks.

tents of
the legionaries

moat

watchtower

HOW DO WE KNOW?

Trajan's Column in Rome is decorated with reliefs showing the Emperor Trajan's military victories in Dacia (Romania).

- How are the legionaries shown on this monument?
- Do you think there are other sources with information about the legionaries?

? WORK WITH THE IMAGE

- What was a century?
- Which weapons did a legionary use? What did he use to protect himself?
- How do you think the following were used?
  - Catapult
  - Watchtower
  - Siege tower
  - *Testudo* formation
- Describe a Roman camp.

THE ITALIAN PENINSULA IN THE 8TH CENTURY BC

Latins
Etruscans
Greeks
Other peoples

Adriatic Sea

Tyrrhenian Sea

Mediterranean Sea

Ionian Sea

The origins of Rome

There were three main peoples on the **Italian Peninsula** after about 800 BC:

• The **Etruscans** lived in the north.

• The **Latins** were in the centre.

• The **Greeks** founded colonies in the south.

In the 8th century BC, the Latins settled around the Tiber River. **Rome** was one of the Latin settlements.

The city of Rome was well protected by hills. It had an excellent strategic location:

• It was in the **centre of Italy** so it was well connected to the north and south of the peninsula.

• **By sea**, it had links with the west and east of the Mediterranean.

From the 6th century BC, Rome took control of the Italian Peninsula. Gradually, it expanded across the Mediterranean, acquiring territories in Europe, Asia and Africa.

The **Mediterranean Sea** was crucial to this vast empire. The Romans called it 'Our Sea' (Mare Nostrum).

The stages of Roman history

Roman civilisation lasted for twelve centuries, from the eighth century BC to the fifth century AD. It is usually divided into three stages:

• The **Monarchy** (753–509 BC)

• The **Republic** (509–27 BC)

• The **Empire** (27 BC–AD 476)

The Roman Monarchy (753 BC–509 BC)

There was a **Monarchy** during the earliest period of Roman history:

• An **elected king** was chosen by **patricians**, who were important, wealthy people.

• A **senate** advised the king. This assembly was made up of **senators** from prominent families.

In the sixth century BC, the **Etruscans** conquered Rome. However, the Romans resisted the Etruscans, and eventually defeated them. The last Etruscan king, Tarquin the Proud, was deposed in 509 BC. This was the end of the Monarchy.

THE TERRITORIES OF THE ROMAN EMPIRE

A TIMELINE OF ANCIENT ROMAN HISTORY

MONARCHY | REPUBLIC | EMPIRE

753 BC   509 BC   27 BC   AD 1   AD 476

 ACTIVITIES

3 Answer the questions:

a Who governed the Romans in the 6th century BC?

b Who were the patricians?

c How did the Roman Monarchy end?

WORK WITH THE MAP

5 In pairs, study the map.
Then ask and answer questions:

• *Was (Greece) part of the Roman Empire?*

WORK WITH THE TIMELINE

4 Answer the questions.

a What were the three stages of Roman history?

b Which stages were before the birth of Christ (BC)?
Which stage began BC but finished later (AD)?

c Copy the timeline in your notebook. Add some
events as you work through the unit.

THINK ABOUT IT

We use the term 'empire' in two different ways:

• The Roman Empire was all the territory ruled
by the Romans.

• The term also refers to the Roman system
of government between 27 BC and AD 476.

Military standard. SPQR meant 'Senatus Populusque Romanus' (The Senate and the People of Rome).

 **ACTIVITIES**

1 What were the main institutions in the Roman Republic? What were their functions?

2 The Republic and Roman expansion

The Republic (509–27 BC)

A **Republic** was established after the expulsion of the Etruscans. It had three main institutions:

- The *comitia* were assemblies where Roman citizens voted laws and elected magistrates.
- **Magistrates** were elected to hold political authority for one year. The leading magistrates were two **consuls**, who were in charge of administration and the army.
- The **Senate** was the most important institution. It directed the magistrates and decided foreign policy.

Patricians and plebeians

Society was divided into the following groups:

- The **patricians** were a minority from a group of rich, powerful families. They claimed to be descendants of the founders of Rome.
- The **plebeians** were the other free groups, like merchants, craftsmen and peasants.
- There were also **slaves**, who were prisoners of war or the children of slaves.

At first, only the patricians had political rights. However, the plebeians also demanded rights. The **Tribune of the Plebeians** became their representative in the Senate. From the fourth century BC, plebeians could be magistrates and senators.

Expansion across the Mediterranean

Under the Republic, Rome acquired many new territories:

- It conquered all the **Italian Peninsula** between 500 and 250 BC.
- It fought against **Carthage**, the dominant power in North Africa. Rome was victorious in the **Punic Wars** (264–146 BC).
- In the second and first centuries BC, Rome conquered **Greece** and the **Eastern Mediterranean**. It also expanded into other parts of Europe.

Provinces were created to make Roman administration more effective. Each province was ruled by a **governor**, and paid taxes to Rome.

The consequences of expansion

The Empire had a great impact on the Roman Republic:

- **Economy**. The conquests created great wealth in produce, slaves and taxes.

- **Politics**. The Senate did not control the governors in the provinces very well, so corruption spread.

- **Society**. A few people had nearly all the wealth. Inequality caused social discontent and revolts.

The end of the Republic

In the first century BC, the Republic was weakened by corruption and internal **conflicts**. The power of the army grew. However, important generals opposed each other and civil wars broke out.

The general **Julius Caesar** was victorious in one of these wars, and was proclaimed dictator. But in 44 BC he was assassinated by senators who were sympathetic to the Republic. His nephew Octavian won a new civil war. The Republic ended when Octavian became the Emperor **Augustus** in 27 BC.

Julius Caesar.

⊠ WORK WITH THE MAP

2 Study the map and the text and answer the questions.

  a Which modern countries are the equivalents of the regions shown on the map?

  b Did the Roman Empire have any natural frontiers in the north?

  c In which period was most territory conquered?

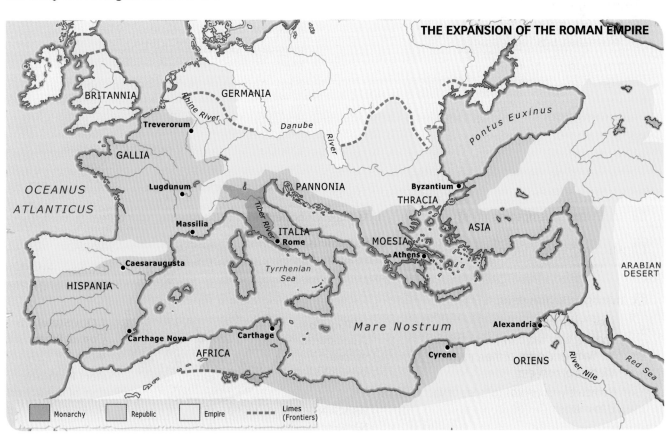

THE EXPANSION OF THE ROMAN EMPIRE

Legend: Monarchy · Republic · Empire · ----- Limes (Frontiers)

IMPERIAL GOVERNMENT

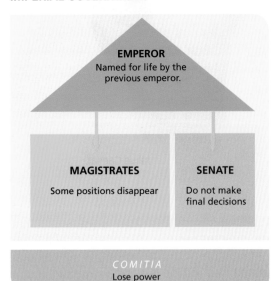

EMPEROR
Named for life by the previous emperor.

MAGISTRATES
Some positions disappear

SENATE
Do not make final decisions

COMITIA
Lose power

 ACTIVITIES

1 Use the internet to find one piece of information about each of the following emperors. Share your information with your classmates.

- Augustus
- Caligula
- Claudius
- Trajan
- Nero
- Hadrian

WORK WITH THE IMAGE

2 What were the emperor's titles?

3 Which regions did Trajan probably conquer?

4 Investigate Roman coins.

  a Look on the internet for photos showing a Roman coin. Make notes on the name and dates of the emperor, the type of coin, etc.

  b Compare your photos to those of your classmates.

Augustus, the first emperor

In 27 BC, **Augustus** introduced a new form of government: the **Empire**.

- The **emperor** held the highest political, military and religious authority. He directed foreign policy, dictated laws and decided taxes.

- The **Senate** still existed, but could only confirm the emperor's decisions.

The position of emperor was not hereditary. However, many emperors were related to each other, so **dynasties** were created.

Pax romana

The empire was stable and prosperous in the first and second centuries AD. There were several capable emperors like Vespasian, Trajan and Marcus Aurelius.

- Rome had a well-defended frontier, and there was little social unrest. The Romans called this the **pax romana** ('Roman peace').

- **Romanisation**: the conquered peoples adopted the law, customs, beliefs and language (**Latin**) of the Romans. Many public works and buildings were constructed throughout the empire.

- At first, only the male inhabitants of Italy had full rights. But from AD 212, all free men living in the empire became **citizens**.

A coin from Emperor Trajan's reign.

DAC(ico): Conqueror of the Dacians.

GER(manicus): Conqueror of the Germanic peoples.

AUG(ustus): Augustus (a sacred person).

TRAIANO: Name of the emperor.

P(ontifex) M(aximus): Religious leader.

TR(ibunum) P(lebis): Tribune of the Plebeians.

CO(n)S(ule) VI: Consul for the sixth time.

P(ater) P(atriae): Father of the fatherland.

IMP(erator): Military leader.

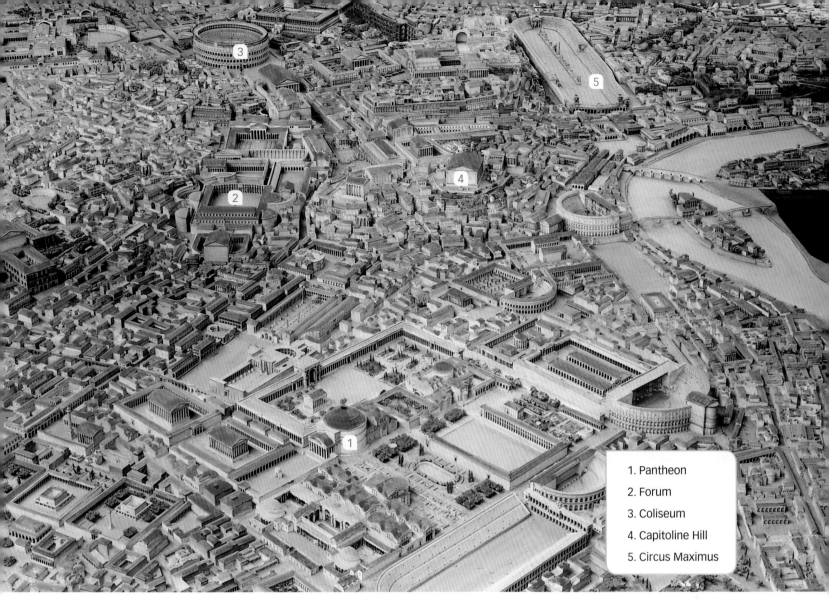

A RECONSTRUCTION OF ANCIENT ROME

1. Pantheon
2. Forum
3. Coliseum
4. Capitoline Hill
5. Circus Maximus

The crisis of the third century

The Roman Empire faced a severe **crisis** in the third century:

- **Wars**. Germanic tribes invaded from the north, and the Persians attacked in the east.

- **Political authority**. Many emperors only ruled for a short time, and were then deposed or assassinated.

- **Economic crisis**. Trade declined because it was no longer safe to travel. But taxation increased because the emperors needed to finance the wars.

- **Ruralisation**. Cities were no longer safe, and urban residents had to pay high taxes. Consequently, many people went to live in the countryside.

WORK WITH THE IMAGE

5 Did Rome look like the capital of an empire? Why?

6 Use the internet to find out more about the buildings in Rome. Do any of them still exist today?

THINK ABOUT IT

From *The Aeneid* by Virgil (70-19 BC)

Roman, remember to rule the peoples of the Earth
By your strength – for your destiny is this:
To make peace and impose the rule of law,
Defeat the proud and spare the conquered.

- Think of a good title for this text.

- Is Virgil's description similar to how the great powers see their role in the world today?

A *DOMUS*

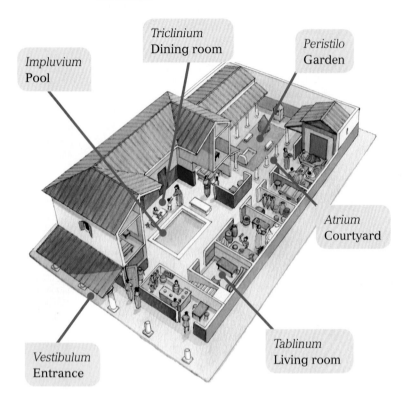

Impluvium
Pool

Triclinium
Dining room

Peristilo
Garden

Atrium
Courtyard

Vestibulum
Entrance

Tablinum
Living room

WORK WITH THE IMAGES

1 With a partner, discuss what the people are doing in each illustration. What are the different buildings used for?

PUBLIC BATHS (*THERMAE*)

Roman society

Roman society was very unequal:

- **Citizens** had the right to vote and stand for public office. Only male adults could be citizens.
- **Women** did not vote, but they could own property and manage businesses. Poorer women worked in shops and the fields, or looked after other people's children.
- **Slaves** had no rights. They became free if their owner gave them their freedom.

Daily life

The Romans got up very early. They washed and had breakfast, and then started work. They finished work at midday, and had leisure time after lunch.

The Romans met their friends and listened to speakers at the ***thermae***, or public baths. They also went to shows at the theatre, circus and amphitheatre.

Where did the Romans live?

In **cities**, the Romans lived in two types of houses:

- Wealthy Romans lived in a ***domus***. It usually had one floor, and was built around a central courtyard. There were paintings on the walls, and mosaics on the floors.
- ***Insulae*** were blocks of small apartments for poor people. They were usually badly constructed buildings made of brick and wood. Fires were frequent and dangerous.

In the **countryside**, there were large farms called **villas**. The owner and his family lived in a mansion, and there were small huts for the peasants and slaves.

ACTIVITIES

2 Compare the position of the following groups.

- Freemen and slaves
- Citizens and non-citizens
- Women and men

The economy

- **Agriculture**. Most land belonged to wealthy people who employed peasants and slaves. The main crops were **wheat**, **grapes** and **olives**. The Romans used wine and oil presses, mills, and **irrigation**. The landowners lived in villas, which were large rural houses with a storehouse, cellar, and animal pens.

- **Crafts**. Potters, weavers, and other craftsmen had workshops in cities, where they made and sold their products. There were a few big industries, like ship building.

- **Mining**. The Romans mined gold, silver, iron, tin and lead. Salt was used to preserve food, and there were salt mines along the Mediterranean coast. Salt mining was hard work, usually carried out by slaves.

- **Trade**. There was trade inside the Empire, and also across its frontiers:

  - The use of a single imperial **currency** promoted trade.

  - There was also a network of excellent **roads** and **ports**.

  - **Oil** and **wheat** were exported from the Iberian Peninsula to the rest of the empire.

  - **Spices**, **silk** and **cotton** were imported from Asia.

  - **Slaves** were bought and sold in slave markets.

WORK WITH THE MAP

3 What were the main sea routes and land routes for trade?

4 Copy and complete a table on Roman products.

Food and drink	Minerals, precious metals	Other produce
.....	.....	.....

5 Study a modern atlas. List the modern countries where resources were found in Roman times.

Resources	Country
salt	....
olive oil	....
wheat	....
gold	....
amber	....

MAIN TRADE ROUTES AND PRODUCE IN THE ROMAN EMPIRE

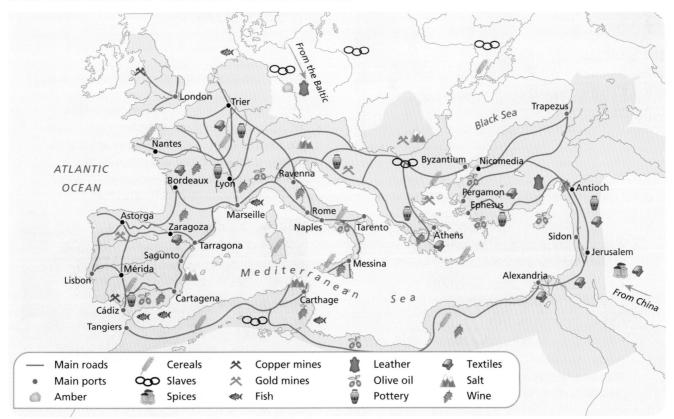

A ROMAN CITY

Circus

Amphitheatre

Aqueduct

Temple

Forum

Victory arch

Insulae

Shop

Domus

Roman cities

Cities were the main centres of Roman authority and influence. The Romans founded new cities, and older cities grew. **Rome** was the capital of the empire. At its peak, it had a population of a million inhabitants.

Most Roman cities had a rectangular layout of parallel streets. There were two main streets:

- The *cardo* ran from north to south.
- The *decumanus* ran from east to west.

A **forum**, or main square, was located in the centre of the city. The forum was the centre of political, social and cultural life. It had arcades, and was decorated with statues of the emperors. Important buildings, like the **Temple of Jupiter** and the **Basilica**, or public court, were located around the forum. There were also shops, markets and craftsmen's workshops.

Roman cities had all kinds of facilities, including public baths, theatres, fountains and drains.

🔑 DID YOU KNOW?

Pompeii

Pompeii was a city in the south-west of Italy. In AD 79 the volcanic eruption of Mount Vesuvius covered the city in ashes and lava. Many people were killed. The city was buried under the ground, and air and moisture could not reach the houses and objects. Consequently, everything was incredibly well preserved. Today, the site provides extraordinary information about everyday life in Roman times.

✂ ACTIVITIES

1 In groups, use more than one website to find images on Pompeii:

- Its **buildings**: its theatres, public baths, the Temple of Isis, private houses...
- Its **art**: frescoes, mosaics...
- Its **people**: evidence on their activities and how they died...

Select the best images for a poster or computer presentation on Pompeii.

Architecture and engineering

The Romans built large scale **monumental** buildings for public use. They also carried out many **practical** engineering projects, like aqueducts, bridges and roads:

- The Romans used **stone**, like the Greeks. But they also used **cement**, **concrete** and **bricks** so their constructions were extremely solid.

- The Romans were influenced by Greek architecture. However, they added other features like the **arch** and **vault**.

Theatre. Mérida, Extremadura.

BUILDINGS		FUNCTION
RELIGIOUS	Temple	Religious rituals
POLITICAL AND ECONOMIC	Curia	Senate house
	Basilica	Commercial exchanges and court
SHOWS	Theatre	Plays (tragedies and comedies)
	Amphitheatre	Gladiator fights
	Circus	Chariot races
CARE OF THE BODY	Gymnasium	Sports training
	Public baths	Baths and social life
COMMEMORATIVE MONUMENTS	Columns	Commemorate military victories and other events
	Victory arch	
PUBLIC WORKS	Roads	Communications
	Bridges	Cross rivers
	Aqueducts	Transport drinking water

Amphitheatre. The Coliseum in Rome.

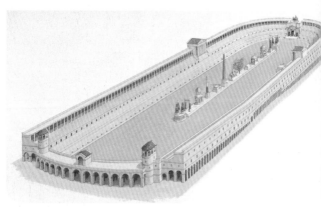

Circus.

 ACTIVITIES

2 Study the table. Investigate three types of Roman building and prepare illustrated fact files:

- What did they look like? (Look for photos on the internet.)
- How were they used?

Exchange your information with your classmates.

3 Why do we say that Roman architecture was both practical and monumental? Give examples.

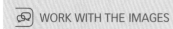 WORK WITH THE IMAGES

4 Which type of event took place in each place?

Polytheism

For many centuries, the Romans were **polytheistic**. They were **tolerant** of the religion of conquered peoples, and sometimes worshipped their gods themselves:

- They adopted all the **Greek** gods, but changed their names.
  The most important Roman gods were **Jupiter**, **Juno** and **Minerva**, who were known as the **Capitoline Triad**.

- The Egyptian goddess **Isis** was worshipped throughout the empire.

- The **emperor** was also a god.
  All the inhabitants of the empire had to honour the cult to the emperor.

The Romans consulted **augurs** (priests) before they took important decisions. *Lares* and *Penates* were gods that protected the house and family. They also believed in the spirits of their ancestors.

Classical culture

Roman civilisation was strongly influenced by the Greeks and other Mediterranean peoples. Roman culture was adopted throughout the empire.

Today, Greek and Roman civilisation is called **'classical culture'**; it had great influence even after the empire had disappeared. For example, **Latin** was the main language of the Roman Empire. Later, it grew into several modern European languages.

DID YOU KNOW?

Roman mosaics

The Romans made mosaics from small pieces of stone, glass and tile. They decorated the floors and walls of buildings with scenes from daily life, or the adventures of gods and heroes.

A Roman mosaic from North Africa.

ACTIVITIES

1. Look on the internet for a 'List of the Roman and Greek gods'. Complete a table in your notebook with the names of ten important gods.

Roman name	Greek name	God of...?
Jupiter	Zeus	Ruler of the gods; sky, lightning
Minerva	....	....
Juno	....	....
....	....	....

2. Investigate Romance languages.

   a With a partner, discuss which of the following languages are descended from Latin:

   - Italian
   - Catalan
   - Castilian Spanish
   - German

   b Write 'Romance Languages' in an internet search engine. Check your answers, and find three more languages based on Latin.

The origins of Christianity

In the first century AD, the followers of **Jesus of Nazareth** founded **Christianity**. This religion was based on the following ideas:

- There is only one God. (Christianity is **monotheistic**).
- Everyone is equal before God.
- People should love and forgive each other.
- People who follow Christianity will be granted **eternal life** after death.

After Jesus' death, the **apostles** spread Christian ideas. The Christians were **persecuted** by the Romans because they refused to worship the emperor. However, they still practised their religion in secret.

Christianity, an official religion

In AD 313, the emperor **Constantine** allowed Christians to practise their religion. Christianity spread rapidly throughout the empire.

In AD 380, the emperor **Theodosius** declared that Christianity was the only religion in the empire. All other religions were prohibited.

The **Pope** was the Bishop of Rome, as well as the main leader of the Christian Church. **Councils** were regular meetings to maintain the principles of Christianity.

Catacombs in Rome. When their religion was prohibited by the Romans, the Christians buried the dead in these secret underground passages.

ACTIVITIES

3 Why were the Christians persecuted? When did their situation change?

4 What were the main ideas of Christianity? Was it different from earlier Roman religion?

THINK ABOUT IT

Which early Christian beliefs, symbols and practices are still found in the world today?

DID YOU KNOW?

Christian symbols

The early Christians used symbols in paintings and on their tombs. This was a way of referring to their beliefs when they practised their religion secretly.

The **fish** also represented Christ.

A **monogram** was a combination of letters representing Christ.

A **dove with an olive branch** – a symbol of divine peace.

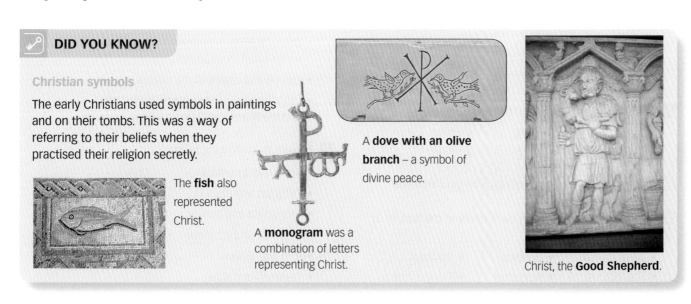

Christ, the **Good Shepherd**.

ACTIVITY ROUND-UP

1 Copy and complete the diagram.

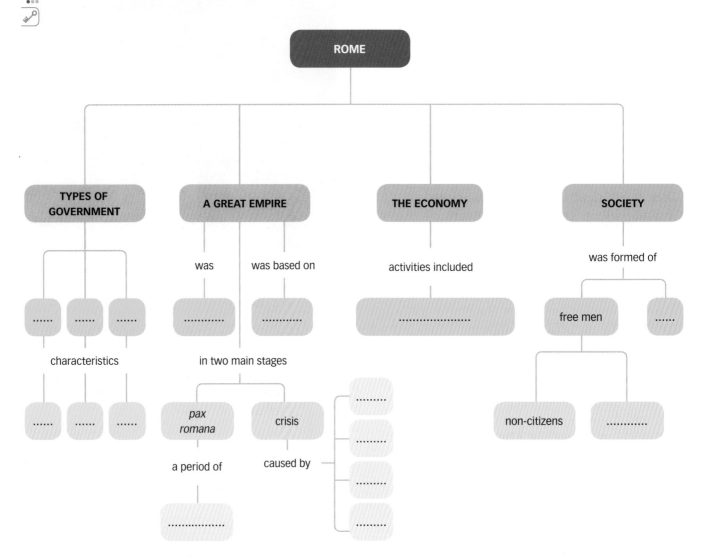

2 Draw a timeline of Roman history. Identify each stage, using a different colour.

753 BC   AD 476

3 What happened on each of the following dates?

- 753 BC
- AD 476
- AD 395
- 509 BC
- 48 BC
- 27 BC

4 Put the dates in the correct place on your timeline.

5 Explain the importance of each figure in the history of the Roman Empire.

- Julius Caesar
- Theodosius
- Hannibal
- Augustus
- Romulus
- Constantine

6 Trace or copy a map of the Roman Empire. (You can use one of the maps of the Roman Empire in this unit.)

- Colour the Roman Empire in the period when it had most territory.
- Identify the capital of the empire.
- Label Hispania, the Mediterranean Sea and the Rhine and Danube Rivers.

7 Explain the following terms:

- Senate and *comitia*
- Patrician and plebeian
- Magistrate and consul
- Province and governor
- Villa and *domus*
- Freeman and slave

8 Compare the forms of government in the three stages of Roman history.

	Monarchy	Republic	Empire
Who controlled the government?	....	....	....
Did citizens elect the government?	....	....	....
What was the role of the Senate?	....	....	....

9 Copy the social pyramid in your notebook and place each group in the right place.

Plebeians
Slaves
Patricians

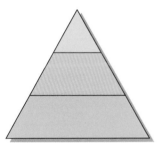

• Where are women on this pyramid? Why?

10 Copy and complete the following text. Listen to the recording and check your answers.

In 27 BC, the Roman _____ ended when Augustus became emperor. The emperor held political, military and religious authority. The _____ still existed, but it only confirmed the emperor's decisions. In the first and second centuries AD, Rome had a well-defended frontier, and there was little unrest. This was called the _____ _____ , or 'Roman peace'. In a process known as _____ the conquered peoples adopted the customs and beliefs of the Romans, and spoke _____ . At first, only the male inhabitants of _____ were full citizens, but after AD 212, all free men living in the empire became citizens.

In the _____ century AD the Roman Empire faced a severe crisis as a result of wars, political instability and economic difficulties. Trade declined and many people went to live in the countryside. (This process was called _____.) Despite all these problems, the empire lasted until AD 476.

11 Did the Romans have the same gods as the Greeks? Were there features of Roman religion that were not connected to the Greeks?

THE LEGACY OF ROME

The Romans have contributed many things to western civilisation:

• **Languages.** Many European languages (Italian, French, Romanian, Castilian Spanish, Galician and Catalan) have a Latin origin. Many of the words that we speak come from Latin words.

• **Laws.** Roman law has influenced the legal system in much of Europe.

• **Cities**. Many important modern cities were originally founded by the Romans.

• **Historical monuments.** These are part of our cultural heritage.

• **Roads.** Many modern roads follow the same routes as in Roman times.

• **Architecture.** New materials included cement and concrete.

• **Agriculture.** The Romans introduced new crops and agricultural techniques.

• **Christianity.** This new religion spread throughout the Roman Empire.

12 Which Latin words have you learned in the unit?

13 What are Roman numerals? Do we still use them?

14 Look carefully at the Roman calendar of Rome.

• Which Spanish days of the week and months of the year come from Latin?

• Which English days and months also have a Latin origin?

Days of the week	Months of the year	
Lunae dies	1. *Martius*	7. *September*
Martis dies	2. *Aprilis*	8. *October*
Mercurii dies	3. *Maius*	9. *November*
Iovis dies	4. *Junius*	10. *December*
Veneris dies	5. *Julius*	11. *Januarius*
Saturni dies	6. *Augustus*	12. *Februarius*
Solis dies		

15 Look for information about the Roman Theatre in Mérida. How is it used today? Is this a good use of the theatre?

🔑 THINK LIKE AN HISTORIAN. **Analyse photos and texts**

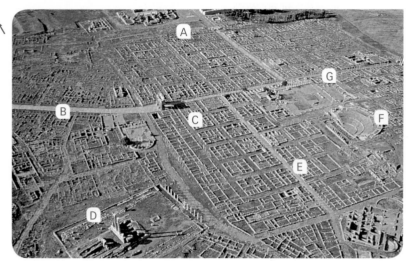

The ruins of a city

1 Identify the following parts of the city on the photo. Explain your answers.

- Cardo
- Decumanus
- Forum
- Houses
- Temple
- Theatre
- Victory arch

The assassination of Julius Caesar

2 Remember what you already know:

- Who was Julius Caesar?
- How did he come to power?
- When was he assassinated?

3 Check you understand the following words

- omen
- priest
- sacrifice
- stab
- conspiracy / conspirator

4 Get information from the text:

- How many conspirators were there?
- Who were the leaders?
- When did the assassination take place? Why then?
- What were the reasons for the assassination?
- How did Caesar die?
- What were Caesar's last words?

5 Are there any details in this account that are difficult to believe? Why?

6 Look on the internet for a short video showing the death of Caesar. Is it similar to this description? Does it look accurate?

Caesar's words and actions made people think that he wanted too much power. For example, he received many honours like Consul, Dictator for life and Censor. A great statue of him was made, and there was a gold chair for him in the Senate.

About sixty people were in the conspiracy against Caesar. Cassius, Marcus and Brutus were its leaders. Together, they discussed where to attack him. When it was announced that the Senate would meet in the senate-house on the Ides of March [15 March], they decided that this was the best time and place.

Some omens warned Caesar about his fate. A priest made a sacrifice which showed that there was great danger. On the night before his murder, Caesar dreamed that he rose above the clouds and joined hands with Jupiter. Caesar's wife Calpurnia dreamed that the house was falling down, and that they killed her husband.

The conspirators surrounded Caesar on the Ides of March. He was stabbed 23 times. When Caesar saw Brutus with the conspirators, he said: 'You too, my son'.

SUETONIUS, *The Twelve Caesars*
(adapted)

INVESTIGATE. **Gladiator fights**

Gladiators were people who fought against each other, or against wild animals, in Roman amphitheatres. Many of them were prisoners of war, but others were condemned criminals. There were even professionals! There were several categories of gladiator according to the weapons that they used.

The Romans loved to go to gladiator shows in the amphitheatre. The combats were held after the working day so that everyone could go. Entrance was free because the shows were financed by rich families to increase their prestige and influence. The Emperor Trajan organised combats that lasted 123 days after he defeated the Dacians. 10,000 gladiators fought in them!

A	Helmet
B	Shield
C	*Gladius* or sword
D	Greave

Gladiator. (This kind of gladiator was called a Samnite.)

A scene from the film Gladiator.

THE COMBAT

1 **Parade of the gladiators.** If the Emperor was present, the gladiators saluted him: 'Hail Caesar, those who are about to die salute you'.

2 **Drawing lots** determined the order in which the gladiators fought. The spectators liked to bet on the result.

3 **The fight**. When a gladiator fell down wounded he raised his left hand to the gallery. If the person presiding over the fight, usually the emperor, raised his thumb, the gladiator was pardoned and given medical help. But if he turned his thumb down the gladiator was killed.

GLADIATORS

1 Form groups. Together your will write a booklet. The booklet should answer the following questions:

1. What was a gladiator?
2. Where were gladiators from?
3. Where did they train?
4. What types of gladiators were there?
5. What were their weapons?
6. What were combats like?
7. What were the prizes?

2 Look for information. Find extra information and illustrations on the internet, using the keywords 'Gladiator Ancient Rome'. Visit several websites, and include links to the websites at the end of your booklet.

3 Organise your information. Use several sheets of paper, and write the title of each section at the top of a page. Decide how the text and illustrations should go on each page, and who will work on each section.

4 Write and illustrate your report.

5 Discuss your opinions with your group. Complete your booklet with a joint conclusion. If you do not agree about everything, think about ways to contrast all your opinions:
Gladiator combats were very popular because... / On the other hand, they were very cruel... / However, ...

FIND OUT ABOUT:

- The Pre-Roman peoples
- The colonisers and Tartessos
- The Roman conquest of the Peninsula and the territorial organization of Hispania
- The Romanization of Hispania

LEARN HOW TO:

- Compare lifestyles

Roman roads

Roman roads were an extraordinary engineering achievement. A network of roads connected Rome to the most remote regions of the empire. Legionaries, merchants and other travellers went along them. Today, many roads in Spain follow routes that were traced 2,000 years ago.

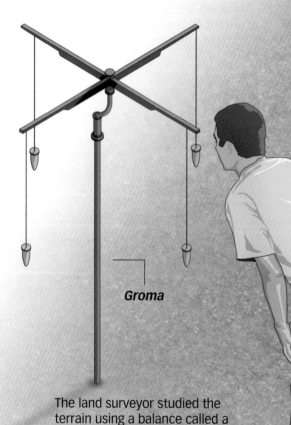

THE LAND SURVEYOR

The land surveyor made measurements and traced the route.

First, they dug the ground. They used a thick layer of stones for the foundations.

Groma

The land surveyor studied the terrain using a balance called a *groma*.

They made very straight roads.

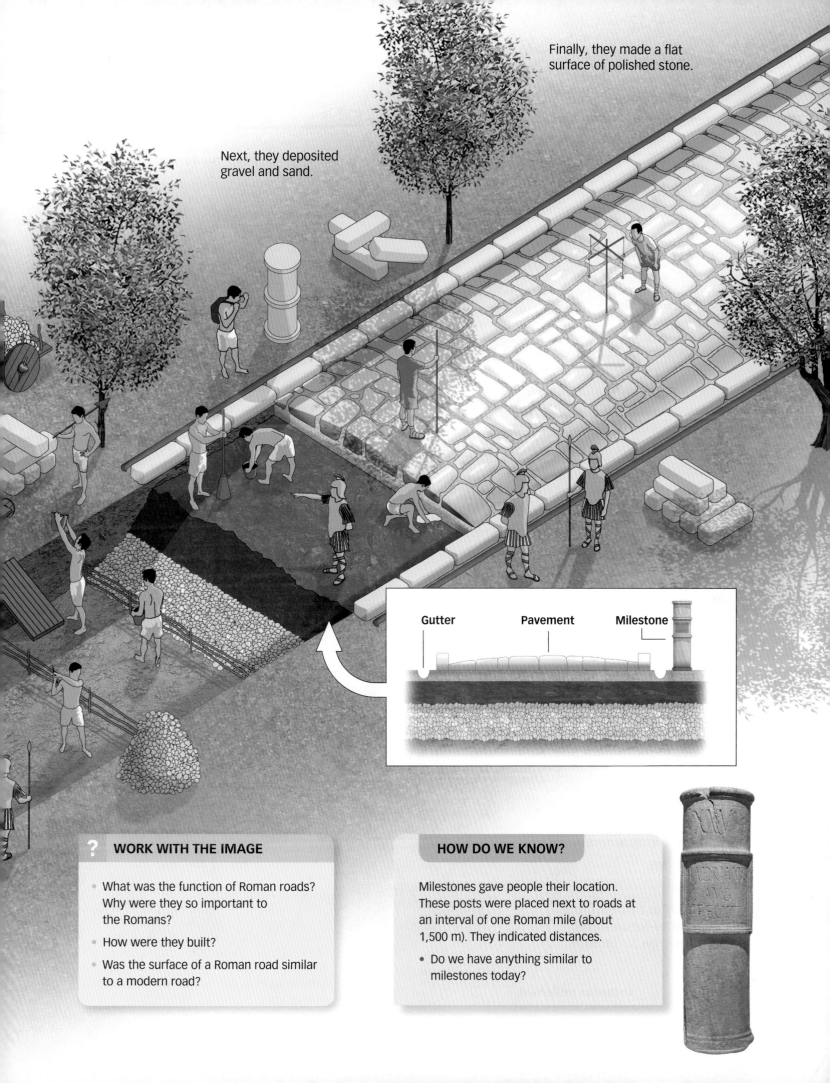

Finally, they made a flat surface of polished stone.

Next, they deposited gravel and sand.

Gutter   Pavement   Milestone

? WORK WITH THE IMAGE

- What was the function of Roman roads? Why were they so important to the Romans?

- How were they built?

- Was the surface of a Roman road similar to a modern road?

HOW DO WE KNOW?

Milestones gave people their location. These posts were placed next to roads at an interval of one Roman mile (about 1,500 m). They indicated distances.

- Do we have anything similar to milestones today?

The Iberians

The **Iberians** lived in the east and south of the Iberian Peninsula from the eighth century BC.

- **Social organisation**. The Iberians lived in settlements with defensive walls. They were organised in **tribes**, led by **chieftains**. They had a hierarchical society.

- **The economy**. They grew cereals, vines and olives, and raised livestock. They were good craftsmen, and made iron tools and swords, pottery and textiles. They had a currency, and traded precious metals.

- **Religion**. The Iberians worshipped mainly female deities. They cremated the dead.

- **Culture**. They acquired writing through contact with the Phoenicians and Greeks. They created fine sculptures like the *Lady of Elche* and the *Lady of Baza*.

THE PRE-ROMAN PEOPLES OF THE PENINSULA

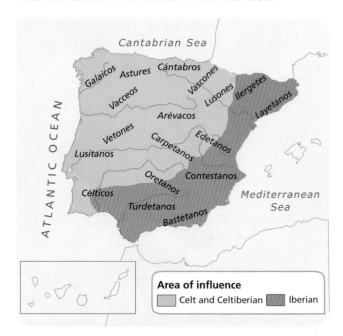

Area of influence
Celt and Celtiberian | Iberian

WORK WITH THE MAP

1 Which Pre-Roman people were in the area where you live today?

 THINK ABOUT IT

Comparing lifestyles

When we compare the culture and lifestyle of two historical peoples, we look at:

- Where they lived
- Their social organization
- Their economic activities
- Their beliefs
- Their art

Do we look at the same things when we are comparing two societies in the 21st century?

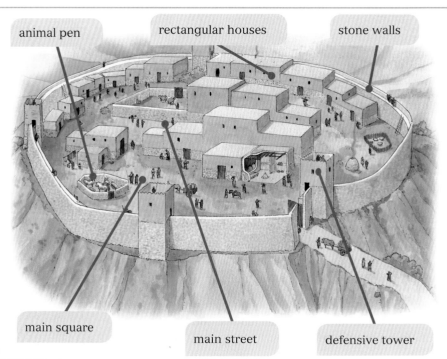

animal pen   rectangular houses   stone walls

main square   main street   defensive tower

An Iberian settlement.

The Celts

The **Celts** arrived on the Iberian Peninsula from central Europe in about 1100 BC. They settled in the centre, north and west of the peninsula.

- **Social organisation**. The Celts lived in settlements with defensive walls called *castros*. They were organised in **clans**, which were based on family ties. Several clans formed a **tribe**.

- **The economy**. The Celts were **self-sufficient**: they consumed what they produced, and did not trade much with other peoples. They did not have a currency. They grew cereals, and had some livestock. They were expert jewellers, and made bronze and iron weapons. They also made pottery and textiles.

- **Religion**. They worshipped the stars, and some natural forces. Their priests were called **druids**. Like the Iberians, the Celts cremated the dead.

- **Culture**. They did not have writing, and they had little contact with most Mediterranean cultures. They made large sculptures of bulls and pigs called *verracos*.

🔎 DID YOU KNOW?

The Lady of Elche is an Iberian statue from the 4th century BC. It is a portrait of a woman with a very elaborate headdress. Originally, it was highly colourful. It was probably influenced by Greek culture.

- Look on internet for photos and information about the Lady of Elche, the Lady of Guardamar and the Lady of Baza. Describe and compare them.

✎ ACTIVITIES

2 Compare the Iberians and Celts in the following areas:

- Society
- Economy
- Religion

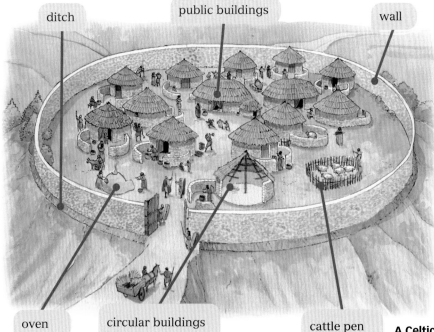

ditch   public buildings   wall

oven   circular buildings   cattle pen   **A Celtic settlement.**

💬 WORK WITH THE IMAGES

3 Compare the two settlements.

a Why do you think the settlements were surrounded by walls?

b Were the settlements built following a plan, or at random?

c What shape were the houses?

d Which economic activities did each people practise?

2 The colonisers and Tartessos

In the first millennium BC, three Mediterranean peoples established **colonies** in the south and east of the Iberian Peninsula: the Phoenicians, Greeks and Carthaginians.

The Phoenicians

The **Phoenicians** were from city-states in the eastern Mediterranean. Their merchants looked for trade opportunities and raw materials.

The Phoenicians established **trading posts** across the Mediterranean after 1000 BC. On the Iberian Peninsula, Gadir (Cádiz), Malaka (Málaga) and Abdera (Almería) were founded by the Phoenicians.

The Phoenician goddess Astarte.

The Greeks

The **Greeks** were the great commercial rivals of the Phoenicians in the Mediterranean region.

They settled on the east coast of the Iberian Peninsula from the eighth century BC. They founded **colonies**, like Hemeroskopeion (Denia) and Emporion (Empuries).

Arethusa, a water nymph.

The Carthaginians

The **Carthaginians** came from the city of Carthage in North Africa, and were the successors of the Phoenicians. They gained control of Phoenician settlements and founded new ones, such as Carthago Nova (Cartagena) and Ebyssos (Ibiza).

Pegasus, symbol of the city.

Unlike the Phoenicians, the Carthaginians were not just interested in trade. They conquered the south of the peninsula, and expelled the Greeks in the sixth century BC. In the third century BC, the Romans expelled the Carthaginians.

A Greek coin from Emporion.

What was the influence of the colonisers?

The colonisers had great **influence** on the peoples of the Iberian Peninsula, especially those who lived near the Mediterranean Sea:

- They introduced new **crops**.
- They improved **mining** techniques.
- They introduced **writing**, in the Phoenician and Greek alphabets.
- They introduced the use of **coins** as currency.

ACTIVITIES

1 Which cities in Spain have kept the names given them by the colonisers? Which names have changed completely?

ATLANTIC
OCEAN

| Phoenician territory | Greek territory | Tartessos |
| ● Metropolis | ● Phoenician settlement | ● Greek settlement | ● Carthaginian settlement |

Rhodes
Emporion
Alalia
Athens
Sidon
Tyre
Kition
Panormos
Hemeroskopeion
Ebyssos
Syracuse
Sexi
Carthago Nova
Carthage
Gadir
Abdera
Malaca

Mediterranean Sea

Red Sea

THE COLONISERS AND TARTESSOS

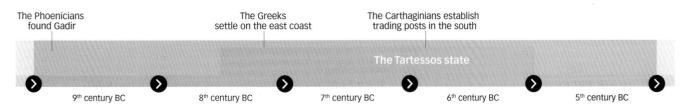

The Phoenicians
found Gadir

The Greeks
settle on the east coast

The Carthaginians establish
trading posts in the south

The Tartessos state

9th century BC   8th century BC   7th century BC   6th century BC   5th century BC

TIMELINE OF THE COLONISERS AND TARTESSOS

Tartessos

Tartessos was the first state to be created on the Iberian Peninsula. It was at its peak between the late eighth century and the sixth century BC.

It was based in the Guadalquivir valley and the south-west of the peninsula.

- **Government**. We know that Tartessos was a **monarchy**, but we have little information about its rulers.

- **The economy**. The Tartessians mined metals, which they traded with the Phoenicians and Greeks. In exchange for copper, silver and tin, they received oil, jewellery and ivory. They were fine craftsmen.

- **Culture**. There was a strong Phoenician influence in Tartessos. They adopted many of their religious beliefs.

WORK WITH THE TIMELINE AND THE MAP

2 Which peoples colonised the Iberian Peninsula between the 9th and 5th centuries BC?

3 Name Phoenician, Greek and Carthaginian settlements on the Iberian Peninsula and the Balearic Islands.

4 Where was Tartessos? Who did it trade with?

A Roman amphora. This was used to store and transport wine, olive oil and other products.

3 Roman Hispania

The Roman conquest

In the 3rd century BC, the Romans and Carthaginians reached an agreement about their frontiers on the Iberian Peninsula. But the Carthaginian general Hannibal broke this agreement when he conquered **Saguntum** (Sagunto), a city allied to Rome. This marked the beginning of the **Second Punic War** (218-201 BC).

At first, Rome only intervened to end Carthaginian influence. But over two centuries the Romans conquered the whole peninsula:

THE CONQUEST OF HISPANIA

First stage (218-197 BC)	**Second stage (154-133 BC)**	**Third stage (29-19 BC)**
• The Romans conquered the **Mediterranean coast** and occupied the Ebro and Guadalquivir valleys.	• The Romans occupied the **Central Plateau**, where they met resistance from the Lusitanians and the Celtiberians. The Celtiberian settlement of **Numantia** fell after a long siege in 133 BC.	• The Romans conquered the **north** of the Peninsula during the **Cantabrian Wars**. However, some groups, like the Vascones, were never conquered.

ACTIVITIES

1 Why did the Romans conquer the Iberian Peninsula? Was there any resistance?

2 Look for maps of Roman provinces on internet. Copy and label maps of the Iberian Peninsula, showing the original provinces, the provinces in 27 BC, and the provinces in the 3rd century AD.

Roman government in Hispania

The Romans called the Iberian Peninsula **Hispania**. They divided it into **provinces**, and appointed a **governor** as the head of each province.

• They originally created two provinces: **Hispania Citerior** and **Hispania Ulterior**.

• In 27 BC Augustus organised the territory into three provinces: **Baetica**, **Lusitania** and **Tarraconense**.

• In the 3rd century AD, there were five provinces: **Baetica**, **Lusitania**, **Tarraconense**, **Gallaecia** and **Cartaginense**.

Romanisation

Hispania adopted the lifestyle and culture of the Romans in a process called **Romanisation**:

- **Latin** became widely used.
- Roman **religious beliefs** spread through Hispania. After the second century AD, **Christianity** became the main religion.
- The Romans built new **cities**, or developed existing cities. They became important centres of Roman life and culture.
- Regions were linked together by a network of Roman **roads**. There were works of engineering, like the aqueduct in Segovia.
- The use of Roman **currency** made it easier for people to trade with each other.
- The Roman **legionaries** were in contact with local people. Many legionaries stayed in the region after they retired.

Romanisation was rapid and complete on the Mediterranean coast. It was slower in the regions where there was more resistance to Roman rule. Hispania became one of the most strongly Romanised territories in the empire.

Society

The society of Roman Hispania was divided into free people and slaves:

- **Free society**. Patrician families from Rome owned large estates. Wealthy local families also belonged to the elite. Below them, the plebeians were craftsmen and small farmers.
- **Slaves** worked in agriculture, domestic service and the mines.

The economy

The Romans used the resources of Hispania and introduced their own **techniques**:

- **Agriculture**. Cereals, olives and vines were grown. Roman innovations included irrigation and a new type of plough.
- **Crafts**. Pottery, textiles and glass were manufactured.
- **Mining**. Metals such as gold, silver and mercury were mined.
- **Trade**. Hispania exported wheat, olive oil, salted fish, precious metals and slaves. It imported luxury items.

MAIN CITIES AND ROADS OF HISPANIA

 ACTIVITIES

2 What was Romanisation? Give examples.

3 Which products did Hispania export? Which did it import?

 WORK WITH THE MAP

4 With a partner, compare the map to a modern map of Spain. Which cities existed in Roman times?

THE KINGDOM OF THE VISIGOTHS (LATE 6ᵀᴴ CENTURY)

🔎 WORK WITH THE MAP

1 What route did the Visigoths take on their way to Toledo?

2 Which territories did Leovigild conquer?

3 Which territories belonged to the Byzantine Empire in the late 6ᵗʰ century?

This 10ᵗʰ century codex shows a council in Toledo.

The Kingdom of the Visigoths

Like other regions in the Roman Empire, Hispania was greatly affected by the migrations of **Germanic tribes**. In 409, three of these tribes (the Suevi, the Alans and the Vandals) invaded the Iberian Peninsula.

In 415, the Western Roman Emperor came to an agreement with the leaders of the **Visigoths** (a tribe that had entered the empire in the late 4ᵗʰ century). The Visigoths forced the Vandals and Alans to leave for North Africa, and pushed the Suevi towards the north-west of the peninsula. In return, they were granted land in southern Gaul (modern France), where they founded the Kingdom of the Visigoths. **Toulouse** was its capital.

In 507 the Franks expelled the Visigoths from Gaul. The Visigoths entered the Iberian Peninsula. **Toledo** was the capital of their new kingdom.

There were important developments from the late 6ᵗʰ century onwards:

• King **Leovigild** (568-586) conquered the kingdom of the Suevi and acquired other territories.

• His son **Reccared** (586-601) converted to Catholicism, which became the religion of the whole kingdom.

• Under **Recceswinth** (649-672), the laws of the kingdom were unified.

In the late 7ᵗʰ century, there were continual conflicts between the kings and the nobility. The kingdom ended when the Muslims invaded the peninsula in 711.

Political organisation

The Visigoths had an **elected monarchy**, which led to frequent struggles for control. The king was advised by a body called the ***Aula Regia***. **Dukes** and **counts** governed the provinces.

Religious and political decisions were taken at **councils**. The King, the Aula Regia and the clergy all participated.

Church of San Pedro de la Nave (Zamora). A. Exterior. B. Interior.

Society and the economy

Only about 100,000 Visigoths settled on the Iberian Peninsula and they formed a small **minority** of the population. There were about five or six million Hispano-Romans. This helps to explain why the Kingdom of the Visigoths was greatly influenced by the language, culture and religion of Hispania.

Nobles and **clergymen** occupied the highest political office and owned much of the land. But most of the population were **peasants**. There were **free peasants**, who had small plots of land, as well as **slaves**, who belonged to the nobles or the Church and worked their land.

Agriculture was the main economic activity and only a small minority of the population lived in cities. The Visigoths were expert **craftsmen** of jewellery and weapons.

Culture and art

Culture and art were closely linked to the Church. Leading intellectuals included Saint Leander, Archbishop of Seville, and Saint Isidore, who wrote the *Etymologies*, which summed up the knowledge of the time.

Small **churches** were built using regular sized blocks of stone. The Visigoths used the **horseshoe arch** and the barrel vault. There was little decoration, except for the capitals and friezes. The churches of San Juan de Baños, in Palencia, and San Pedro de la Nave, in Zamora, are important surviving examples of the architecture of the Visgoths.

The votive crown of the Visigoth King Recceswinth was made of gold and precious stones.

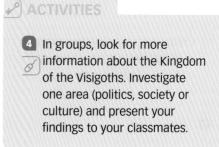

ACTIVITIES

4 In groups, look for more information about the Kingdom of the Visigoths. Investigate one area (politics, society or culture) and present your findings to your classmates.

1 Copy and complete the diagrams.

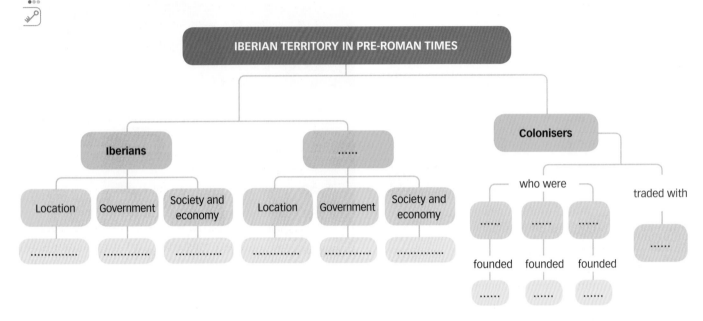

IBERIAN TERRITORY IN PRE-ROMAN TIMES

Iberians
- Location ....
- Government ....
- Society and economy ....

......
- Location ....
- Government ....
- Society and economy ....

Colonisers
- who were ...... founded ......
- ...... founded ......
- ...... founded ......
- traded with ......

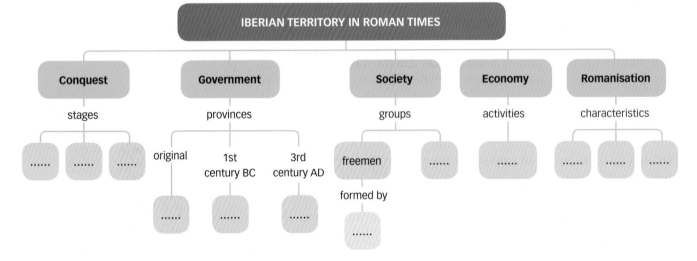

IBERIAN TERRITORY IN ROMAN TIMES

Conquest — stages — ....

Government — provinces — original ...... / 1st century BC ...... / 3rd century AD ......

Society — groups — freemen (formed by ......) ......

Economy — activities — ......

Romanisation — characteristics — ....

2 Put the following events in chronological order.
- End of the Second Punic War
- Foundation of Gadir
- Cantabrian Wars
- Beginning of the Roman conquest of Hispania
- Foundation of Carthago Nova
- End of the Roman conquest of Hispania

3 Create a timeline of the stages of the Roman conquest of Hispania. Write the dates of the beginning and end of each stage.

218 BC   19 BC

4 Complete a map of the Iberian Peninsula in pre-Roman times. Label it following this key.

- Iberian influence
- Celtic influence
- Carthaginian settlement
- Phoenician settlement
- Greek settlement

5 Explain the following terms:
- *castro*
- Carthaginian
- chieftain
- Tartessos
- trading post
- *Aula Regia*

6 What was Romanisation? Give examples from different fields, such as the economy, society, religion and art.

7 Copy and complete the following table in your notebook.

	Iberians	Celts
Location	......	......
Settlements	......	......
Society	......	......
Economy	......	......
Beliefs	......	......
Funerals	......	......

8 Answer the questions.

a Why were the Phoenician trading posts and the Greek colonies established on the coast of the Iberian Peninsula?

b Why did the colonisers have links with Tartessos?

c Why did the Romans conquer the Iberian Peninsula?

d What did the legionaries contribute to the Romanisation of Hispania?

THE LEGACY OF ANTIQUITY

The **Phoenician** and **Greek colonisers** left us:

- Some **crops**, like the vine and olive tree, which are still very important today.
- The use of **money**.
- The **alphabet**.

The **Romans** left us:

- **Latin**. Intellectuals like Seneca and Martial spoke Latin. Modern Romance languages like Castilian Spanish, Catalan, Valencian and Galician are based on Latin.
- **Roman law**. This was the basis of later legal systems.
- **Christianity**. This religion reached the Iberian Peninsula in Roman times.
- **Cities**. There were cities in Pre-Roman times, but the Romans founded new cities and changed existing ones. They built new constructions, like aqueducts and bridges.
- **Roads**. Many modern roads follow the same routes as Roman roads.

9 Are the following sentences true or false? Correct the false sentences in your notebook. Then listen to the recording and check your answers.

a The Iberians lived in the north and west of the Iberian Peninsula.

b The Celts made large sculptures of bulls and pigs called *verracos*.

c The Phoenicians established trading posts across the Mediterranean after 1000 BC.

d The Carthaginians came from the city of Emporion in North Africa.

e The colonisers introduced writing in the Latin and Greek alphabets.

f Saguntum was the first state on the Iberian Peninsula.

g Many Roman legionaries stayed in Hispania after they retired.

The Roman aqueduct in Segovia.

10 Study the photo and answer the questions.

a What construction is this? What was it used for?

b Have any other Roman buildings survived in Spain?

11 Investigate. Look for the modern names of these Roman cities, and say which Autonomous Community they belong to.

- Bilbilis
- Caesaraugusta
- Segóbriga
- Emerita Augusta
- Saguntum
- Pompaelo
- Tarraco
- Lucus Augusti
- Complutum
- Valentia
- Toletum
- Italica

12 Investigate Latin.

a Does anyone still use Latin today?

b Find three words in a modern Romance language that come from Latin.

THINK LIKE AN HISTORIAN. **Look for information**

Analyse a map

1 Study the map and answer the questions.

a When did the Roman conquest begin? When did it end? How long did it take?

b How many stages are shown on the map?

2 Now compare the information from this map with what you have learned in the unit.

a Where was the first conquered area? Was it Iberian or Celtic? Were there any colonisers in this area?

b Where was the last conquered area? Was it Iberian or Celtic? Were there any colonisers in this area?

Cantabrian Sea

Asturica Augusta

Numantia

Emporion

Barcino

Saguntum

Olisipo

Emerita Augusta

Corduba

Carthago Nova

Mediterranean Sea

Gades

ATLANTIC OCEAN

▮	Territories conquered by 197 BC
▮	Territories conquered by 154 BC
▮	Territories conquered by 29 BC
▮	Territories conquered by 19 BC

Write a biography

A **biography** is a person's life story – the main events in their life. To write a biography, we need to do the following:

1. **Look for information**. It is best to use more than one source and compare them.

2. **Make notes** on key events.

3. **Write a fact file** with the information you have collected. Add photos and illustrations.

Lucius Annaeus Seneca

- Personal life:
- Main events:
- Historical importance:

3 Look for information on Seneca the Younger, who was a great philosopher and dramatist. Find out:

- Where and when was he born?

- Which Roman Emperors did he know?

- Did he have a role in public life?

- What were the names of some of his works?

- Why and how did he die?

- Organise your information in a fact file.

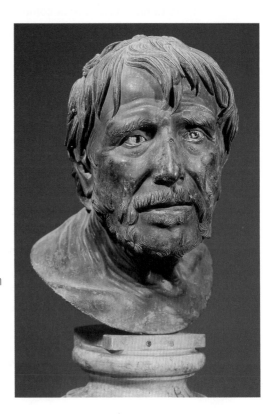

GROUP WORK. **A journey through Hispania**

How about a journey back through time to visit Roman Hispania?
It's not difficult thanks to the fine state of many surviving
Roman monuments...

Walls of Lucus Agusti. These were built between
the 3rd and 4th centuries AD. They were 2,266 m long,
and had 85 circular towers.

The ruins of Baelo Claudia. This city traded
with North Africa.

Aqueduct in Emerita Augusta. The aqueduct carried
drinking water to the city from the Prosperpina marshes.
Some arches were more than 24 m high.

1. Look for good websites with information
   about Roman Spain and share your information
   with your classmates.

2. In groups, choose one of the Roman monuments
   shown on this page, or choose another monument
   from Roman Hispania.

   Look for information about it:
   - When was it built?
   - What was it used for?
   - What condition is it in today?

Prepare an illustrated poster on the monument
you have chosen.

3. In groups, decide where you will go.
   Prepare an itinerary.
   - Where will you begin your journey? Where will
     you finish?
   - Which present-day Autonomous Communities
     will you go through?

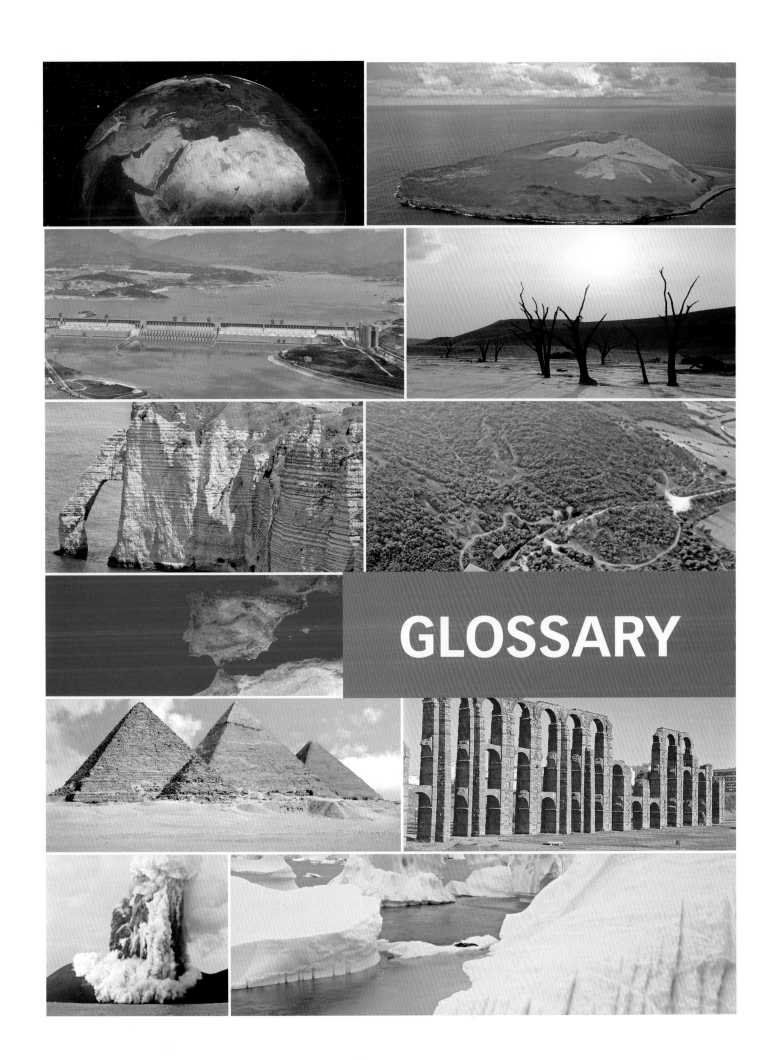

GLOSSARY

Geography glossary

Abyssal plain: a vast underwater plateau.

Alluvial plain: a fertile plain where a river has deposited sediments.

Altitude: the elevation of a point in relation to sea level.

Anemometer: a device that measures wind speed.

Anticyclone: high atmospheric pressure that causes dry and stable weather.

Aquifer: a large store of natural underground water.

Archipelago: a group of islands, like the Balearic and Canary Islands.

Atmosphere: the layer of gases surrounding the Earth up to an altitude of more than 1,000 km.

Atmospheric pressure: the weight of air at the Earth's surface.

Basin: a natural depression that is lower than the land around it.

Bay: a small gulf.

Biodiversity: the variety of plant and animal species in their natural environment.

Biosphere: the ecological system in which all living things exist.

Canopy: a layer of thick leaves and branches in a rainforest.

Cape: a strip of land extending into the sea.

Cardinal points: the directions of north, south, east and west.

City map (or street plan): a map that helps us to find our way around a city.

Climate: the typical state of the atmosphere in a place over a long period of time.

Climatology: the scientific study of the climate.

Climograph: a graph representing average precipitation and temperatures in a place over a period of time.

Cone: the raised land around a volcano caused by the accumulation of lava and rocks.

Continental drift: the theory that many millions of years ago a single super-continent broke up to form smaller continents that gradually moved apart.

Continental shelf: a large underwater plateau surrounding a continent.

Continental slope: an inclined area leading down from the continental shelf into a deeper part of the ocean.

Continental water: the water found in rivers, lakes, glaciers, and groundwater.

Core: the deepest layer of the Earth.

Course: the direction in which a river flows.

Crust: the solid layer of rock at the Earth's surface.

Cyclone (or hurricane or typhoon): a very strong wind that causes storms in tropical latitudes.

Dam: a barrier that turns the water from a river into a reservoir.

Deciduous forest: a forest made up of trees, like oaks and beeches, which lose their leaves in the autumn.

Deforestation: the cutting down of trees in a forest and the use of the land for other purposes.

Delta: a triangular area near a river mouth, where the river deposits sand and stones.

Deposition: the placing of eroded material in areas where sediments accumulate.

Depression: low atmospheric pressure that causes unstable weather and rain.

Desertification: the transformation of fertile land into a desert.

Earthquake: a violent movement of the Earth's crust along the boundary of a tectonic plate.

Emergent: a very tall tree in a rainforest.

Endangered species: a species of plant or animal that faces a high risk of extinction.

Epicentre: the point on the Earth's surface where an earthquake is at its strongest.

Equatorial: characteristic of the regions close to the Equator.

Equinox: the time (around 23 September and 21 March) when the Sun's rays are vertical at the Equator, marking the beginning of autumn and spring.

Erosion: the process by which rocks and soil are broken up and moved around.

Estuary: the area around the river mouth, where the river flows into the sea.

Fault: a break in rigid rock caused by pressure at the boundary of a tectonic plate.

Flow: the volume of water that a river carries.

Fold: a bend in the surface of the Earth's crust caused by pressure at the boundary of a tectonic plate.

Fresh water: water that has a low level of salinity compared to saltwater.

Front: the area where a mass of cold air meets a mass of hot air, which often causes precipitation.

Geographic coordinates: the latitude and longitude of a place indicating its exact location on the Earth's surface.

Geoid: a slightly flattened sphere like the Earth.

Glacier: a mass of ice created by the accumulation of snow.

Global warming: the increase of temperatures at the Earth's surface as a result of greenhouse gases produced by human activity.

Graphic scale (or bar scale): scale represented as a bar divided into segments.

Greenhouse effect: a natural process by which a mixture of carbon dioxide and water vapour prevents solar heat from leaving the Earth's surface.

Groundwater: water that is stored beneath the Earth's surface.

Gulf: an area of the sea that is partly surrounded by land.

Humanized: transformed by human activity.

Humidity: the amount of water vapour in the air.

Hydrosphere: all the water that exists on Earth.

Hypocentre (or focus): the point beneath the Earth's surface from which energy is released during an earthquake.

Ice cap: a mass of ice covering a large land area.

Iceberg: a mass of floating ice.

Inland sea: a lake containing saltwater.

Island: an area of land surrounded by water on all sides.

Isthmus: a strip of land connecting a peninsula to a continent.

Lake: a permanent mass of water that has accumulated in an inland basin.

Latitude: the distance between a point on the Earth's surface and the Equator.

Lava: magma when it reaches the Earth's surface.

Leap year: a year that has 366 (and not 365) days because an extra day is added at the end of February.

Lithosphere: the solid outer layer of the Earth.

Long profile: a graph of a river that shows its length, the places it flows past, and its altitude.

Longitude: the distance between a point on the Earth's surface and the Greenwich meridian.

Magma: hot liquid rock beneath the Earth's surface.

Mantle: the middle layer of the Earth.

Map: a flat representation of all or part of the Earth's surface.

Meadow: an area of grassland in a temperate zone.

Meridian: an imaginary semicircle running in a north-south direction from the North Pole to the South Pole.

Meseta: the large, highland plateau in the centre of the Iberian Peninsula.

Meteorology: the scientific study of weather.

Mid-ocean ridge: an underwater mountain ridge.

Moor: an uncultivated area where bushes and short grasses grow.

Mountain: a steep natural elevation of the Earth's surface.

Mountain range: a group of mountains that are connected to each other.

Numeric scale: scale expressed as a fraction.

Ocean: a huge mass of water surrounding a continent.

Ocean current: a large body of water, similar to a river, that flows through the oceans.

Ocean trench: a long, deep crack in the ocean floor.

Parallel: an imaginary circle running round the Earth in an east-west direction.

Peninsula: an area of land that is mainly surrounded by water.

Plain: a large area of flat land.

Plateau: a high raised plain.

Polar: situated inside the Arctic and Antarctic Circles.

Prairie: a grassland where high grass grows.

Precipitation: the falling of water to the Earth as rain, snow or hail.

Rain gauge (or pluviometer): a device that measures precipitation.

Rainforest: dense forest found in equatorial and tropical regions.

Relief: all the features, like mountains and valleys, which make up the Earth's terrain.

Remote sensing: the collection of data about the Earth's surface from satellites.

Reservoir: an artificial lake.

Revolution: the movement of the Earth around the Sun.

Ría: a coastal inlet found in Galicia.

River: a continuously moving body of water that flows into an ocean, a sea or another river.

River basin: the area occupied by the main river and its tributaries.

Rotation: the movement of the Earth on its own axis.

Salinity: the amount of salt dissolved in water.

Saltwater: water (like seawater) that has a high level of salinity.

Savannah: a large plain of grassland in a tropical region.

Scale: the difference between the size of something on a map and its size in the real world.

Sea: a large mass of water that is smaller than an ocean and partly enclosed by land.

Seawater: the water found in oceans and seas, which has a high level of salinity.

Sediments: the soil and minerals that accumulate in the lower course of a river.

Seismic wave: the form in which energy is released from beneath the Earth's surface during an earthquake.

Solstice: the time (around 21 June and 21 December) when the Sun's rays are vertical at one of the tropics, marking the beginning of summer and winter.

Steppe: a grassland where low grass grows.

Stratosphere: the part of the Earth's atmosphere that contains the ozone layer, which absorbs harmful radiation from the Sun.

Sub-continent: a large landmass that forms part of a continent but is considered a separate region, like North or South America.

Subtropical: characteristic of the regions where the tropical and temperate zones are close to each other.

Sustainable development: the use of natural resources in a way that does not cause long-term damage to the environment.

Taiga: a landscape in the northern hemisphere covered by coniferous forests.

Tectonic plates: great blocks of the Earth's crust that move apart or slide against each other.

Temperate: characteristic of the mild climate found between the tropical and polar regions.

Thematic map: a map that provides visual information on a subject like climate or population.

Tide: the rise and fall of the water level in oceans and seas.

Time zone: one of 24 zones around the Earth that have the same time.

Topographic map: a map that shows the main features of relief, like rivers and mountains.

Topographic profile: a graph that represents the relief of a region.

Tornado: a column of air that spins rapidly.

Transportation: the movement of eroded material by agents like water and wind.

Tributary: a river that flows into another river, and not the sea.

Tropical: characteristic of the regions close to the Tropic of Cancer and Tropic of Capricorn.

Troposphere: the lowest layer of the Earth's atmosphere.

Tsunami: an earthquake on the ocean floor that creates huge waves.

Tundra: a very cold landscape where only a few plants grow.

Vent: the main channel of a volcano.

Volcano: an opening in the Earth's crust through which magma rises to the Earth's surface.

Water cycle: the continual movement of water between the oceans, the atmosphere and the Earth.

Watershed: a territory in which all the rivers flow into the same ocean or sea.

Wave: an undulation of the surface of sea water caused by the wind.

Weather vane: a device that shows the direction of the wind.

Weather: the state of the atmosphere in a place at a particular time.

Wind: a mass of moving air caused by differences in atmospheric pressure.

Acropolis: a walled area high above Greek cities, where the main temples were located.

AD (from the Latin **Anno Domini**): referring to dates later than the birth of Christ.

Agora: a public square in a Greek city where the market was held.

Akkadians: a people living in the south of Mesopotamia.

Amphitheatre: a circular Roman building where gladiator fights were held.

Amphora: a tall Greek or Roman container with two handles that was used to store and transport liquids.

Apella: an assembly in Sparta that consisted of all free men over 30 years old.

Aqueduct: a work of engineering that transported water to Roman cities.

Arch: a curved architectural element covering the gap between two pillars or walls.

Archaeology: the scientific study of the material remains of the past.

Archaic period: the earliest period of Greek history between the 9th and 6th centuries BC.

Archon: a chief magistrate in Athens.

Ardipithecus: an early primate with some hominid characteristics that appeared 4.4 million years ago.

Assyria: a region in the north of Mesopotamia.

Australopithecus: an early hominid that appeared about 4 million years ago.

Basilica: a Roman public building where trade took place. (It was later a Christian place for religious celebration.)

BC (or Before Christ): referring to dates before the birth of Christ.

Bipedal: able to walk upright on two feet.

Black land: the Egyptian term for the area near the River Nile that was covered by dark fertile mud.

Boule: a council in Athens made up of 500 citizens.

Cardo: an important road running from north to south through a Roman city.

Castro: a walled Celtic settlement.

Catacomb: an underground gallery where the early Christians buried their dead.

Cave art: prehistoric paintings and engravings on the surface of caves, often representing animals.

Celtiberians: a group of Celtic-speaking tribes who lived in the interior of the Iberian peninsula before the Roman conquest.

Celts: a people living in the north, centre and west of the Iberian peninsula before the Roman conquest.

Centaur: a creature in Greek mythology that had a human head and a horse's body.

Circus: a Roman public space where chariot races were held.

Citizen: an adult male who had political rights in Greece and Rome.

Clan: a group of people who believed they shared the same ancestors.

Classical period: the period of Greek history between the 5th century BC and the mid-4th century BC.

Colony: a settlement established by a city or a state far from its frontiers.

Consul: a leading Roman magistrate.

Cuneiform: a type of writing developed in Mesopotamia by making signs on clay tablets.

Cyclops: a one-eyed monster in Greek mythology.

Decumanus: an important road running from east to west through a Roman city.

Delian League: a union of several poleis under the leadership of Athens.

Democracy: "rule by the people", a form of government developed in Athens in which all citizens participated.

Dolmen: a megalithic tomb consisting of a series of vertical stones supporting a large flat horizontal stone.

Dome: a hemispherical construction covering the upper part of a building.

Domus: a home for a single family of wealthy Romans.

Drachma: a silver coin used by the Greeks.

Dynasty: a succession of rulers who all belonged to the same family.

Ekklesia: an assembly of all the citizens in Athens that voted laws, decided foreign policy and elected magistrates.

Ephor: one of the five leading Spartan magistrates.

Fertility goddess: a Neolithic clay statue that was believed to favour good harvests.

Forum: a square in a Roman city with public buildings, and where goods were bought and sold.

Gerousia: a council in Sparta formed by prestigious, older citizens.

Gynaikonitis: a space reserved for women in a Greek house.

Hand axe (or biface): a Palaeolithic tool that was used to cut meat and carve wood.

Hellenism: the culture of the territories conquered by Alexander the Great. (It was mainly Greek, but with a strong eastern influence.)

Hellenistic period: the period of Greek and Middle Eastern history between the mid-4th century BC and the 1st century BC.

Hero: in Greek mythology, the son of a human with a god or goddess.

Hieroglyphs: a system of writing developed in Egypt using signs to represent words or sounds.

History: the period of time since the invention of writing about 5,000 years ago.

Hominid: an early primate with some human-like characteristics.

Homo antecessor: a hominid whose remains were found at Atapuerca (Burgos).

Homo erectus: the species of hominid that learned how to use fire.

Homo habilis: the species of hominid that developed the first tools.

Homo sapiens: the species to which modern humans belong.

Hoplite: a Greek soldier who fought on foot.

Hunter-gatherer: a person who lived from hunting animals and gathering plants.

Iberians: a people living in the south and east of the Iberian Peninsula before the Roman conquest.

Ice age: a long period when the climate was extremely cold. (There were several ice ages in Prehistory.)

Insula (plural: insulae): an apartment building where less wealthy Roman families lived.

Kore: an Archaic Greek standing sculpture representing a woman.

Kouros: an Archaic Greek standing sculpture showing a warrior or athlete.

Lares: Roman household gods.

Latin: the language spoken in the Roman Empire.

Legionary: a Roman soldier who fought on foot.

Levantine art: Neolithic cave art that was created in eastern Spain.

Mare Nostrum: "Our Sea", the Roman term for the Mediterranean Sea.

Megalith: a monument built with large stones.

Menhir: a megalithic monument consisting of a single vertical stone.

Mesopotamia: the region around the Tigris and Euphrates rivers.

Metal Age: the period in Prehistory when people started to make metal objects.

Metallurgy: the technique of making tools, weapons and jewellery from metal.

Metic: a foreigner who lived in Athens.

Metope: a square panel with reliefs in a Greek temple.

Milestone: a column next to a Roman road that indicated distances.

Monotheism: the belief in a single God.

Mosaic: a decorative surface made from small pieces of stone, glass and tile.

Mummy: a dead body that was dried to ensure its conservation in Egypt.

Myth: a story about gods or heroes that helped people to understand the world.

Naos: the main hall of a Greek temple, where the statue of a god was kept.

Neanderthal: a species of hominid that appeared nearly 200,000 years ago. They were the first to bury their dead.

Necropolis: a Neolithic cemetery where the dead were buried with their personal objects.

Nemes: striped head clothing worn by a pharaoh that symbolised the power given by the gods.

Neolithic: belonging to the period in Prehistory that began about 10,000 years ago, when agriculture and livestock farming were developed.

Neolithic Revolution: the important social and economic changes that took place during the Neolithic period.

Nomads: people who went from one place to another in search of food and shelter.

Oligarchy: "rule by the few", which was the form of government adopted by poleis like Sparta.

Olympic Games: a famous Greek sports competition, which was held in Olympia every four years in honour of the god Zeus.

Olympus: the mountain where the gods lived in Greek mythology.

Oracle: a message from the gods that was interpreted by a Greek priest or priestess.

Order: an architectural set of rules.

Ostracism: a Greek practice of voting to decide which leading politician should go into exile for ten years.

Palaeolithic: belonging to the earliest period in Prehistory, which began about 5 million years ago.

Panathenaic procession: a procession celebrated in Athens every year in honour of the goddess Athena.

Papyrus: a kind of paper made from a plant.

Patrician: a member of one of the leading Roman families.

Pax romana: "Roman peace", the Roman term for the period of stability and peace in the first and second centuries AD.

Peloponnesian League: a union of several poleis under the leadership of Sparta.

Penates: Roman household gods.

Pharaoh: a monarch of Egypt who held absolute power and was considered a god.

Plebeian: a free Roman citizen who was not a patrician.

Polis (plural: poleis): a city-state in Greece that had its own government, laws and army.

Polytheism: the belief that there are many gods.

Pre-Hellenic: referring to the civilisations, like Knossos and Mycenae, which existed in the eastern Mediterranean before the emergence of Ancient Greece.

Prehistory: the period of time between the emergence of the early hominids and the invention of writing about 5,000 years ago.

Pyramid: a large triangular construction used as a tomb for an Egyptian pharaoh.

Red land: the Egyptian term for dry desert areas.

Relief: a sculpture on a flat surface.

Republic: a system of government in which there was no single ruler or monarch.

Romanisation: the assimilation of Roman culture by the conquered peoples of the empire.

Sanctuary: a sacred place.

Sarcophagus: an ornamental box containing a dead body.

Scribe: an official who could read, write and count.

Sedentary: living in a single place in a settlement with walls or fences.

Senate: an important assembly of leading figures in Rome.

Slave: a person with no rights who was bought and sold by wealthy people.

Social pyramid: a diagram that represents all the groups in a society.

Sphinx: a mythical creature with a human head and the body of a lion.

Stone circle: a megalithic monument consisting of several menhirs arranged in a circle.

Strategos (plural: strategoi): a general in the Athenian army.

Sumerians: a people living in the south of Mesopotamia.

Tartessos: an early kingdom based in the south-west of the Iberian Peninsula.

Temple: a building where religious worship took place.

Thermae: Roman public baths, which were for both bathing and meeting people.

Trading post: a settlement where goods were traded.

Tribe: a group of people with shared customs who lived together.

Vault: an arched roof covering the space between several walls or pillars.

Venus statuette: a small Palaeolithic sculpture of a woman used as a fertility symbol.

Victory Arch: a Roman arch that commemorated a military victory.

Villa: a large Roman house in the country.

Ziggurat: a stepped pyramid in Mesopotamia on which a temple was built.